SHE LOVED
A
WICKED CITY

LAWRENCE EARL

SHE LOVED

A

WICKED CITY

The Story
of Mary Ball, Missionary

1962

McCLELLAND AND STEWART LIMITED

FOR
DEWI AND ROBIN
AND JANE

LIST OF ILLUSTRATIONS

AUTHOR'S FOREWORD

THIS is a book that refused to remain unwritten.
Let me explain.

One day, in the long ago of 1951, Dewi Morgan phoned me
in London to say that he wanted me to meet a woman medical
missionary who had just returned from a quarter of a century
in a remote outpost of North China. Her name was Mary Ball
and her story (my friend said) would make a fascinating book.

Had I followed my first inclination at that moment, there
would have been no beginning to *One Foreign Devil*, for Dewi
was a Church of England clergyman, occupationally interested in
mission work while, at best, I was indifferent to it. Even as he
spoke of her, I formed a mental image of Mary Ball: a dried-
up do-gooder who, twenty-five years earlier had transplanted
some frustration of love and life into an escape that had taken
her to a monotony of time in a strange land. I don't know
what prompted me to say that I'd meet her for an investigative
chat.

Oddly, because I recall so much else about her so clearly, I do
not remember where we met. Was it in Dewi's Tufton Street
office? In my own, near Fleet Street, where at that time I was
working as a magazine editor? Or at the flat in Brompton Road
where I then lived? But I remember Mary, translucent-skinned,
conservatively-clothed, gentle—who smiled and at once fell into
step to answer my first probing stock questions and burst like a
strangely beneficent bomb into my awareness as a fully-developed
personality I suddenly wanted to know much better.

From that point, we together launched into nearly three
solid months of questions and long answers, memories, geographi-
cal details and word-pictures of people and places and events that
carried us to and beyond far-distant Tatung, the ancient walled

town on the edge of Mongolia that Mary still thought of as home.

To say that my originally imagined picture of her had been in error is to say far too little. In her quiet, efficient, unaggressive, marvellously straightforward way, Mary was a force of nature. Some power of spirit drove her on. Slender as a willow wand, red-haired, quick to smile and to appreciate, she gave the impression of having great strength not only of mind and heart but of body as well, though I soon perceived that she had drawn so unselfishly upon her by-no-means bottomless physical resources over the years that she was now far from being a well woman. . . .

And Dewi Morgan had been quite correct: hers was indeed a fascinating story. I wanted greatly to get it down on paper.

It was not long after our interviews came to an end that Mary suddenly died. I had not yet begun the actual job of writing because the situation at the hospital in Tatung in regard to the indigenous Christians on the staff had not at that time become fully clarified and the Society was anxious not to cause them any embarrassment. Then the news of Mary's death moved me to abandon, at least for a while, all thought of shaping a book out of the more than one hundred thousand words of notes I had taken. My heart was no longer in it.

I buried the notes in a drawer of my study desk, forgetting them but not Mary. The years passed. Every now and again my wife, Jane, would ask when I intended to begin the Mary Ball book, for she too had known and could not forget her. But by now I was inwardly convinced that the book would never be written.

In the Spring of 1960, taken ill and moved by a high fever to murky actions, I slipped out of bed one day to rummage through my desk where, like a squirrel, storing nuts, I had saved all my old notes and manuscripts. I tore them up in a frenzy of tidying, filling my waste-paper basket with the scraps. Soon after, I went to my native province of New Brunswick, Canada, to convalesce.

While there, I had a letter from a London publisher. He had been talking to Dewi Morgan about the Mary Ball story and was keenly interested: would I write the book for him? Now, at last, after nearly ten years and with this renewed expression of interest, I was again eager to do it. But had I destroyed the Mary Ball notes with the others? If so, the entire project was lost for ever.

I cabled Jane, who had stuck at her post as London correspondent of the Toronto *Telegram*. After a disturbed night of worrying, back came her reply: MARY BALL NOTES OKAY HURRAH JANE.

In my return to London, I set to work, but discovered that the passage of time had altered my view of the shape the book ought to take. I wanted further research and additional information. Fortunately, with the kind help of the S.P.G., I was able to round up many of Mary's colleagues who had known her in China and were most generous in finding the time to help me. Some of these are still in far places—Mrs. Claire Birse, in Northern Rhodesia, Sister Isabel Mary, O.S.A. (formerly Isabel Garnett), in Mindanao, Miss D. M. Disney, in South Africa and Miss D. E. Mitchell, in British Columbia—but others had long since returned to England: Mrs. Edith Bryan Brown, Mrs. R. C. H. Swain, Dr. Mary Dunn, Miss Etheldreda Fisher, Lieut-Col. and Mrs. George Lancashire of the Salvation Army, and A. J. D. Britland.

I thank them all. And I thank especially, too, Miss Helen Mosse, who was Mary's good friend at S. P. G. headquarters and Mrs. William Siems (née Margaret Ball), for their most valued assistance. In their separate ways, they all helped with the book that refused to remain unwritten.

L.E.

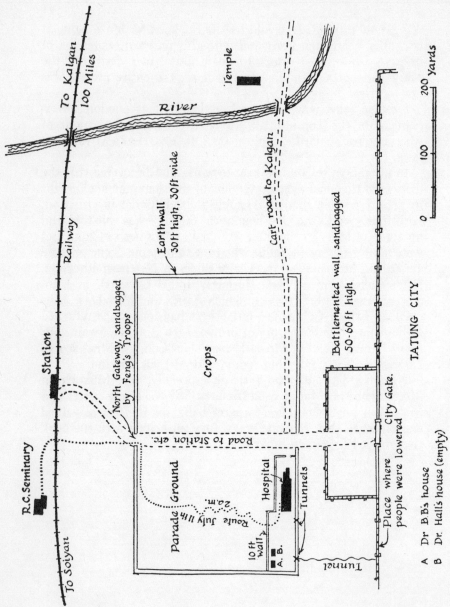

To Kalgan
100 Miles

To Kalgan

Railway

River

Temple

Station

R.C. Seminary

To Soiyan

Earthwall
30 ft high, 30 ft wide

Cart road to Kalgan

North Gateway, sandbagged
by Feng's Troops

Crops

Battlemented wall, sandbagged
50-60 ft high

Road to Station etc.

Parade Ground

Route July 11th

2 a.m.

Hospital

Tunnels

10 ft wall

A. B.

A. B.

Tunnel

Place where
people were lowered

City Gate.

TATUNG CITY

0   100   200 Yards

A   Dr B.B's house
B   Dr. Hall's house (empty)

CHAPTER I

MARY was scrubbing up, late in the afternoon, when Nursing Sister Preece panted in, swinging a hot draught through the doorway. Preecie was no longer a young woman in that July of 1950, and it was easy to see that she was excited.

She said in a breathless rush: "Mary, can you come downstairs right away?"

Quite deliberately, Mary rinsed off the suds and their sharply antiseptic smell. She had always considered it part of her job as matron—as more than matron in this outpost hospital—to keep the staff calm in times of crisis.

"Now then, Preecie. Is it *that* important? I'm waiting to deliver Mrs. Lin's baby."

The elderly nursing sister was really quite flushed. Tendrils of damp, greying hair clung to her forehead. "I think it is. It's—it's the letter from Peking."

"From the Bishop?"

"Yes."

"Have you seen it, then?"

"I've seen it. We've been told to apply at once for our exit permits."

Mary nodded. Then she said, briskly: "Well, I'm afraid I can't come just now."

With the nursing sister gone, Mary allowed herself a momentary shiver. This was what she had been dreading ever since the Communists had taken over northern Shansi in 1948. Yet, now that it had come, she could scarcely believe it; for to say that she did not wish to leave Tatung was reducing truth to absurdity. She wanted to stay on so passionately it was an aching prayer under her skin. How could she leave the city—the wild and wicked city—she had grown to love and the hospital which had

13

been her life's mission for twenty-five years? It was unthinkable. All the same, she could not ignore the Bishop's letter. The situation in Peking must be much worse than she had supposed.

She almost always stood with uncompromising erectness, but with a conscious effort she brought her shoulders back still further. Then she thrust, elbows forward, into the delivery room.

Miss Chao, the pretty Chinese nurse who had given her so much trouble, came over to her, trousered legs whispering against one another. "It is time, Teacher Ball."

Mary nodded. There was no ostramalicia to complicate Mrs. Lin's case, and it would be a perfectly straightforward delivery. This, at least, was nothing to worry about. How many babies had she delivered since she had come to Tatung? How many patients had she treated in the remote villages when she had gone out for her week-long swings by mule cart? How many opium cases, wolf bites, wounded soldiers had she tended? How many nurses had she trained?

Yes, and how many regimes had she survived? Surely there must be some way to survive this one, a way to stay on at the hospital, serving the Shansi people and God!

As soon as she was free to do so—scant moments after the first lusty squalling of the hospital's newest boy baby—Mary went down to read Bishop Scott's letter for herself.

At nine that evening they gathered in the living room of Superintendent Philip Li: Mary, the Superintendent, Nursing Sister Preece and Mr. Fox, the S.P.G. chaplain. Mary, seated beside Preecie on a small white-and-blue covered couch, let her eyes wander round the room. The Superintendent, across from her, seemed far removed, gazing into space; and, a few feet to his right, Mr. Fox drummed on his knee with his one good hand. Between the two men was a small table: on it—in a brass tray —cups, a pot of tea, a large thermos of hot water.

Then Mrs. Li entered in a grey silken robe. She bowed, saying nothing, and began to make the tea. Still no word was spoken. And, when Mrs. Li had finished her chore, she retired as silently as she had come.

Then the air of suspended reality was shattered. The Superintendent sighed. He held his two hands palm up and raised them slowly, in a gesture almost of pain, to his forehead. After a moment he separated his hands and brought them down as far as his ear lobes, which he tugged quite violently.

With a small, embarrassed, unhappy laugh, he finally said: "This is an unthought of thing. An unthought of thing!" He passed the tea around in the small, fragile cups which had no handles. "Have you decided?" he asked.

Mary held the warm, nearly translucent cup in her fingers. "There is nothing to decide, is there? The Bishop says we should put in for our exit permits."

"You have decided," the Superintendent said unhappily. "I think the exit permits may take some time, and you will have to give reasons."

Mr. Fox looked surprised. "Reasons to *leave* the country? I understood that the idea behind the entire operation was that we are being forced out."

The Superintendent created a subtle gesture of apology with his hands, arms and shoulders.

"I suppose I can say I want to go because of my age," Miss Preece volunteered wryly. She was in her early sixties.

"And since I have already requested a transfer," Mr. Fox said, "I can say that my work here is finished."

They all looked enquiringly at Mary.

"I can't think of a thing," she said, not wanting to. "I certainly can't use my health—or my age." The prayer that she would not have to go beat within her like a pulse.

The Superintendent said mildly: "Did you not say some months ago that a member of your family had died?"

"Yes, my brother-in-law."

"Then put 'death in family' in your application. It would be an acceptable reason, I think."

When they put in their applications, the man at the local Bureau of Foreign Affairs said they would probably have their permits within a week. Mary doubted that they would come so soon, but just the same she handed the keys to the stores cupboards over to Mrs. Li, who would be matron in her place, and had the inventories translated into Chinese.

When, by the week's end, the permits had not come, she checked with the Foreign Affairs Office. She checked on the seventh, on the twelfth and on the twentieth of July and there was no word. She certainly did not mind for herself—the longer she could stay on the better—but she was anxious for the others.

On the morning of the twenty-second, she again asked for news and was told that the applications had been sent along to Kalgan, and from there to Peking. But, later that day, the same official got in touch with her.

"We cannot find any sign of your application forms," he said, quite blatantly. "Obviously you have not applied for exit permits at all. You must apply again."

Her angry protests were quite unavailing, and mixed incongrously with her anger she began unreasonably to hope that she would not, after all, have to go.

Then she began to wonder: why had the Foreign Affairs Bureau changed its tune? Knowing something of the thought processes of the Chinese Communists, Mary believed she could guess the reason. Foreigners were always suspect to them, and now that hostilities had broken out in Korea, doubly suspect. Perhaps the timing of the applications had been unfortunate; perhaps suspicious officials even thought that the three foreigners at the hospital were British spies, anxious to escape now that their work was done and war was actually at hand.

The following forenoon, after the outpatients' clinic, Dr. Francis Li, the Superintendent's cousin and now consultant at the hospital, asked Mary to walk with him in the garden. It had rained earlier, but the sun had come out since so that while it was still fresh in the garden it was rapidly becoming warmer.

"What is it, Francis?" Mary asked. She had known him for a long time and she was aware that he had something special on his mind.

He said: "Miss Ball—" He hesitated, shaking his head. Then

he said: "Do you think you could possibly stay on and help us here?"

For an instant she lost the stern grip she had kept on herself. Her hand caught at her throat; but she recovered quickly. "You know that is impossible. You know they will not let me stay."

Then the Chinese doctor smiled. "We all want you to stay, all of us at the hospital. I have been making enquiries in the city with the authorities to try to find out what would be required of you—and of us—if you agreed to stay. You see, there is really nobody who can take on all your many responsibilities of running the hospital."

It was quite true, of course, that Mary had been much more than her title as matron implied; for she had accumulated responsibilities over the years, accepting them gladly—taking charge of the training of nurses, ward work, all foods and stores, laundry. She had taken over the financial side of running the hospital, assisted at operations, given anaesthetics, supervised maternity work. ("She really was the boss of the hospital," Dr. Mary Dunn, who once worked with her there, has reported. "There was no doubt of that.")

But Mary said to Dr. Li: "You will find someone."

The doctor was a tall man for a Chinese: very close to six feet. Mary tried to remember what he had looked like when he first came to the hospital, but the changes had come so gradually over the years that she really could not say positively that he had changed at all. He still had his shy and hesitant manner. He was still slender and quite youthful in appearance: or was that because she thought of him as youthful from long ago?

"Everybody in Tatung knows you," he said, "and the city people are sad to think that you consider going. I guarantee that if the people of the city were asked, they would want you to stay on."

Now, for the first time, a truly practical hope was alive in her.

"You said you had spoken to the authorities, Francis?"

"Yes. And in the first place your application to remain would have to be passed unanimously by the hospital workers' union. It would be passed."

"And what else?"

"After that, by the doctors' union, and then approved by several Government offices."

She saw that he was hesitating. "There is more?"

"Yes, there is more."

"Tell me, Francis."

"There are two things you would have to agree to carry out. You would have to give up your British nationality and become, instead, a Chinese citizen. And, I must warn you, after the age of sixty they would have no work for you."

"And the second condition?"

"You would have to become a professed Communist and give up your faith in God."

They stopped walking round the garden. They were very old friends and had gone through many troubles together. The recent history of China had swept over them and they had shared this vast experience and had helped one another when they were able; but now Francis could no longer help her. He had gone as far as it was possible—and Mary was immeasurably grateful.

She had nearly always before known precisely what she wanted and what to do; and all the often turbulent passage of her life had led unerringly to this agonizing moment of decision which was hers alone to make.

*   *   *

CHAPTER II

S H E had come out of a convulsed, often desperately unhappy childhood—a puny, lost little girl; but her first memories were of joyous entanglements with a great, black, chest-deep beard and the sound of booming laughter. The beard, as well as the laughter, belonged to William Henry Ball, her father, who from the moment of her premature birth had installed Mary as his favourite child. Before her had come Francis Henry, Annie Elizabeth, Emily Helen and George Armitage: after her, Margaret.

It is Margaret who recalls Mary in her earliest years as "a poor, frightened little soul who used to cower under the table as if for protection against the world". But her father was Mary's real bulwark. She adored him. Once, she was always to remember, he had held her on his knees and confided that if he could have had his first choice of a parish it would have been in China. Instead, he had been appointed as an Anglican missionary to work amongst the Basuto tribes people in the Orange Free State, and had later written back to England for Elizabeth Armitage, a Sunday school teacher, to join him in the dark wilderness as his wife.

His beard, like a prophet's, was biblical and grand, but Mary remembered him better for his jolly sense of humour. She often chuckled, looking backward, at the way it had bubbled to the surface at the most unexpected times. Once the reverend gentleman had suddenly noticed in the midst of intoning a High Church ceremony, with his Basuto parishioners around him, that not all the ceremonial accoutrements—some of them makeshift—were in their proper place. Without interrupting the rhythm of his ecclesiastical chant, he intoned: "Oh dear, oh dear, where am de incense pot?" and the quick, chanting reply came in Bantu accents: "Couldn't bring it, baas: it was too dommed hot!"

But with the sudden death of Mary's mother, at the early age of thirty-eight, the Ball family's era of peaceful calm came tragically unstuck. The Boer War in South Africa did nothing to reestablish a secure atmosphere for the six youngsters. Francis Henry, the eldest boy, became a bugler in the British Army; and, for a time, Mary, Annie Elizabeth, George, Emily Helen and Margaret were sent to a farm called Ben Lomond where a kindhearted young woman—Annie Fraser—acted as a sort of fostermother to them; but in 1902 the family went to Tottenham, in England, to live with relatives.

There, Mary's father made two unnerving discoveries: that he had a valvular disorder of the heart which affected his breathing and that a clergyman could not take over a living in Britain if he had been ordained elsewhere, without first having two years there as a curate.

The first discovery made it imperative that he should find for his health's sake some less damply dismal climate and the second that he could not afford to maintain his six children by himself remaining in England. He took Francis Henry with him and went off to the New World—first to a church in Ontario, and later to churches in Miami, Florida, and Monroe, North Carolina.

The other children, Mary amongst them, he left for safe-keeping in the hands of a maiden aunt who had accumulated for herself an incredible range of Victorian complexes and the constantly recurring delusion that all unmarried males who visited the house instantly fell in love with her but were too shy to propose marriage. Doubtless, in her own mind, her intentions towards the children were high-mindedly pure, but the narrowly bitter boundaries behind which she hemmed in her life made her treatment of them—certainly in today's terms—unduly harsh.

Mary, delicate of health and vastly sensitive, suffered most. Soon her hidden upheaval—almost unbearably missing her loved father, being brow-beaten by the aunt and a particularly astringent schoolteacher—revealed itself on the surface with an attack of St. Vitus Dance.

Into this period of anguish, when she was not quite eight years old, came a moment of almost blinding enlightenment, for which a psychiatrist of today might have found the promptings in her past loves and existent yearnings, but for which Mary herself much later accounted in more mystic terms. The moment came at a morning prayer service in Tottenham when she heard a line read from St. Luke: "Thou, child, shalt be called the prophet of the Highest."

Mary whispered excitedly to Annie Elizabeth beside her: "It must be *me* they're meaning."

"Huh!" Annie Elizabeth snorted. "It isn't you, Mary. It's St. John."

But Mary was convinced and nothing whatever could alter her stand. Years later, she was to amplify her feelings.

"It was a call for me to become a missionary. The call comes in waves—first strong, then it seems to stand in abeyance, and finally it becomes so strong it is unmistakable." Thus, from the age of seven, her inner self had begun to feed on an awareness of her special destiny.

Mary's father, for whom her young heart yearned, came on a visit to Tottenham in 1910. He must have felt ill-equipped as a widower, who had not sought to remarry, to create a satisfactory new home for his daughters, but he did collect his younger boy, George, and took him back to North Carolina. One last time he visited the girls, in 1914. Then the first World War cut him off from them.

Francis Henry, still in the United States, after being first a tutor in a southern military academy, then a chartered accountant, then an Episcopalian minister in Oregon, rushed across the Canadian border to join the Princess Patricia's Light Infantry. Soon he sailed for an anticipated glory which was to be debased sadly in its actuality. In France, he was gassed, shell-shocked and wounded by shell fragments. Young George, distant and therefore undisillusioned, was keen to join up as well, but for some time his father held him back by reiterating that one son sent into action was enough.

By 1917, George's eagerness overcame the parental check-rein. He became an American infantryman and, early the next year, went overseas. *The Monroe Journal* for June twenty-fifth, 1918, recorded: "The city aldermen ordered the American flag on the Court House Square to be lowered at half-mast in memory of Lieut. George A. Ball, the first Monroe citizen to die in France for the glorious cause of democracy."

Perhaps this blow was too heavy for his father's damaged heart, for William Ball died shortly after. The double helping of grief nearly shattered Mary, but after it had eased a bit her resolve hardened to trace her adored father's footsteps into the mission field in South Africa, where she remembered him best.

"She wanted to follow Daddy in his profession," sister Margaret was to say, long after. "She felt she could never do the preaching part, but rather could do things for people—like healing the sick. That's why she went in for nursing. Her great singleness of purpose gave her a kind of dedicated biblical approach, though she was anything but cold or austere."

And Mary was bound and determined to create out of herself the best instrument for her purpose. Soon she was taking general training for nursing at Addenbrooke's Hospital, in Cambridge, went on to Malvern to do sister's work—and became assistant matron in the process—and from there departed to take midwifery at North Middlesex Hospital.

Wherever she applied herself everyone recognized her as outstandingly intelligent, willing and hard-working. Indeed, she was driven from within to give always of her best, never losing sight of her intent.

After completing a course on anæsthetics at the London Homeopathic Hospital, she offered herself to the Society for the Propagation of the Gospel in Foreign Parts (often simply called the S.P.G.), an Anglican body which, in the beginning of the seventeen hundreds, had sent its first missionaries to North America to convert the red-skinned Indians and the black-skinned slaves and to give religious comfort to the colonists.

When she was asked her preference of working locale, Mary plumped enthusiastically for South Africa. She felt very close to her father at that moment, and she made a remarkably good impression on the Miss Whitmore who was probing her with questions. A note was written after her name into the permanent S.P.G. records: "Expected to be a missionary since about seven. Some preference for South Africa. Desires preparation. Very sensible and understanding."

Then, and later, Mary appeared to have a special, native genius for digging herself into the sensibilities of others. Etheldreda Fisher, a missionary friend, some years afterwards commented on this ability in a tone of wonder. "When we were both home in England doing deputation work, we'd stay as guests at people's houses. I would tip the maid when I left, but with Mary it was quite different. The maid would dig into her savings and force the money on Mary to further her work. Without seeming even to try she just charmed people into giving."

Of course, the S.P.G. accepted Mary's application to serve. She took her theological training at the Deaconess's House in Clapham. In September, 1924, she began a course in African phonetics at the School for Oriental Studies, fighting her way bravely through the tongue-clacking and the strange rhythms. Then a great blow fell. She was told that her destination had been changed to Singapore.

Mary stopped her language course. She tried hard not to let the change of plans upset her, but the keen edge of her anticipation was dulled. Then another change was thrust upon her: this time appointing her to China. Her joy was revived. Hadn't her father first set his sights on the Orient? In an oddly oblique way she felt that now she could truly carry on in his place.

She embarked with great enthusiasm on a course of Chinese, but had hardly begun to puzzle over that difficult tongue when her sailing date to Peking was suddenly set for early in the New Year. She was not told where her ultimate destination was to be, but she remembered having heard Bishop Frank Norris, of the Diocese of North China, speak at Caxton Hall when on a London visit some weeks before. The Bishop had said that in January the S.P.G. would be sending a nursing sister to the Mosse Memorial Hospital in a remote town near the border of Mongolia. The town's name was Tatung. Mary rushed to the S.P.G. library to look it up but could only find that it had been the scene of a massacre some years before, when all the Christian missionaries there had been slaughtered, and their families with them. She made the mistake of mentioning this to her next eldest sister.

Emily Helen, distressed by the information, tried to dissuade Mary from going, but was reminded gently of the call which Mary had first clearly heard at the prayer meeting in Tottenham, more than twenty years before.

"Yes, but you *know* Annie Elizabeth isn't well," Emily Helen protested desperately. "What if anything should happen to one of us—if one of us should die? Would you change your mind about going then?"

Mary sighed, patting her sister's arm.

"I can't stop now," she said. "Not for anything."

And she did feel that it was true: her course at last was set and no earthly force could change it.

*　　*　　*

CHAPTER III

I F Mary arrived in Peking with a passion to embrace her future, she learned in very short order to curb it. On her first day, she had an invitation to lunch with Bishop Norris, who had preceded her back to his post in China.

The Bishop asked her to remain after his other guests had gone. In his sixties, he was a tall man with thinning hair far turned into grey. Behind the lenses of his gold-rimmed spectacles, his eyes seemed uncompromising and stern.

"Come into my study, Miss Ball," the Bishop said, and motioned her to a chair.

He sat himself behind his desk and drummed his fingers on the wooden top, looking bleakly at Mary. What he saw must have caused him to doubt her as much of an acquisition to his rota of diocesan workers, for certainly she did not have the look of a woman with the stamina for a full load of work or responibility.

She was, as a Salvation Army friend later described her, "like a piece of pale, carved jade, flawless and fragile, her skin absolutely transparent." She was five feet six inches tall, but so slender as to appear frail. Her hair was an almost frivolously bright red. Her eyes, steady and gentle, sometimes seemed hazel and sometimes brown.

The Bishop cleared his throat.

"It's been reported to me that since your arrival you've said something you may now care to deny: that you were going to Tatung."

Mary's eyebrows shot up.

"I certainly won't deny the truth," she said. "I did mention it." She felt more and more like a small girl called to account for leaving jam prints on the kitchen wall.

"And what gave you the impression that you were going there?"

"Well, you see, I had letters of welcome at the boat from Dr. Bryan Brown and Dr. Hall. They both seemed to think I was going to join them at the Mosse Memorial Hospital." Dr. Bryan Brown was superintendent of the hospital at Tatung and Dr. Hall was his assistant.

"*They* don't make such decisions," the Bishop said brusquely.

Mary accepted this with a nod. She was concerned at the Bishop's line of questioning, not understanding what lay behind it.

"But there was another thing," she said. "I'd heard you speak at the medical mission meeting in London when you said that a nurse was going out to Tatung in January."

"Well?"

"I suppose I jumped to conclusions since I was the only nurse going out at about that time."

It seemed to her that the Bishop's lips twitched ever so slightly at the corners.

He said: "I see. Well, I want you to remember this: that you may never get to Tatung. It's a most difficult post and not everyone is suited to work there." She was still waiting when he looked up at her again from some far-removed thought. "Good afternoon, Miss Ball," he said, with an impersonal nod of dismissal.

Mary settled down to a crash programme of studies at the language school in Peking. A day or two after completing it, at the end of July, she was surprised to get word from the Bishop to proceed with all haste to Tatung. It was an emergency case. A Mrs. Porteus, visiting there, had contracted scarlet fever. Since she was the wife of an S.P.G. priest, a special responsibility was felt towards her.

Mary's destination was about two hundred miles west and slightly to the north of Peking, a distance multiplied by the country's disorganization. Rail services were, at best, haphazard. Thus it took two wearisome days for her to reach Tatung. Even at that, as she was soon enough to learn, she had managed on the route to catch up with and leave forever behind the Bishop's telegram announcing her arrival.

As a result, no one waited to meet her at the station, miles outside Tatung's incredibly massive walls. With a certain hesitancy, and a lick at her lips, Mary approached a rickshaw coolie. She was still unsure of her Chinese, but she tried to compensate by speaking slowly and distinctly.

"Do you know a foreign place where they look after the sick?"

"I know, I know!" The rickshaw man grinned his delight at having understood the foreign devil, the incredible foreign devil with red hair. "I have been there," he added, and he pointed out the direction.

Leaving her luggage at the station, Mary made her way to the hospital, a grey brick building which had been completed only three years before. It, too, was located outside the town proper—though just outside—in its own compound within the crumbling walls of what had been Tatung's Manchu city until it had been razed in 1912.

Remembering the Bishop's warning that it was a "most difficult post", Mary was delighted at sight of the hospital. It was solidly built of brick, three stories high. Entering, she noted its polished wooden floors and how clean everything was kept; and she was soon to learn that it was modernly equipped with such unexpected amenities as central heating and high-pressure sterilizers. From all sides it had been impressed on her that Tatung was a backward and immoral city—a frontier outpost. Now, seeing the hospital, she felt that surely the difficulties must have been greatly exaggerated on every count.

As soon as she identified herself to the matron of the hospital and made known the purpose of her visit, Mary was regretfully informed that she had arrived too late to fulfil it. Mrs. Porteus, suddenly worsening, had died the day before. And, even at that moment, the Bishop was on his way up from Peking to officiate at the funeral.

But, she thought, she might just as well wait for his arrival and perhaps go back to Peking in his company. Ivan Nikulin, a

White Russian who was the hospital's engineer, gallantly offered to go to the station to pick up her luggage. Indeed, he appeared to be delighted that she had decided to stay, even if only for a few days. He was a tall young man and quite slender and really very charming and good-looking, Mary reflected as she thanked him for his kindness.

After the funeral, the Bishop took her aside.

"Well, Miss Ball?" He held his head quizzically aslant, his eyes searching hers. "How do you like it up here?"

"Very much," she told him. "The air seems so bracing in the hills, and the garden is so full of flowers." The city was on the Mongolian plateau, several thousands of feet above sea level. In the near distance, craggy mountains stood up still higher against the sky.

The Bishop merely nodded. It was quite clear to Mary that he still had his doubts about her.

That evening, Dr. Giles Hall, the fair-haired assistant superintendent, sought her out.

"Miss Ball, have you ever seen an opium-poisoning case?"

"No, doctor."

"Then you'd better come with me."

He led the way down to the reception hall of the outpatients' department.

It was quite a large hall, crowded now with Chinese men and women and echoing to their excited chatter. As she passed amongst them, Mary almost gagged at the cumulative stench of unwashed bodies. But when she caught her breath, it was not because of that.

In the thick of the crowd, held up forcibly by two coolies, was a young Chinese woman, barely out of her 'teens.

She was naked to the waist, her torso painted a deep red. Her black hair fell in dishevelled strands across sickly yellow cheeks. The two men took turns in calling out to her, trying to tease her into answering back.

Profoundly shocked, Mary fought to conceal her dismay.

"She was brought in from one of the city's brothels," Dr. Hall told her.

"Attempted suicide?" She tried to sound clinically professional, though her state of mind was far from that.

"Yes—she took an overdose of opium." The doctor added with a frown: "This is typical of a good deal of our work here. You've heard that Tatung is the wickedest city in China?"

"I've certainly heard it said."

"If you had been here as long as I have, you wouldn't doubt it, Miss Ball. Ninety per cent of the city's population has venereal disease. Many have gonorrhea and syphilis at the same time."

"Then all the city's hospitals must be kept terribly busy," Mary commented.

The doctor's short laugh was ironic. "There is none but ours. Except for Dr. Bryan Brown and myself, there are no qualified doctors, either."

It hardly seemed possible. Mary wondered how one small hospital of sixty beds could be made to cope with the needs of nearly one hundred thousand people.

She said abruptly, "This poor soul—has she been given treatment?"

"Emergency treatment," the doctor said. "Her stomach has been pumped and now she has to be kept on her feet and on the move."

She followed the doctor out of the outpatients' department. As they were climbing the stairs, he said: "There's another thing. Even though we're the only hospital, most of the city people won't come to us—look on us as foreign devils, not to be trusted. So far, the only women patients who have come to us from the city have been—like the one you just saw—out of the local brothels."

Dr. Hall, nodding, excused himself to go on about his rounds. Presently the Bishop came looking for Mary.

"Well, have you changed your mind about liking it here?"

"Oh, no!" She was still disturbed. She still carried in her memory a picture of the sadly tormented young woman who had found life too harsh to go on with.

"There is much more to think about than the bracing air and the flowers," the Bishop said dryly.

"Yes; there is a great deal to be done." She added with some passion: "Why haven't the city people accepted us? Why don't they trust us?"

The Bishop sighed. His eyes searched into hers almost with approval. "Do you happen to know why we built the hospital in Tatung?"

Mary shook her head.

"Back in 1917 they had a most serious epidemic of bubonic plague here," the Bishop said. "The city had no means of combating it. After the plague, after many hundreds had died, the Shansi Government asked us to build a hospital here. They gave us the use of this land and we built the hospital on it.

"But before that, while the plague was still raging, a team of doctors was sent up from the Peking Union Medical College to help fight it. They had to use drastic measures. To prevent the plague spreading, the dead were wrapped in sheeting by the doctors and taken out by medical teams to beyond the wall and burned.

"Normally, the Chinese here take great pains to send off their dead in their approved manner. They dress the body, often in several layers of clothes, to provide for all weathers in the hereafter. They leave food by the body so it will not go hungry. And they burn a paper to tell heaven that a soul is coming, believing that otherwise it will float in a perpetual purgatory.

"But our teams of doctors had made these ritual precautions impossible to carry out. This set the whole town against foreigners and—when it was built—against the hospital run by foreigners."

The Bishop sighed softly. "The people here desperately need all the help we can give them. . . . You do see the problem?"

"Of course," Mary said. "We must find the way to win back their trust before our real work can properly begin."

Now, at last, the Bishop smiled at her.

"Exactly. Perhaps it will not come about in my life-time, but —did you know—it is the long-range policy of the S.P.G. eventually to have the hospital staffed and run entirely by the Chinese themselves."

He cleared his throat, almost formally.

"Miss Ball," he said, "I'd be most pleased if you would stay here and help out. I can promise you this: that you will find the local people very strange at first and difficult to work amongst, and you will find it very hard at times to compromise with your own conscience. But if you can bend without breaking, I know you can help us to win our way in the end."

* * *

CHAPTER IV

T HE city, itself, was very near to the northern tip of Shansi
Province. It was close to the Great Wall, close to Mongolia,
close enough to the great wasteland of the Gobi. Once, it had
been the capital of the dreaded Ghengis Khan; and, when it was
known as Tenduc, Marco Polo visited there.

To Mary, the city seemed to have survived nearly intact out
of its own distant past. It still had its ancient Drum Tower from
which the drums beat at sundown for the city's great gates to
shut and its Bell Tower from which the bells tolled at dawn for
them to open again; though, now, the drums beat and the bells
tolled in the—after all—not so infrequent times of martial
law.

The city had a feeling of great remoteness, but it was on the
ancient trade routes to India and even Arabia and other far
places, so that it pulsed with a mystic movement which also
made continuity with the passing centuries. Trains of sneering
camels still came through the mountains from Tibet, from Mongolia, and from the distant desert places. They came as well from
the coal mines where sweating men bent to their pick-axes almost
in sight of Tatung's parapets.

The camel caravans came, heavily laden with lime and sulphur
and rare wools and coal and the rock-hard bricks of tea which
were used as a kind of inter-tribal currency. They came and they
paused, adding colour to the grey brick city, and passed through
to the inner world of China.

In the city, in the barracks on and behind its walls, lived
the mercenaries, the troops of the garrison. Beyond the city,
along the trails of commerce, preyed the roaming bands of cut-
throat brigands.

And, in the city, gambling was a raging fever; there was a

32

brothel in nearly every compound; and smoking of opium was indulged in as freely as cigarettes in the England which now seemed more than a world away. "In their utter lack of medical services," Mary wrote to a friend at home, "the people have no way to kill pain but opium. No wonder that they have become addicted to it!"

She was sometimes exhilarated and often appalled by her almost daily discoveries. She felt an urgency to learn all she could of the city and its people, and in that search she found another reason why foreigners were held at arm's length.

The reason was a middle-aged, stubbily-built and doubtless well-meaning American woman named Anna Holt, who had come fervid-eyed to Tatung in 1924 to set up her own funda-mentalist mission. She never seemed to want for money. When-ever the need arose, she merely rubbed her lamp and a Far Western genie provided funds.

Thus, when she found the compound she wanted in the heart of the city, with plenty of land and the shell of a former granary, she could lay down cash for the lease. When she wanted the granary rebuilt into a church with capacity to seat five hundred, she had it done and called it The Holiness Mission.

Her apparently limitless source of funds enabled her to take a risky short cut, also, in building a congregation: she bought one with food. 'Rice Christians', they were called in China; and after enticing them into her fold by gifts, Miss Holt put them through concentrated Bible courses.

Most convincingly, she often had dreams of 'spiritual instruc-tion'. When she began The Holiness Mission, she believed in baptism by immersion: rubbed her lamp and had a large tank for the purpose put into the church in place of an altar. Later, she reported, she had had one of her dreams. An angel had told her that baptism by immersion was unnecessary.

After that, her meetings were conducted so as to develop in emotional pitch to a climax of shouting and frenzied movement. Now she was convinced that unless her converts were completely overwhelmed by 'the visitation of the Holy Spirit' they were not converted at all.

Her very success in this ultimately brought about her downfall in Tatung. An elderly Chinese preacher had joined Miss Holt's fundamentalist group; and one night, soon after he had come into her camp, she had preached on the text from St. Luke: "He shall give his angels charge over thee, to keep thee: And in *their* hands they shall bear thee up, lest at any time thou dash thy foot against a stone." Developing her theme, she worked herself and her congregation up to fever pitch. Finally, in his transplanted frenzy, the elderly preacher shouted that the Holy Spirit had moved him. He would *prove* that what Miss Holt said was true.

Before he could be stopped, he rushed out to the south wall of the city and threw himself over. The wall was forty or more feet high and no miracle saved him. He was instantly killed.

From that moment, Anna Holt's rice converts turned their backs on The Holiness Mission. The five hundred seats remained unfilled. The city had found further justification for its antagonistic stand in regard to the foreign devils.

Yet Mary felt that in the long run it was not so much the Anna Holts but the indigenous problems she must learn to understand and to live with.

"This is a city of mixed influences," she wrote home. "There is the Mongol influence, from beyond the Great Wall, where one woman can have as many husbands as she chooses; and the Chinese influence, where a man with money can get as many wives as he can afford to keep. Women and children are often bought and sold and this, too, is merely taken for granted.

"Immorality hangs over the city like a thick fog which seems to penetrate every sphere of life. Peking people and even our Shansi nurses say Tatung is worse morally than any town they know.

"I don't know what we can do about the girls engaged in brothels. Probably our greatest difficulty would be in making contact with these girls, and I know that if one wishes to leave her master the difficulty arises that the man is unwilling to let her go. Not long ago a girl was in hospital suffering from venereal disease. She was anxious to leave the life she had been forced into. We tried to get the girl released, but our efforts were rewarded by the brothel master taking her out of our hands. In an hour, all trace of her had vanished. We never saw her again.

"Superstitions of all kinds prevail. A woman brought her little boy to the outpatients'. He had a scar on his head, just where the anterior fontanel would have been.

" 'What is the scar?' I asked.

" 'That is where we let the devil out,' the mother replied. 'When he was born he had a devil which kept tapping at this place in his head. We made a hole and let the devil out so he could not cause the child to have fits and die.'

"It was, of course, merely the pulsing of the brain she could see. I have noticed quite a number of children with the scar since.

"How can I ever learn to understand these people and hold back at what seems such barbarism? But I shall *have* to learn if I am to be effective in my work. It seems very strange to me to have to call on God to help me keep from crying out against un-Christian ways!"

The matron at the hospital at the time of Mary's arrival was Isabel Garnett, a dark-complexioned woman of middle age who wore a chronic look of anxiety that came from vision even her thick-lensed eyeglasses could not altogether help.

But, a week after Mary came to Tatung, Miss Garnett left for a long furlough in England. A New Zealand nurse, Kathleen Hall, took her place, only to be sent off herself within a month to take over the S.P.G. hospital in Ho Chien, south of Peking.

Thus Mary became acting matron before she had settled in, and certainly while she still had a great deal to learn.

One special problem she soon had to cope with arose from a disease dreaded by the local women. In its advanced stages, it made normal childbirth impossible. It resulted in a seemingly endless chain of still births—Mary heard of one woman who had ten—and in countless tortured deaths during impassable labour.

The disease was ostramalicia, a calcium deficiency ailment; and it had its origins in the faulty diet due to an extreme poverty that made existence itself marginal. In an area where there was seldom enough food to go round (and where girl children were barely tolerated by their fathers) it was always the men who called the tune and the women who finally paid the piper. They had to be satisfied with what was left after their male masters had chosen the best of a poor larder. Considering that even the men had to make do during the long winters on salt vegetables, this left the women badly off indeed. Only during the Chinese New Year, the Dragon Festival and the Moon Festival did any meat appear in the kitchen.

When a woman became pregnant, she was further deprived by the selfish new life forming within her womb. Her small store of calcium went into its shaping bones. Then it was that the deficiency became acute.

First thrown out of pivot by her peculiarly mincing walk (caused by the still universally practised foot-binding) the mother's pelvis soon became grotesquely malformed. Sometimes, if she was one of a lucky minority, she was able to bear one or even two children in the normal way, though invariably they suffered from pre-natal rickets; but with each confinement the disease worsened. If the first normally-born baby was a girl, she began life on the calcium-deficient milk of her mother (though a boy rated a hired wet nurse). Thus the vicious, woman-wasting cycle seemed destined to sustain itself forever.

A short time after Mary became acting matron, the hospital had its first woman patient from the city who had not been the inmate of a brothel—a Mrs. Wong. She had come to have a baby by Cæsarean section because of the common local complaint.

Before this confinement, Mrs. Wong had given normal birth to two sons, and with such a record to fall back upon she did not feel unduly insecure when, this time, her baby was a daughter— in spite of the local prejudice against girl children.

But when her husband came to see how she was progressing and learned of the sex of the latest offspring, he flew into an unreasoning rage and stormed out of the hospital.

Next day, he returned, bringing with him a broad-faced Mongol merchant named Tsai. And, later, when Mary stopped at Mrs. Wong's bedside, she found the poor woman's face streaked with the tracks of tears.

"Why are you so unhappy?" Mary asked sympathetically.

The woman, moaning, turned her face away.

"What is it, Mrs. Wong?" Mary prompted. "Are you in pain?"

At last, in a voice broken by sobs, the woman cried out: "He sold me, he sold me!" And, after a fresh storm of weeping: "He has taken the two boys and now I have to go to a new home!"

Mary, finding no practical way to console or help her, recognized this as one of the countless frustrations the Bishop had promised her; but it was far more than a mere frustration for Mrs. Wong, who cried quietly to herself for two days. At last, numbed and weary, she told Mary that she had resigned herself to her future.

"*Mei yu fa tzu,*" she murmured. "There is no way out."

When her impassive new husband, Tsai, came to collect her, he brought his three other wives. His number one wife ranged her eyes over her newest rival as if she had just been delivered from the cattle market.

"What is the use of having an invalid in the house who cannot work?" she sneered.

Tsai said nothing. No doubt he was reflecting with some satisfaction that this new woman had already proven her fertility, while none of his three wives had been able to give him a single child. Since they had each failed in the duty they owed him, what matter if they were hurt by what he did?

Soon after this, perhaps because the news had spread of Mrs. Wong's successful delivery, despite her acute ostramalicia, another woman came from the city asking for a Cæsarean section.

She had, however, waited to put her trust in the hospital until much too late: she had been several days in labour before applying. As a result, she died of septicaemia on her third day in the women's ward.

Unfortunately, her husband, an ignorant man, failed to take into account his wife's tardiness in seeking the help of the foreign devils. He took her body out of the mortuary and laid it out on the ground in the hospital garden.

He cried out for the Chinese people going to and coming from the hospital to approach and see his dead wife with their own eyes.

He cried out for them to come, and when they came he waved his arms supplicatingly towards heaven and cried: "Chih ke wai kuo jen chih ssu la wo ti tai-tai. These foreigners have killed my wife." Then he entered the outpatients' waiting room and climbed up on a bench to denounce the hospital and its foreign doctors.

"This is what they do," he wailed, rolling his eyes. "They have killed my wife."

Mary could have wept. Instead of gaining, they seemed to be losing ground.

At a little past noon of a busy day late that autumn, Mary was surprised to see Anna Holt come into the hospital and look around with jerkily anxious movements of her head. Catching sight of Mary, she hurried to her and asked to see Dr. Bryan Brown. She seemed out of breath, as if she had been pushed by some powerful inner command.

"I'm afraid the doctor has gone to lunch," Mary told her. The Superintendent lived in a separate house in the hospital grounds.

Miss Holt appeared to take this as a far more serious frustration than it seemed. She seemed momentarily at a loss, running a hand nervously over her greying hair.

"It's very important that I see him, Miss Ball," she said. "Very important, you see. Do you think Mrs. Bryan Brown would understand if I interrupted his lunch?"

Mary did not much like the thought of inconveniencing Mrs. Bryan Brown at lunch time, for she was an amiable woman who had four very young children with priority demands on her attention. But Anna Holt had a purpose in her eyes that would not be delayed.

"I suppose if it's really important . . ." she began, and Miss Holt was on her way. As Mary watched the chunky figure hurrying towards the Superintendent's house, she could not help but wonder what it was this time that the fundamentalist missionary was up to; and could not help but hope that it would not result in a further lowering of prestige—low enough already—of Tatung's 'foreign devils'.

When Dr. Bryan Brown returned from his lunch, he hurried to speak to her.

"Miss Ball," he asked, "did you by any chance happen to see Miss Holt earlier?"

He was a tall man, with penetrating dark eyes and, during the warmer months when he kept himself clean-shaven looked more the successful banker or businessman than the medical missionary. But he was more than ordinarily sensitive to cold weather and at this time had just begun to grow a beard to help him withstand Tatung's below zero winter.

"Yes, she came down to the outpatients' before she went to see you," Mary answered. "I hope she wasn't a bother."

"No, no, no," the Superintendent said, shaking his head in remembered disbelief. Then he scratched at the stubble of his new beard. "It's the most amazing thing! She's had another of her dreams. In this one she has been told to make haste and leave the city and shake the dust from off her feet. Those were her words! She seems to believe that disaster is coming, but doesn't appear to think her message applies to any but herself. . . . She wanted me to take on her compound in the city!"

"'Take it on', Dr. B.B.? How do you mean?"

He shook his head again, still caught up in amazement.

"She wanted to *give* it to me, personally, for my own use. Of course, I told her I couldn't accept. I suggested that the S.P.G. might buy up the remainder of her lease and make use of the buildings." His voice trailed off and he looked at Mary oddly.

"I wonder. . . . Miss Ball, do you think it could be possible?"

"Could *what* be possible, doctor?"

"That the disaster is the one that has already occurred to her—not one that is to come?"

Mary thought of the Chinese preacher who had thrown himself to his death over the city's wall.

"I wonder," she mused. "I think you may be right."

And, whatever the reason, by the year's end Anna Holt had indeed shaken the dust of Tatung from off her feet and returned whence she came—the Pacific coast of the United States of America.

An obstacle which kept Mary from reaching far into the Chinese mind was her still faulty grasp of the language. She was often forced to grope for words and to detour around what she wished to say. Besides, the general vocabulary she had memorized in Peking had omitted many words in everyday use in the hospital.

Fortunately, a big-boned Mongol girl nurse named Bridget Tung spoke English fluently and was eager to help.

Often Mary would catch up with Miss Tung in the wards. "What do you call this?" she would ask, touching a sheet.

"*Ta tan tzu.*"

Mary would repeat it.

"And this?" She would indicate a padded quilt.

"*Pei wo.*"

"*Pei wo,*" Mary would say. "*Pei wo. Pei wo.* And what is the word for 'heart'?"

"The word for 'heart' is *hsin,*" Miss Tung would tell her earnestly.

"Thank you, Bridget," Mary would say, and she would go about her duties, muttering the new words under her breath until she felt that they were firmly fixed in her mind. But, because she was not yet confident of her ability fully to understand all that was said to her—especially in the peasant dialect known as 'earth talk'—she tried to have Miss Tung with her whenever she thought an error in communication with a Chinese patient might have serious consequences.

And she had another reason: she had become aware that some of the city people were not above trying to use her ignorance to further their own personal ends.

But surely the main problem was not in the long view insurmountable, Mary thought. If the people in the city mistrusted foreigners so much that they would not come to the hospital when they should, then she had better go to them. It might take time, but she would start by making purely social visits: perhaps that would make them see that she was not quite the red-haired foreign devil they thought her. Perhaps if she could prove to their satisfaction that one foreigner was harmless, they might reason that others might be harmless, too; and then, perhaps, they would think of the hospital when they were ill not as a place to shun but to come to for help.

One sunny autumn morning, still crisp with the previous night's frost, she went into the city to call on a Miss Chang with whom she had become friendly; and she noticed that part of the compound was decorated with paper pennants and bunting. Over a cup of tea, she asked what the decorations signified.

Miss Chang smiled. She was a gentle young woman and her smile was softly pleasant with white teeth partly showing.

"There is to be a wedding here today," she said in her murmuring voice. "Would you like to meet Almond Blossom, the bride?"

Mary said she would, and was at once taken to her, a small and pretty girl dressed for the ceremony in an embroidered scarlet satin costume and coral tiara. She was seated, head bowed and eyes downcast, on the family *k'ang*—the wide brick bed with its built-in oven for cold nights. Beside her on the bed was her mother-in-law, wizened at forty, all in black satin with her black cap encrusted with seed pearls.

"How old are you, Almond Blossom?" Mary asked, seeking an opening.

"She's eighteen, she's eighteen," the mother-in-law interjected; for at such a time the bride was not supposed to speak for herself.

Trying to repair her error, Mary addressed herself to the older woman.

"You have a beautiful daughter-in-law," she said.

The woman snorted. "She is very ugly indeed!"

It would have been grossly impolite for her to admit otherwise.

Mary thought that the girl looked utterly disconsolate, never glancing up, never letting so much as the flicker of an expression cross her face, which had been painstakingly prepared for the ceremony: first with a heavy layer of white powder and over that a bright rouge. A bare square of skin had been plucked in her front hair. It would be kept that way all her married life.

Mary wished the bride and mother-in-law happiness and left them. On the way back through the compound, Miss Chang pointed out the groom, a lad of about sixteen, pacing restlessly back and forth in the courtyard.

"He must not see Almond Blossom before they are married," she whispered.

"Is that why he looks so sad?"

"Oh, no!" Miss Chang giggled softly. "He is *supposed* to be sad now because he is leaving his youth behind."

Several weeks had passed by, when Miss Tung hurried into the men's ward to find Mary. She said that a Mr. Fang had come to the outpatients' department to ask for 'the foreign woman doctor'.

"He means you, Miss Ball," the girl nurse said.

"Did he say what he wants?"

"Yes: for you to go quickly with him as his wife is very sick."

When she reached the outpatients' department, Mary was startled to discover that the Mr. Fang was the bridegroom. She also felt within herself a faint flutter of hope. Was her visiting in the city beginning to reap its reward?

"What is the matter with Almond Blossom?" she asked Fang.

He wrung his hands. "She has swallowed opium." He looked singularly young and frightened. Mary's heart went out to him in sympathy.

"Then call rickshaws quickly," she told him, and dashed off to throw the things she might need—including a stomach pump —into a bag. She remembered how miserable Almond Blossom had appeared to be on the day of her wedding and fleetingly wondered what, in her short span of married life, had made existence seem so intolerable as to inspire a suicide attempt. Mary knew by now that the life of the women of North Shansi was very hard and that they too often sought this escape from it, but each time she heard of such a case she was plunged into fresh sadness.

When her bag was ready, Mary on the fly asked Miss Tung to go with her into the city. They drove off, out of the hospital compound, through the North Gate and down the bustling Great North Street full of oxen, mules, carts, and turned off at the lane leading into the compound where she had met Almond Blossom.

As they came to the gateway and climbed out of the rickshaws, Miss Tung said in a stage whisper made purposely loud for Fang's ears: "You see the burnt ashes from the paper, Miss Ball?" She pointed to a small heap of ashes near the compound entrance. "She is already dead."

Fang had not paused to listen. In nervous haste, he was already within the compound. Mary and Miss Tung hurried quickly to catch up with him, then followed him into the room where Almond Blossom, arrayed incongruously in her scarlet wedding dress, was stretched out on the k'ang with a handkerchief over her face.

Beside the bed was a dish. It was filled with small pieces of steamed bread, each one marked with a scarlet dot.

Turning angrily upon Fang, Miss Tung snapped: "Why have you brought us when your wife is already dead?"

"Oh, she's not dead; she's not dead," the boy whined, his eyes darting away from her accusing stare. "Why should I worry you if she had already died? All I want is for the doctor to give her an injection and she'll be well again."

He snatched the handkerchief from his wife's face and turned to Mary, showing his back to Miss Tung.

"Give her the injection!" he pressed desperately.

"I can't do that since she's dead," Mary said, shaking her head sadly. By now she knew enough of local laws and customs to make a shrewd appreciation of Fang's motives—which she was later able to substantiate.

He had quarrelled, violently and bitterly, with his young wife; and as a result of the quarrel she had killed herself with the usual overdose of opium. In such cases in China, the law could be used to establish guilt and exact punishment; and the boy husband had been plunged into an agony of fear, of virtual certainty, that Almond Blossom's parents would bring a suit against him to determine responsibility for her death. He had leapt at the idea of transferring the blame—and the lawsuit—over to the foreign hospital.

Mary wondered in despair: *Will this always be their only use for us?*

She was ready to seize upon any ray of hope which might lead to the hospital being accepted more by the people of Tatung. And when, early in October, Dr. Bryan Brown returned from a visit to Peking, he brought news that gave promise of making a chink in the darkness. A Chinese doctor would soon be joining the hospital staff—a Dr. Francis Li.

"He is a protégé of the Bishop's," the Superintendent explained, almost apologetically. "When the Bishop was headmaster at the *Chung Te* School in Peking, Li was one of his pupils; then, as a scholarship boy, he went on to Peking Union Medical College. After qualifying, he assisted at a small Peking hospital, but he didn't get on there. In fact, he quit medicine to return to Liu Hua Tien, in Ho Pei Province, where his family had land. He farmed for a year or two.

"The Bishop felt badly at his waste of medical training. When I asked for more help up here, he suggested Li—I fancy to see how he'd work out in a country hospital after his Peking failure."

"About how old is he now?" Mary wanted to know.

"Somewhere in his late thirties, I would judge. The Bishop asked me particularly to give you this background about him. He also said to tell you that Dr. Li is of a very independent mind: we'll all have to be very patient with him."

"I quite understand," Mary said, remembering that the Bishop had confided to her the long-range plan for the hospital's future: that it would one day be handed over to an all-Chinese staff. She wondered if Dr. Li was to be the first hesitant step in that direction. "Is there anything I can do to prepare for his coming?"

"Well, though Dr. Li is married and has children, he isn't bringing his family to Tatung for the present. I wonder if you'd mind finding a room for him and getting some furniture together for it?"

Buoyed up by the prospect of Dr. Li's coming, Mary set aside a semi-basement room for him, next to that of Mr. Liu, the catechist, and made sure that it was adequately furnished. Bearing in mind the Bishop's message, she resolved that no matter how difficult Dr. Li might prove to be, she would get along well with him.

But when he arrived, she liked him at once.

He was, in fact, quite shy, hiding behind his Oriental reserve. His sensitive face was long and thin, but firm-jawed; and he was quite tall for a Chinese, almost six feet, and carried no excess weight. His movements were almost languid. But he seemed at times to hold himself altogether aloof, and then he appeared to take notice of no one around him even when making his ward rounds in his black Chinese gown.

Since his special interest was surgery, Dr. B.B. (as Mary had come to refer to Dr. Bryan Brown) soon made him his assistant at operations and put him on the surgical cases in the outpatients' department.

Yet, despite his reserve, Dr. Li appeared to have a mystic quality which made others take instinctively to him. Mr. Nikulin, the Russian engineer, greeted him with an effusion of smiles. Mr. Liu formed an instant admiration for him. And when Dr. Li showed Mr. Chang, a rough and uneducated Shansi peasant, how to take blood counts and perform certain other tests, the new laboratory assistant shone up to the Chinese doctor like an over-eager puppy.

One side to his nature troubled Mary a little: if the new doctor was withdrawn in respect to his personality, the same could also be said of his attitude towards the practice of his profession. "But Francis believed in the inevitability of gradualness," she was to say in his defence, years later. "He was also a strange mixture of old and new, ancient and modern. He had had very good training under first-class doctors, but he combined this with what he had picked up from the ancient Chinese medical traditions."

There was a wild, low scrub bush in the Tatung area that bore bright red berries: these he crushed for juice and made into tonics. He brought in *Ma Huang* grass, from which he extracted ephedrine for the treatment of respiratory ailments. And he clung to the centuries-old Chinese practice of using the dried and powdered membrane from the human afterbirth as a specific for the ailments peculiar to women, especially menstrual disorders. This last remedy he did not use in the hospital, but only for treating the private patients which he was allowed to have.

But it was her discovery that Dr. Li was at times extraordinarily casual towards some of his duties that disturbed Mary. Soon after coming to the hospital he performed a Cæsarean section on a Mrs. Shang. Three days later, checking up on her wound, Mary found it to be considerably inflamed. She hurried downstairs to knock at Dr. Li's bedroom door.

"*Lai.* Come in."

Opening the door, she found him cross-legged on a brightly-coloured mat—a large yellow tiger with a lolling red tongue against a fawn background. He was wearing his usual black robe and a round, black satin Mandarin hat; and he was smoking a pipe of vile-smelling tobacco.

"Dr. Li, I'd like you to come and see Mrs. Shang's wound. It's not looking at all well."

He nodded, but did not rise, and kept puffing quickly on his pipe.

He said: "Well, I don't (puff) think I need (puff, puff) to come and see Mrs. Shang's wound. If I look at it (puff, puff) I can do it no more good than you can. You'd better (puff) just put some iodine on it and (puff) dress it again."

"But, doctor—"

"You can do it (puff, puff) just as well."

And he would not come: she could not persuade him. Nor did she mention his refusal to Dr. Bryan Brown. She thought she had begun to comprehend the Chinese trait of leaving so many subtle things unsaid and she hoped that Dr. Li in some inscrutable way was paying her a compliment. But she knew that it was equally possible that he was merely lazy.

Nevertheless, his very presence in the hospital gave her more of the opportunities she wanted the better to know the people outside. It was, for instance, because of him that she dared wangle from two Swedish evangelical missionaries of the China Inland Mission an invitation to accompany them far into the hinterland for several days. The destination was T'uan Pu, a village a hundred and twenty Chinese li—about forty miles—from Tatung. Mary took Nurse Tung to help her and they set out, the two Swedish ladies on horseback, Mary and Bridget in a mule-drawn cart.

"We came to T'uan Pu at four o'clock of the second afternoon," Mary reported later, "and at once the news spread of our arrival. Everyone was so friendly it was difficult not to offend by refusing to eat all the queer dishes we were offered."

Next day, nearly the entire village crowded round Mary and her assistant, demanding to be examined. After a hasty consultation, the two women decided to charge two coppers each in order to weed out the merely curious, and this did somewhat stem the tide. But one old lady paid her money and then whispered confidentially: "I have no illness—I've just come to see!"

Mary let her have a good look round and she went happily away.

"I feel as if we're running a peep-show!" Mary said to Miss Tung with a wry smile.

Most of the patients they examined had serious eye trouble and many were far past medical help, but the two women washed their eyes and did what they could. Because of the colder weather, quite a number of the villagers had bronchitis. Nearly all were afflicted with scabies. Mary and Miss Tung stayed from the Tuesday to the Friday and saw sixty patients, all of whom were clearly grateful for such unaccustomed attention.

"We recommended several to come to the hospital," Mary reported when she got back, "but I doubt whether they will. The distance is great for them and the expense beyond their means. Yet they now know, as many did not before, that we do have a hospital here."

And she wrote home: "This has been a wonderful experience for me—to have the opportunity to assist those far from medical help, to get to know the people better, and to help overcome some of their fears. I do want to go into the villages again."

But then the cruel winter of the northern plateau sealed off the villages from the city. It came howling in with its knife-edged winds and temperatures plummeting down to fifteen below zero, bringing quite a number of frost-bite cases to the hospital.

For the first time in her life, Mary was often lonely. Not that she found her work any the less absorbing, but she came to realize then that every human must lean on friends for strength through understanding and warmth through sympathy. What she missed most was a woman friend to talk to—someone with a background not far removed from her own. There were the doctors' wives, of course—Mrs. Bryan Brown and Mrs. Hall—but they lived in houses separate from the hospital and in any case were preoccupied with their own families.

That year, as never before, she ate her Christmas dinner without company. She had given Bridget Tung, the only trained girl nurse, time off to spend her Christmas at home. The Bryan Browns—she later learned—had assumed that the Halls, who were soon to leave for a prolonged stay in England, had invited her to join them for the traditional feast; and the Halls, in the midst of packing for their departure, had assumed the same of the Bryan Browns.

Early in the New Year, the Halls left; and, for the while at least, Dr. Francis Li moved up into the post of assistant superintendent.

*　　*　　*

CHAPTER V

THERE were times during her first Tatung winter when it seemed to Mary that the bleak and bitter season would never end; but by March the snows began to thaw and late in the month she was in the city when, echoing down the muddy main street, she heard an excited call: "*Shuan shusi lai-la!* The mountain water has come!"

It was a cry of purest joy, caught up by others and relayed by them from compound to compound; for it meant that the hard winter had at last really spent itself and melting snow waters were rushing down the rocky steeps, swelling the small streams and roiling the rivers. And it meant that the farmers could at last begin the new season's work, for they would use the water to irrigate their fields of millet which in this austere northern land substituted for rice as the principle subsistence crop.

It was a season of hoping and yet a season of lurking death.

As protection against the freezing winter the Mongols of the district had worn their sheepskin clothing with the fur side soft and warm against the skin; but now the springtime sun was reactivating the crawling hordes of body lice that the unwashed fur had also kept cosy all the winter long.

To deal with that immediate problem, the Mongols now turned their clothing fur side out. Insect parasites by the million dropped to the ground. Then they scurried after new bodies to infest.

The lice were typhus carriers. No one could be sure of escaping them or the often fatal fever they delivered together with their uninvited selves.

But in that contaminated spring of '26 a more fearful plague was abroad. In the outer perimeter of a China still divided, greedy war lords had for some years been preying for power and booty upon one another; and now the pace of their grand-scale banditry quickened, spurred on by a new threat—the Nationalist attempt at consolidation—which might soon succeed and so put a damper on their freelance lawlessness.

With the young Chiang Kai-shek already setting into motion his Northern Expedition, the war lords knew they had to hurry to get their licks in first. One of them was Feng Yu-hsiang, the so-called 'Christian General' who lusted after the booty to be won in northern Shansi by his hymn-singing soldiers.

For some time now there had been a crackling of rumours in Tatung that Feng's army was approaching. Ivan Nikulin, the hospital's stateless engineer, came back from the city one early April day flushed with excitement. He caught at Mary's elbow.

"Miss Ball, have you heard the latest news about the war?"

"What news is that, Nik?"

"Fighting is to break out in three days time!" the engineer announced solemnly.

"And what makes you so sure?"

"Why, everybody's saying it." He was really quite wrought up: Nik's Slav emotions were never very far from the surface. "Everybody's saying it in the city—it must be so."

"Now, calm down a little, Nik."

He stared at her, his face more flushed than ever and his eyes feverishly bright.

"Calm?" he said. "You've never seen it before as I have—the shooting and the killing. How can one be calm in times like these when one hasn't even an embassy to ask protection from?"

"You shouldn't let the rumours upset you, Nik," Mary told him with a soothing smile. "Time enough to get excited when the fighting really begins—if it ever does."

"It will begin in three days," Nik said stubbornly. But he had calmed down a little in spite of himself.

The three days passed and another three and still another. The attack did not come but the 'three days' rumour persisted in the city and from time to time Nik repeated it to her, never failing in his faith that the rumour was true.

And each day there were new signs that the fighting was in fact not long to be delayed. Reinforcements of Shansi troops came to the city and trainloads of them paused at the station beyond the walls of the hospital compound and passed on to other centres. The townspeople lived in a miasmic fear of coming disaster. Of each new fact they made a stepping stone for wild guesses and conjectures.

When sandbags were filled and piled in readiness at the city's gates, Tatung men gathered in buzzing clusters to ask one another whether the bags were meant to keep Feng's mercenary forces from entering or to prevent the defending mercenaries from running away. They debated whether there was enough food in the city in case of siege. They speculated if there would be bombing from the air. They discussed whether or not the ancient walls could withstand direct hits by heavy guns.

"A walk into the city the day before yesterday was very interesting," Mary wrote in a letter home. "The chief street was lined with soldiers, looking very clean and smart in their grey padded clothes, and wearing bright blue puttees. A great official had just arrived from Tai Yuan, the capital of Shansi. All the inns, schools and available shops and even temples are filled with soldiers.

"Food and other commodities are going up in price, and the shopkeepers' stores are getting low because of the want of supplies, which are not getting here from Peking.

"Indeed, even from the hospital itself we can see the gathering signs of war. The operating room windows give us a fine view of the soldiers' parade ground, next to our compound, where all the usual drills and goose steps are often on display. The arms of the Shansi men are a wonderful mixture of modern field-guns and old-fashioned spears such as you see in pictures of the Crusaders —but of very little use, I should think, in war today against the better-equipped soldiers of Feng's army. Each day we are told that 'in three days time' the fighting will start, so that we are beginning to get used to the idea and take but little notice."

Then a rumour reached Mary's ears that she could not ignore: that the city's gates were to be closed and no one was to be allowed in or out. She was responsible for the hospital's food supply. If the city were sealed tight, where would supplies come from?

She decided to stock up, but when she went to make the necessary arrangements she was told that the officer in charge of the city's commissary had just ruled that no one person could take more than a pound of foodstuffs beyond the wall in any one day. At once, Mary organized the hospital staff, giving each member of it instructions to visit the city every day and bring out his pound of rations. This, of course, was no better than a stop-gap: it would not build up the hospital's reserves: but it was all that could be done.

Thus food loomed very importantly in Mary's calculations just then. It was uppermost in the minds of all.

Perhaps the pressure of this common worry was what made Dr. Li momentarily drop his reserve. One afternoon he sauntered in his customary languid way into the office where for the tenth time Mary was going over the inventory of hospital supplies.

She looked up, sighing. If the war really did come to Tatung, there was no doubt about it: they would be caught short of food unless unforeseen sources were discovered. Mary's clear skin was pale against her Cambridge blue nurses' dress; there were tell-tale shadows of beginning weariness under her eyes.

"Yes, Dr. Li?"

Rather hesitantly, he put a pound packet of rice on the desk. He pushed it towards her.

"I had a friend in the city who gave this to me," he said, dropping his eyes. "Since it was in addition to the pound I was allowed, I had quite a business to get it through the guard at the gate." He shrugged to belittle what he had done, smiling wryly; he looked at her but then his eyes flicked away again. "I told him it was for the foreign lady at the hospital—so I thought you ought to have it."

"I really can't take this. . . ."

"It is yours, Miss Ball." There was a new firmness in Dr. Li's voice, and Mary realized then that he had brought the rice as a gift for her in the first instance and had no intention of letting his plan go awry. The low spirits which had been hovering over her suddenly lifted. She could no longer doubt that Dr. Li both liked and respected her; at least *one* Chinese had been won over.

"I am pleased to accept," she said, picking up the small packet of rice with a smile. "I'm really very grateful for this."

"No, no," Dr. Li said, embarrassed. "It is really nothing at all." He backed quickly away, losing his languor.

Half an hour later, he passed by her in a corridor with his head held high, a black lacquer walking-stick limply in his hand, pretending as hard as he was able not to notice her.

It was in such an atmosphere—when the talk of war and the fear of war and the confused preparations for war had been stirred into a restless vapour over Tatung—that Etheldreda Fisher arrived at the hospital, on April 13th, for a purely social visit with Mary. She had come up from Peking with the Rev. P. M. Scott, who had been assigned to take over for the S.P.G. Anna Holt's onetime Holiness Mission—now known as *Nan Tang*, the South Hall.

Miss Fisher's announced intention was to remain as Mary's guest for one week—no more—taking the time off from her duties as vice-principal of a Peking theological college for Chinese women. She was a small and tidy woman in her early thirties, fresh-faced and attractive; and she was always ready to reach out for laughter. It was that infectious gaiety which had first attracted Mary when she had attended Peking's language school. In that city the two had become friends.

Until the moment of Etheldreda's appearance at the outpost hospital, Mary had not realized quite how much she had come to miss the companionship of women of her own age and background, if only to discuss the pleasures and problems of the work that absorbed her. She was fond of Edith Bryan Brown, but the Superintendent's wife was preoccupied by her own different interests. Thus Etheldreda's arrival buoyed Mary up on a kind of delight she tried to forget was only temporary. The week would surely flit by all too soon.

She could not have calculated that War Lord Feng would immediately force a drastic change in Etheldreda's plans. In fact,

little Miss Fisher's train was the last one out of Peking: on April
14th, the 'Christian General' and his advancing forces cut the
line halfway between Peking and Tatung.

When the news reached the hospital and Mary passed it on to
her friend, Etheldreda frowned, cleared her throat, tilted her head
back—and suddenly grinned.

"Well, if I can't go, I shall have to stay," she said.

She might not have treated the news of her enforced stay so
lightly had she known how long it would last and what dangers
she would be compelled to face during it.

The north gate of Tatung was situated diagonally across a field
about a hundred and fifty yards wide which separated the city
wall from the hospital compound. Out of it passed the road
which led north, through the walled area (and the soldiers'
drilling ground) that was once the Manchu city, to the railway
station beyond. The chances were that when Feng's men came it
would be by rail; they would swoop to the attack from the
direction of the station; and then the hospital would be in a
particularly vulnerable position, squeezed between the attackers
and the defenders. This self-evident situation had long ago
occurred to the Chinese members of the hospital staff. They
certainly knew that they would be safer almost anywhere else.

Thus it was greatly to their credit that the male nurses turned
down an offer to join the Shansi army as 'doctors' at higher than
hospital pay. Only the dispenser defected, and Mary, shrugging
her slender shoulders—added his duties to her many others.

Yet the offer helped bring the reality of war closer to her, even
against the counterpoint of Nik's continuing 'three days until
the fighting begins' forecast, which by now had become a running
hospital joke.

Towards the end of April, a delegation of Shansi medical corps
officers made a formal call to ask if the Mosse Memorial Hospital
would take in wounded from the front. In exchange, they offered
—for some time in the indefinite future—supplies of food. Dr.
Bryan Brown and Mary conferred, then quickly agreed to the
proposal.

They would still have done so even had they then known—as they were later sadly to learn—that the promise of food would never be implemented.

Now Mary had to find extra beds, and extra room, to take care of the expected influx of Shansi wounded. She solved the space problem easily enough by transferring all the girl nurses-in-training and all the women patients to the house on the hospital compound left empty by the departure of Dr. Hall and his family. What to do about extra beds was more of a poser, which she finally settled in desperation by having boards put across trestles. Then she and the others waited for the wounded to come.

The first of these was not, as it turned out, a battle casualty. Indeed, Chiang Hsing Pang was a Shansi peasant-turned-soldier of surpassing ignorance in the tools of his new trade. He had taken a grenade to bed with him, the bed being a k'ang hot from its built-in oven. When, not unnaturally, the charge exploded, he suffered severe wounds in his legs, an arm and his head.

Fortunately, the victim recovered—but not before every member of the hospital staff had heard him muttering over and over again his half-bewildered, half-angry protests at the grenade for having so cruelly repaid his kindness.

After all, hadn't he gone out of his way to take it with him to his hot bed on a cold night?

At long last—not until the third week in May—word came that Feng's advance guard was approaching the city. Miss Tung came to Mary on her own behalf and that of the nurses-in-training. She was beside herself with fear.

"Please, Miss Ball," she begged, "arrange for us to go into the city! We can put up with the thought of dying, but we think it would not mean merely death."

"I'll see what I can do," Mary promised. Then she saw that she had not said enough. "Don't worry, Bridget; I'm sure it can be arranged."

She went at once to consult Dr. Bryan Brown and found him quite disturbed at the probable events to come.

"I quite agree," he said, tight-lipped, when she repeated Miss Tung's request. "I'm worried about Edith and the children as well. We most certainly must send them all in. I'll drop a line to Mr. Scott and ask him if he can care for my family and the girl nurses."

Meanwhile, Mary was wrestling with her own conscience. There was Etheldreda Fisher's safety to consider. She dreaded losing her only close friend: she had grown accustomed to their shared confidences, to Etheldreda's laughter and her disarming way of poking fun at herself. As soon as she left Dr. Bryan Brown, Mary sought her out.

She said: "Look here, I've been thinking things over. Do you have any idea what it may be like here if Feng's army attacks the city?"

For once, the smaller woman was quite serious.

"I've thought about it," she admitted.

Mary swallowed. She knew that what she had to say would likely mean that she would have to face the hard time ahead without her friend. "We're quite likely to be caught in the middle —between the two firing lines," she said.

Etheldreda frowned, nodding.

"Anyone who stays," Mary continued, "will likely be risking her life."

"I know that," Etheldreda said uneasily.

"Well, then," Mary said. "Don't you think you ought to go into the city with the B.B. family? It's sure to be more dangerous here than there."

Their eyes met and for the moment Mary found that she could scarcely breathe. She, herself, would certainly stay on at the hospital in any case, but she would sorely miss her friend's buoyant company.

Etheldreda was looking quite serious and pale. Then, with a small and tentative smile, she shook her head. "No thanks, Mary: I'll just stay on with you."

Mary found it easy to breathe again.

"You're sure?" she pressed, wanting to be absolutely fair.

"Oh, yes; quite sure."

"All right, then," she said briskly. "I think I'd better lend you one of my nurse's uniforms. The hem might need a bit of taking up, but I do think it would be better if you wore one—don't you agree?"

"Yes, but I think I ought to tell you that I'm terrified at the sight of blood. A nurse's uniform isn't going to change *that*. But I do want to help all I can. . . ." Suddenly her nose crinkled and she burst into a trill of laughter. "You can call me Mary's Little Lamb—I'll follow you around and see what I can learn."

That day, Mary knew for certain that the invading forces were drawing near. She knew it by the muffled rumble of gunfire; and she knew it, too, because the Shansi officers who had been admitted as patients wrapped themselves in hospital bedding and rushed off into the city, despite Mary's angry protests and the hysterical pleadings of bed-ridden other ranks not to leave them behind.

But they *were* left behind, shivering in their blankets with terror, moaning that Feng's men would surely kill them when they came, or dismember them or, at the very least, toss them into dungeons and let them starve. This was on May 19th, a Wednesday.

Late each night Mary snatched at moments to keep her diary up to date.

She wrote: "*Thursday*. Dr. Li was warded with a slight fever, and also two of our men nurses. We sent home as many of our men patients as we could. . . .

"*Friday*. Miss Fisher has taken ill—nothing serious—but this has made the day a very busy one for me as there is a great deal to arrange and we are very short staffed. I have come to depend on her a great deal.

"*Saturday*. We moved Mrs. Bryan Brown and the children to *Nan Tang* where Mr. Scott is living. Etheldreda, looking out of her window, found the procession into the city quite comic. She can find the lighter side of almost anything! No carts could be had as all had been commandeered to carry ammunition and supplies for the soldiers, so after great searching we procured one rickshaw into which Mrs. Bryan Brown climbed with two children. Then came Mr. Scott pushing two children in the pram, then Dr. Bryan Brown convoying them on a bicycle with parcels tied on it like decorations on a Christmas tree. Four coolies with poles carried boxes of clothes and the baby's cot. It was impossible to get into the city without an arm band so we hastily made Red Cross armlets for them all, stamped with the hospital's name. Dr. B.B. must have hated to come back, leaving his loved ones behind, but they will be safer in the city. This evening we got our first battle casualties.

"*Whitsunday.* Before early church, I received a message from Dr. B.B.'s house in the compound saying he was ill and could not come up to the hospital. Miss Hung, our woman catechist, was taken extremely ill. We have small hopes of her recovery. We hear typhus fever has broken out in the city's barracks— seventy cases in one barracks and forty in another. Nothing being done for them, or to prevent the spread of the dreadful disease. Dr. Li is not yet back on duty. We also heard that two B.B. children are ill in the city.

"*Monday.* I was up nearly all last night with admissions. We had a Russian man living on the compound, with Shansi army consent, for five days. He said he was trying to get to Kalgan. This evening he was arrested as a spy, and so added to the general excitement.

"*Tuesday.* Today the women nurses became very frightened, and we felt it best to send them at once into the city. Coolies carried Miss Hung and our two other remaining women patients in on stretchers, ankle-deep in mud all the way. Miss Fisher is now able to get up. She still refuses to go into the city.

"*Wednesday.* Loud, continuous firing all night. Wounded continued to pour in and our staff worked excellently. Both doctors now on duty, although neither feel well. Operations in the morning and afternoon. At ten p.m. we heard the Shansi men are in retreat.

"*Thursday, May 27.* Not a sight or sound of anyone on the plain or the roads early this morning. The city gates are now closed. The day began in an air of expectancy and fear, with the male nurses very frightened and the Shansi soldier patients quite

wild with terror. They thought they had good reason: they had
heard—as we did—that Shansi men had been shot by Feng's men
in other hospitals."

At about ten o'clock that morning of May 27th, Mary was
feeling low in her mind because a patient had just died. She was
busying herself with ward duties when she happened to glance
out of the window. She felt the quick, hot shock of fear as she
saw a scattered group of men darting half-crouched across the
parade ground towards the hospital. Numbering about thirty,
they wore blue-grey uniforms and carried rifles in poised readiness. They were the members of a scouting party, and were not
Shansi men.

The first of them angled sharply through the entrance into
the compound. Mary thought, quite ridiculously, of Nik's 'three
days' forecast and that, at last, it had caught up with him.

Then from the ward behind her Mary heard the small whimp-
erings of animal terror. She turned: the Shansi patients had
covered their heads with their bed clothes, under which they
were shaking uncontrollably. She walked past the beds murmuring words of encouragement, trying to conceal her own anxiety.

At one end of the ward, there was an iron door leading to a
fire-escape. Two screens had been placed against it to keep out
draughts. Without warning, the door was flung open, the screens
clattering to the floor.

A soldier in blue-grey lunged through the open doorway into
the ward. A bayonet was fixed to his rifle.

* * *

CHAPTER VI

THE soldier, pushing blindly at the door from outside, was startled by the clatter of the falling screens; but he was visibly shaken at finding himself face to face with a red-haired, pale-skinned nurse—an authentic foreign devil!

Mary was scarcely less taken aback. To help her gather her wits together, she walked to the door and shut it. She replaced the screens. When she turned back, the soldier was still staring at her with flaring eyes. Describing the tableau later, she said: "If the tension had kept up for one more moment, I should have screamed!"

But, to her great relief, just then a harried-looking Dr. Bryan Brown entered the ward, escorting the remainder of the scouting party.

During the ensuing half hour, it became clear that the plans of the enemy scouts did not include murdering the wounded in their beds. Presently, finding themselves neither bayonetted nor shot, some of the Shansi men popped up wide-eyed from under their blankets to ogle their enemies. At first, they seemed astonished to find them ordinary men like themselves, without horns or blood-stained fangs. One Shansi soldier, who had earlier been the loudest to predict the ghastly end of them all, now found a *soupçon* of courage to tug at the sleeve of the scout officer passing his bed. In a quavering voice he pleaded for food and protection. The officer glibly promised both.

Mary did not know it at the time, but Etheldreda in another part of the hospital had simultaneously been burst in on by one of Feng's scouts.

"He kindly kept his revolver pointed at the floor, asked who the men were and proceeded to walk through the ward with me at his elbow," she reported later. "I said we had no one but

wounded, and he asked if I was Russian. When I said I was
English, he became quite chummy and I suddenly discovered that
I had been very wobbly about the knees. By this time I had
sufficiently cooled down to be immensely amused at the sight of
the men nurses, who the day before had been denouncing the
incoming soldiers as all sorts of rascals: they were now beseech-
ing them to eat and drink and were nearly falling on them in an
endeavour to make friends with them. We went downstairs and
I caught sight of Dr. Bryan Brown piloting more revolvers
around."

Now it was time for the officer commanding the scouts to
come down to cases. He told Dr. Bryan Brown that he had come
to the hospital for two reasons.

"First I had to satisfy myself that you are what you pretended
to be by your Red Cross flags," he said, and paused, looking
around the ward through narrowed eyes.

"I am satisfied," he went on at last. "Second, I must warn you
to shut your gates, for we are going to open fire on the city with
big guns."

Then the scouts very properly and politely withdrew to their
prepared positions near the railway station. A few minutes later
the shells began to fly over the hospital into the city. Some of
them burst around the city's gate, and presently the Shansi
guns replied, trying for the station but occasionally falling far
short so that several shells burst within a few yards of the
hospital.

The situation was certainly parlous; yet Miss Fisher's recollection of the hospital's initiation into No-Man's-Land has a typi-
cally light touch.

"I regret to say that the Chinese male nurses remained in the
basement most of the day. The Russian engineer found the pump-
ing apparatus at the bottom of the fifty-foot well suddenly needed
much attention: I didn't blame him—he didn't know who were
his friends and who his foes. I was glad my duty took me to the
upstairs ward, which had a fine view; and I was rewarded by
seeing a shell burst near the railway station, one in the road outside the hospital and one in the parapet at the very top of the

city gate. Oddly enough, that night Mary and I decided to vacate the top storey, where we had previously slept, for a room one flight down that was, coincidentally, partly protected by the old Manchu wall."

That night, Dr. Bryan Brown also decided to move from his accustomed sleeping place—in the superintendent's house, some hundreds of yards from the hospital—into the main building with the others.

Next morning, Mary grimly called a meeting to discuss the food problem, now critical. There was only one item in reasonably good supply: a stock of two hundred eggs she had bought as long since as March 19th, and which caused Etheldreda to remark, "Chinese eggs are *most* peculiar!" The two Englishwomen decided to ration themselves to two thin slices of brown bread, half a spoonful of sugar, four eggs, very little tea and certain oddments of tinned goods per day. The patients and staff were rationed as well, but out of separate supplies more suited to their dietary habits.

The menus for Mary and herself were now included amongst Etheldreda's responsibilities. She recollected her tribulations wryly.

"Tea had practically given out and though Mary produced a small amount from a picnic tin it had somehow become impregnated with naphthaline. I drank two cups at its first appearance, but when the boy produced the reboiled remains the next morning for breakfast I only drank one cup. I had put milk in it before I discovered how frightful it was; but it would have been a pity to waste the milk. There were a few fruit trees in the garden, but we both agreed that next time we dined at a London restaurant we would not have woody pears stewed without sugar with a flavouring of Nestle's malted milk to try to give them some sort of taste."

The siege of the city went on, with big guns duelling and small arms rattling and the hospital lying vulnerably in between the two forces, unvisited and forsaken—except for short-falling shells and rifle bullets burrowing into the plaster.

One day, Mary had a brain wave.

She said to Etheldreda: "Now, why didn't I think of it before?"

Etheldreda, scrubbing at some laundry, looked up. She brushed a wayward wisp of hair out of her eyes with the back of one wet hand. "Hmm? Think of what?"

"Why, of Dr. Hall's house! I shouldn't be surprised if there's something in the cupboard."

"You mean *food?*" Etheldreda asked, starting to wipe her hands.

"Food was what I had in mind. But I could be wrong."

"I don't know what we're waiting for," Etheldreda grinned.

They dashed out across the garden and into the house the Halls had lived in and began rummaging through the pantry, finding a tin of treacle, a number of tins of tomatoes, a supply of curry powder and several cakes of soap.

Etheldreda's eyes gleamed with pleasure. "What a marvellous find, Mary!"

But Mary was frowning.

"Do you suppose it's all right to take this?" she asked herself aloud.

"Of course it's all right," Etheldreda said. "You know very well the Halls would want us to have it."

"Oh, I don't mean the food part," Mary said. "I'm sure *that* would be all right. We can always replace it after this is over. But not the soap."

"Why on earth not? Goodness knows we've little enough of it left in the hospital. We'll be smelling as bad as—as those peculiar eggs!"

But Mary shook her head stubbornly.

"No," she said, her mind made up. "Definitely not the soap. It's *much* more valuable when it's dry and hardened with age. I could only replace it later with soft new cakes. It wouldn't be fair."

Etheldreda sighed, not sure in her own mind whether to be exasperated by Mary or to admire her. Deciding, she said: "Well, I certainly know one thing."

"What's that, Etheldreda?"

"You, my dear, are one of the real, sea-green incorruptibles!"

"Never you mind what I am," Mary said with a laugh. "At least this curry powder will make those eggs go down without gagging."

Each day the house boy would come into the downstairs room that Mary and Etheldreda were now using as a combined office and living room.

He would say to Etheldreda: "Please, what will you have for food today?"

Etheldreda would cock her head to one side, pretending to consider the matter. Then she would ask seriously: "Well, what did we have yesterday?"

"Yesterday you had curried eggs for lunch; tomato with scrambled eggs for supper."

"Ah! Then today we'll have tomato and scrambled eggs for lunch and curried eggs for supper."

"Nothing else?" the boy would ask, disappointed.

"*Can* there be anything else?"

The boy would sadly shake his head.

"Then hunger is the best sauce," Etheldreda would say, and there, invariably, the discussion would come to an end. Nor did it vary until the eggs, smelling and tasting sulphurously foul, even with the curry powder, eventually gave out.

With shells whistling overhead from both sides of the battle, the identifying Red Cross flag that flew over the hospital assumed a tremendous importance to those who lived under it. The difficulty was to *keep* it flying. A boisterous wind had begun to blow in from the west every afternoon, carrying desert dust as an abrasive additive; an argumentative wind that cracked the flag regularly like a whip. No cloth could stand up for long to that continuous beating; but there was no spare flag.

One night they hauled it down for just long enough to mend a torn edge by machining a new strip of calico along it. Two nights later, down it came again, for the new stitches had burst apart. Still worse, of the twelve cords which had originally attached the flag to the lanyard, only one remained. Nik worked feverishly on repairs. By dawn, the flag was flapping at the pole's tip again;

by afternoon it was cracking hard in the dusty and ill-tempered wind. What could be done about it?

"I have an idea," Mary said, looking up at the flag with great concern. "Why don't we stitch a red cross onto one of our cotton quilts and have it ready as a spare?"

"Why don't we?" Etheldreda repeated eagerly. And they did.

In early June, Dr. Li had a recurrence of his fever and again took to his bed. The second day, Dr. Bryan Brown and Mary did the rounds together and stopped in to see their Chinese colleague. Dr. Bryan Brown, timing his assistant's pulse, asked: "And how do you feel today, Dr. Li?"

At that moment a shell exploded somewhere in the hospital compound. Plaster dust drifted down from the ceiling.

"I think," Dr. Li said seriously, "that I'd feel much better at home."

Mary could hardly contain her laughter; could hardly wait to tell Etheldreda of Dr. Li's unconsciously comic remark.

Mary wrote in her diary: "This morning, across the deserted parade ground, we saw a solitary figure dressed in a bright blue coat and carrying a white flag. I felt very excited: we have been cut off for days. But as the figure came nearer, I recognized the mother of a little girl who had been in hospital over a year, but who had been taken home at the beginning of the fighting. She came nearer and nearer, waving her flag, poor soul, when the soldiers on the city wall started a rapid round of firing at her.

"The poor woman came a little further; then she turned back, running a bit and then halting for fear. We were perfectly frantic, but could do nothing to help. I was certainly thankful when she appeared to make it back to safety without being hit; but I wonder how the child can be—the sweetest little girl!— for the mother to have risked her life in an attempt to reach the hospital.

"There has been more heavy gunfire, and many shells have been bursting over the city, with rifle fire in between. One bullet

crashed through our outpatient department window but no one
was hurt. At about eight in the evening there was a good deal of
shouting of orders given by officers to the soldiers on the city
wall. We could make out enough to know they were expecting
an attack upon the North Gate. I took the hint and made sure
that we had plenty of dressings ready and that the beds were
made, as it seemed likely that we would be getting another rush
of wounded. But the attack did not take place.

"*June 3rd.* Last night we did not have the usual exchange of
gunfire between eight and nine o'clock. However, just after nine
the Shansi men on the wall fired a very loud gun. That was how
we discovered that they were taking advantage of our hospital
for cover, behind which they had somehow managed to raise this
large gun onto the wall. But if it draws return fire from their
enemies, some of the shells are bound to fall short onto the
hospital itself."

What, then, if the hospital were hit by a shell and set alight?
Dr. Bryan Brown and Mary, discussing the danger, agreed that
they should concoct a plan to deal with such an emergency.
Etheldreda and Dr. Li were invited to join them for an exchange
of ideas, and the meeting was called to order.

Dr. Bryan Brown outlined the suggestions he and Mary had
talked over: certain of the coolies should be assigned to fight
fire, certain male nurses should be assigned to carry out patients
too ill to help themselves: every member of the staff should be
appointed to fulfil a specified duty.

"Do you think the arrangements will work?" he asked, turning to Dr. Li.

The Chinese doctor smiled languidly.

"No," he said. "It is impossible: they will not come."

The Superintendent stared at him in disbelief. "You mean the
Chinese staff would refuse to fight a fire or help the patients to
escape it?"

Dr. Li shrugged. "If it is a big fire, they will probably say that
they can only save themselves. They would say: 'What is the
use of bothering about the patients—we might all die then.'"

Mary, shaken, leaned forward in her chair.

"But you can't mean that, Dr. Li! Won't they understand that we simply cannot leave the sick ones behind to burn alive?"

But he said stubbornly: "They will only wish to save themselves."

Finally, Dr. Bryan Brown said: "All right, we must assume that you know your own people best. But tell me this, Francis: if the coolies and nurses all run away, what about you? Will you help to carry out the patients?"

Dr. Li's forehead wrinkled as he thought it over.

"If there is no danger to life," he conceded, "I will be pleased to help."

Mary was greatly depressed by Dr. Li's attitude. She had really become quite fond of him and somehow she felt he had let her down. She wrote in her diary: "If the assistant superintendent —a Christian of many years standing—thinks that way, what can we expect of our nursing staff, who are so young, let alone the coolies? We pray to be spared the experience."

Yet she tried to comfort herself by conceding that it was too much to expect a change in national outlook in a single generation.

The last of their coarse brown flour was all but used up; and there was neither tinned milk left nor any tea. The last few remaining eggs had gone quite putrid, so that even the most liberal application of curry powder could not make them edible.

The food situation was now desperate.

One night, Nik crawled up into the rafters of the hospital loft, inching his way in the darkness by sense of touch. One after another, he caught eight pigeons as they slept. He gave one to Mary, one to Etheldreda, one to Dr. Bryan Brown. He kept one for himself. The others, he turned over to the hospital staff to divide amongst themselves, for they still had a little millet left in their store room to keep them from starving; but it, too, would soon be gone.

Mary and Etheldreda made their pigeons last for four days, at last chewing the bones to pulp and swallowing the pulp down.

And, each night after his original run of luck, Nik crawled hopefully up into the rafters again. Each night now the loft was bare.

The following Sunday, Mr. Liu, the catechist, preached at a short service for the coolies and those patients who were able to attend. He took his text from Matthew 14, on the feeding of the five thousand.

Sealed in as they were between the two opposing battle lines, how could they get fresh supplies of food?

Desperately, Mary searched her mind for ideas. Then she thought of one. She had a large placard painted, addressed to any one of Feng's soldiers who might see it, asking him to take the letter which was stuck on the board to his captain. The letter outlined their difficulties and offered to pay for any food that could be spared. Mary knew that at twilight small scouting parties usually probed past the hospital gate, close to the city's wall. She had the placard taken out at night and tacked to the gate. The next morning but one, the letter had gone.

Just before noon, Mary saw two officers in blue-grey walking towards the hospital across the parade ground. When they came into rifle range of the city wall, bullets whined past the hospital and puffs of dust appeared at their feet. The two officers turned tail until they were out of range, looked back, held a council of war and then withdrew altogether. But Mary was still hopeful that her letter might bring the hoped-for results.

That evening, just before six o'clock, Etheldreda happened to glance towards the city wall.

"I saw a white flag and some men being lowered down the wall with ropes. I called Mary and we counted six men altogether. We roared with laughter at number six—he had long white trousers and seemed extremely uncomfortable at the end of the rope: when he landed he sprawled like a frog!"

Then they both regretted their laughter.

Etheldreda's hand flew to her mouth.

"Mary, I do believe the tall one is P.M.!" she gasped.

As he came closer, they saw that it was indeed Rev. P. M. Scott, the S.P.G. priest.

"What on earth can he be coming for?" Etheldreda added. "The B.B. family must be sick!"

The two women hurried downstairs. Mary called to Dr. Bryan Brown: "Dr. B.B.! Some people have just come over the wall— P.M. is one of them. I wonder how the children are?" The last that had been heard of the Bryan Brown children, they had all been down with measles.

The three of them—Mary, Etheldreda and the Superintendent —rushed out of the hospital to the hospital compound gate and from that vantage watched the small procession come towards them, with Mr. Scott carrying the flag of truce. With him, they now saw, were two Swedish missionaries, a Salvation Army captain and two Chinese Christians. As they approached, Dr. Bryan Brown called anxiously from behind the gate: "P.M.! How are my wife and children?"

"They're all right," the priest called back. "Don't worry about them."

The party continued past the gate in the direction of the railway station, but before they were out of hearing, Mr. Scott called back over his shoulder: "We have peace proposals to make to the troops at the railway station. We'll call in to see you on our way back."

They advanced to a small archway just beyond the hospital compound. As they started through, a shot cracked out viciously from the station side and they dodged back behind a low wall. They waved the flag of truce over the wall and tried again; and this time they went through safely and crossed the parade ground.

All that long night those at the hospital waited for the peace party's return, and all that long night there was no sign of it. By mid-morning, Etheldreda was frantic.

"Do you suppose that something dreadful has happened to them?" she kept asking Mary.

"Of course not—I'm sure they're all right," Mary told her, but she was nagged by her own misgivings.

At seven-thirty in the morning; she was wearily preparing dressings on the third floor, which, though most vulnerable to shell fragments and rifle bullets, also gave the best view. When she glanced out of the window for what must have been the hundredth time she caught sight of movement—men coming towards the hospital from the direction of the station.

She called out excitedly to Etheldreda.

"They're back—they're back at last! Look; there they come!"

"I wonder if they've been successful?" Etheldreda said, worrying at it. "I wonder if they've made peace?" It seemed a long time to her since she had come to stay for the one week. It *was* a long time—two months, now; and if a peace were not agreed upon there was no telling how much longer she would be hemmed in to this nightmarish No-Man's-Land, crouching down in fearful haste when shells whistled overhead and being knocked flat by blast when they burst nearby—and constantly filled with an eroding fear that sapped her strength and even her sense of humour.

The two women made their way to the gate with Dr. Bryan Brown and Dr. Li; but when Rev. P. M. Scott and his party approached, they could see their faces were drawn and discouraged.

"We couldn't get back last night because of the long parleying," the priest told them dispiritedly. "Then, after all that, they told us only an hour ago that the terms proposed by the city were unacceptable." He put a hand on Dr. Bryan Brown's shoulder. "I hate to have to tell you this, B.B.—they warned me they might use poison gas against Tatung. You really must try to get your family out of the city if you can and to Peking."

The unsuccessful peace party returned to the city wall, where they were hauled up again by the ropes. After they saw them safely over the top, the two doctors, Mary and Etheldreda had a meeting to discuss what action the two women should take, in view of the poison gas threat.

Dr. Li was quite upset about it.

"I think these two ladies should not be exposed to poison gas bombs," he said, wringing his hands. "They should go to Peking with Mrs. Bryan Brown."

The Superintendent, who had become quite haggard for worry about his family, turned to Mary.

"Well, Miss Ball? What do you think about it? Do you think you should leave?"

"No," she said, not hesitating. "I don't feel I can leave the nursing staff; but Miss Fisher should certainly consider it, especially since she has an aged mother at home."

Her eyes lit on Etheldreda as she waited for her to reply. She wanted to give Etheldreda every chance to make up her own mind, but she still did not relish the thought of being without the friend on whom she had come to lean more than ever for her help and good cheer.

"I want to do what is best," Etheldreda said, furrowing her brow. "Of course, I realize I'm no real help here. Perhaps I *should* go back to Peking if I can."

Mary's heart sank, but she said nothing further. All the rest of that day she kept thinking of what life at the hospital would be like, under siege, without Etheldreda's companionship.

At this time, the two women were sharing a bedroom on the first floor of the hospital—the upper floors were far too exposed to flying lead—and just as Mary was trying to drop off to sleep that night across the barrier of a dreadful vision of gas bombs bursting over the city and the wind carrying the deadly mist towards the hospital, Etheldreda whispered from the next bed: "Mary—Mary, are you awake?"

"Yes, just."

"I've been thinking and thinking all day about leaving you here alone."

Mary's eyes flew wide open in the darkness.

"Yes, Etheldreda?"

"I've decided I can't possibly do it."

"Are you sure? What about your mother?"

Etheldreda was silent for a moment. From somewhere on the city wall, a rifle cracked, followed by its hollow echo. Then, quite softly, Etheldreda said: "I don't think I'd care to see my mother again if I'd left you."

But, in the end, they *all* stayed where they were, for Dr.

Bryan Brown was unable to negotiate his wife and children out of the city, and, in any case, it developed that none of them could have got through to Peking.

"My wardrobe is a great problem," Etheldreda wrote, in the long, omnibus letter she hoped to post to her mother in England on that future day when the mails began to function again. "Miss Ball has lent me a uniform too small for herself and two white Chinese robes, so I wear and wash and wear again. I have only one pair of shoes, so I occasionally have to clean them on my feet. As we cannot be quite certain that if anything disastrous happened at night the night nurses would remain on duty, we both sleep in half our clothes, ready to go to the wards if necessary in a flash.

"The men in my ward are getting on very well. In fact, we invited five of them to leave the hospital when they can, because our business was to cure them and we have done that. The only one who is not getting on is a beggar-man whose arm had to be amputated.

"Poor old thing! He reminds me of a badly-treated dog, he always seems to be so pitiful. No one knows his dialect so we can't understand most of what he says. Hospital ways must drive him demented; but he has managed to hoard his flour and we really can't allow him to roll up his balls of dough in his sheet and keep them in his bed all day!

"I washed his chest and back this morning and he wept all the time, so I felt it a great triumph that when I cut his finger-nails he asked me to cut his toenails as an encore!"

The hospital was only about a hundred and fifty yards from the nearest point on the city wall, so that whenever there was a lull in the firing, and provided there was no wind, it was possible to shout back and forth and exchange simple messages.

Mary had discovered that one of the hospital coolies had a soldier-brother on the wall, and now she got him to shout across the shell-pocked field to ask him to have some bags of millet and oatmeal lowered down so that a work party from the hospital could pick it up under cover of night.

After consulting his officer, the Shansi man shouted back that the request had been denied.

Mary said to the coolie: "Then ask him if they will promise not to fire on any party we might send to the station to ask for food there."

To this request the coolie reported a favourable reply—provided the hospital foraging party carried a white flag with a red cross on it.

Mary ripped open a white pillow case, and with Etheldreda's help dyed bandages with red ink for the red cross and then sewed the cross on the pillow case. But when she volunteered to carry the flag to the station, Dr. Li protested indignantly.

"For a woman to do things like this is wrong," he said.

Mary stared at him. Would she ever be able to chart the ins and outs of his Oriental conscience?

There followed a prolonged discussion as to who should take the risk of going to the station in search of food. Mr. Liu, the mild and middle-aged catechist, kept repeating that he would be glad to do so. He was a short man and quite rotund—not at all the fictional figure of a hero but, as Etheldreda said later, "If ever a man deserved a Victoria Cross, he did."

At seven o'clock next morning, taking the Chinese cook and one coolie, he set out bravely waving the makeshift Red Cross flag and hopefully wearing a long white gown and white topee as further signs of his peaceful purpose.

"How our hearts and prayers went with them, risking their lives to try to get food for us all," Mary recorded in her diary.

In spite of the promise from the city, as soon as the three men got out into the open parade ground they were fired on from the walls. But Mr. Liu went forward serenely as if he were marching down a church's aisle to the altar. "One felt he was saying to himself, 'I am doing God's work, nothing can touch me,'" Etheldreda said later. The others could not but follow his example.

Finally, the watchers from the hospital's third-storey windows breathed their relief as they saw the small party disappear behind the wall at the far side of the parade ground. They knew then that the foragers were safe from the city soldiers, but they could only pray that Feng's men would see and respect their flag.

Even before the party had set out, Mary was quite aware that the soldiers at the station might not be willing to sell food to Mr. Liu. Talking the possibilities over before he set out, they had decided he should go on to another town a few miles away if he could do nothing at the station—provided, of course, that the troops there allowed him to proceed further. But, just after ten that morning, the three Chinese men returned, "Well in body," as Mary put it, "but sad in heart."

They were met anxiously at the hospital gate.

"Have you any news—any food?" were Dr. Bryan Brown's first words.

"No," Mr. Liu said, shaking his head. "The officer at the station said we were spies from the city and wouldn't let us see the merchants. And they wouldn't let us go further seeking for food."

"Have you anything to suggest, then, about what we ought to do?" the Superintendent asked him.

"Yes, I have: I think if one of you foreigners came with me the soldiers would believe we were not spies," Mr. Liu said.

"You really think that might work?" Mary asked.

"Yes."

She turned to the Superintendent.

"I'd be quite willing to go with Mr. Liu," she told him.

Dr. Li sucked in his breath. "Really," he said, "I must protest against a woman going. It is not right."

"I will go, of course," Dr. Bryan Brown said shortly. "The sooner the better, I suppose. Tomorrow, Mr. Liu?"

"Yes, tomorrow morning, I think," the catechist said.

They had very little food left. If they had one very inadequate meal a day, in three days time there would be nothing at all.

That night was especially noisy, with no break in the artillery and machine-gun duels. Then, at seven in the morning, there was a lull, unnatural-seeming in its suddenness.

"We'd better go while we can," Dr. Bryan Brown said. Like Mr. Liu, he was all in white—a tropical suit and cotton sun hat. Now, in mid-June, the days had become almost unbearably hot. Flies buzzed in the unaccustomed silence.

They set out, and this time as they crossed the parade ground —with everyone back at the hospital expecting the worst—there was no firing at all from the city. In about two hours, Dr. Bryan Brown and Mr. Liu returned, grinning in triumph.

"At noon," the Superintendent announced grandly, "we are to pick up our supplies. They will be left behind the cover of the wall beyond the parade ground. . . ." Then he dropped his grand manner. "Miss Ball, it was marvellous! We were able to buy about forty bags of flour and other meal. The cook and our coolie are collecting it now."

The words were scarcely out of his mouth when the fighting suddenly broke out again, first with the crump-crump-crump of an artillery barrage and then with the staccato wickedness of machine-gun and rifle fire. The wind carried with it the sharp smell of singed cordite.

"No one is going to be able to go out in this," Mary said, worried. She heard the crunching sound of a shell exploding very near at hand and looking across at the city wall saw that the new barracks on the wall had been squarely hit.

"What a jolly place to put a barracks!" Etheldreda said, but her remark did nothing to relieve the tension.

The two women were still making use of a third-floor bathroom at this time and just before noon Etheldreda was washing her hands there, readying herself for a meagre lunch, when a rifle bullet splintered the window and buried itself in the wall inches from her head. For a breathless moment, she leaned back against the wall with her eyes shut. Then, still very pale, she scurried downstairs. A moment later, the firing suddenly came to an end.

Mr. Liu listened for it to continue.

"Now!" he said after a minute or two. "We must be quick!"

Waving his Red Cross flag, he ran out to the middle of the road outside the compound so the Shansi troops could see him

Meanwhile, Nik was already organizing the male nurses and coolies—even the convalescent patients. A minute later they were all sprinting raggedly across the parade ground to pick up the sacks of flour and grain waiting beyond. They brought it all into the compound and slammed the gate shut, breathing hard. As they did this, the firing began again, more violently than ever.

"It seemed almost a miracle," Mary said.

When, in another lull, the cook and the coolie dashed back to the hospital, they brought with them an unexpected bonus of goodies; onions, green vegetables and pork. That evening, for the first time in weeks, they had meat for dinner. The shelling and machine-gun fire continued throughout the night. Sleep proved virtually impossible, but for once nobody seemed to mind greatly.

Just before dawn, a particularly vicious bombardment fell on the city. After it was over, Mary heard Etheldreda giggling to herself in the next bed.

"What's so funny now?" she demanded.

"Oh, nothing really," Etheldreda said, and started to giggle again. "I was just thinking how much I agree with Dr. Li: I think I should feel better at home, too!"

"I think we all should," Mary agreed, smiling in the darkness.

*　　*　　*

CHAPTER VII

THE working of the human mind was most curious, Mary observed; for, now that the harsh immediacy of starvation no longer threatened, other trials and dangers pushed in for a greater share of her awareness—and most of them had been there all the time.

While in Etheldreda's ward of more or less minor ailments nearly all had quite recovered, in the other, eight deaths had occurred during the past fortnight and two more patients were unlikely to survive beyond a few days. Most of these cases had been hopeless from the start, but Mary could not help wondering how much their desperate situation had contributed to the high mortality rate: the tensions and the terrors, the enveloping cacophony of war, the shuddering from shellbursts and thudding of bullets and shattering of glass, the insufficiencies of diet and—worst of all—the eroding suspense. At what moment would the juggernaut assault against the city be mounted by Feng's army, crushing the hospital and its occupants impersonally on its way?

The bodies of the dead had been put in the mortuary, a room cut into the ancient Manchu mud wall. There were no coffins and now that the weather was warmer Dr. Bryan Brown decided they must be buried without delay. The coolies dug graves under protection of night; Nik and Mr. Liu carried the bodies to the burial places on stretchers.

"I went out to help," Mary said later. "Conditions were shocking: rats had got in and mutilated the corpses and they had already begun to smell."

There had been other digging going on during the night—Feng's men creating a zig-zag of communicating trenches across the open parade ground. Then, on the morning of June 17th—as Mary reported—"about two thousand of them burst into the hospital compound through an opening they had cut in our mud north wall. They took over all the houses and outbuildings on the hospital grounds, but Dr. B.B. insisted to their commanding officer that none of his men should come into the hospital. We were, certainly, no longer in No-Man's-Land. Much worse, we were now smack in the middle of the firing line—fair game for the city's guns."

Fair game, indeed: for Feng's men had even opened the hospital gate and erected a machine-gun emplacement there, training it on the outer north gate of Tatung. They swarmed up the thick south wall of the hospital compound, the wall in which the mortuary was cut, and scooped out machine-gun emplacements along the top. The hospital staff was ordered not to leave their building, even for exercises on the compound, unless escorted by a soldier.

It seemed that now, surely, the moment they had all feared was at hand: the moment of the final brutal assault upon the city. Four small biplanes. the air arm of Feng's force, swooped down on the city dropping bombs while Shansi machine-gunners from the embattlements tried frenetically to fend them off.

During all this, Mary and Etheldreda were kept busy chasing rubber-necking infantrymen out of the hospital; while Dr. Bryan Brown and Dr. Li formed a committee of two in a desperate effort to convince the Feng senior officers to reverse their plan of using the hospital grounds for their front line of trenches. The plea earned only shrugs and apologetic smiles and shakings of military heads. New trenches were dug between the hospital itself and the city walls.

"That night was a very disturbed one," Mary recorded. "There was incessant digging of trenches, marching of men and shooting. Soldiers slept everywhere in the compound; some wandered gawking curiously through nurses' rooms, coolie quarters—even into one isolation block. We were kept busy keeping them out of the wards. Early in the morning a bursting shell gave us five rather bad casualties amongst the men, and as another exploded just outside the window of the bedroom shared by Miss Fisher and myself, we thought we had better move down again—this time to the ground floor. We are now sleeping in the nurses' lecture room. A bullet came through the bedroom we had just vacated, lodging itself in the wall at the head of my bed. I'm glad I wasn't in it."

Mary soon learned that a final assault was not on Feng's immediate agenda, but so extraordinary was the nature of the news which supplanted the earlier fear, she hardly knew whether to feel relieved or to find in it an even more terrible nightmare.

Dr. Bryan Brown had been inspecting the grounds with an officer, on the morning of June 21st, for the purpose of placing latrines. He returned to the hospital pale with suppressed excitement.

"They've started to dig two tunnels towards the city," he said in an oddly taut voice. "One of them has been started right in the middle of my tennis court." He managed a sickly smile. "That's goodbye to my tennis!"

"How long will it take them?" Mary asked.

"They say about two weeks. They're putting hundreds of troops on to the diggings." The Superintendent sighed. "I'm afraid there's nothing we can do about it. . . ." Desperately, he sought to change the subject. "How is Miss Fisher feeling now—any better?"

"She doesn't complain," Mary said, feeling sorry for the Superintendent, for she knew he must be sick with worry for his wife and children. "Her fever isn't high; but I think it's good for her to get some rest in bed—she was getting so tired and looking so white."

Mary did not know it, but at that moment Etheldreda was faithfully adding to the omnibus letter she was writing to her mother. By now, it had become a very fat letter indeed.

"Just a line because it is Sunday," she wrote, sitting up against her pillows. "Miss Ball has put me to bed with a slight temperature and I dare not let her catch me writing: she says I'm not to. Mr. Liu preached this morning on 'He that loseth his life for my sake shall find it'. It can not be so very often that a man lives his sermon as he has been doing."

But, by the following Tuesday, she had recovered her good cheer and her health. "I am up again. It appears to have been sand-fly fever—the effect of sand-fly bites. I am afraid it added a few years to Miss Ball's age as I have such an awful propensity for picking up the various things killed by Keating's Powder, not to mention bugs Keating is too polite to name: she had begun to think I might be going in for one of the diseases *they* convey.

"I have returned to an appetite on the right day! I had a new-laid egg for my breakfast; roast beef, baked potato, stewed fresh apricots and custard for my lunch. Our kitchen folk have hob-nobbed so successfully with Feng's men that we can buy anything we like, so we are going back to normal meals.

"Miss Ball's imp of a cook-general, whom we sent to the station for supplies on Friday, could not get what he deemed sufficient there, so he took the train to Fengchen and returned today with beef, pork, five live chickens, a sack of potatoes, jam, tea, salt, sugar, two kinds of cooking fat and two hundred eggs—not a bad effort for a boy of seventeen! To think that we had been prepared to be very annoyed with him, as we thought he had gone off on a spree!

"We are settling down to the new state of affairs of actually being a part of the front line. The attackers have mounted four or five machine-guns on the south wall and are now driving tunnels under the wall in order to (pause, while I chivvy a soldier out of our bedroom!) reach the city wall and blow it up.

"Relations between us and them were strained for the first day or two; we, of course, bitterly resent the abuse of our Red Cross flag, and they suspect us of siding with the enemy. But we are absolutely in their hands. Still, I suppose any other Chinese army would be taking everything on the premises, so our relations have become more friendly. They are supplying coal for the engine-house, having 'requested' us to keep it going night and day to supply electricity for their tunnels. However, they are really awfully good and have given more meal for the hospital and will buy cigarettes for the patients.

"I am much better for two days in bed and have slept twelve hours out of the last twenty-four. In the previous four days and nights, Miss Ball and I have slept a total of sixteen hours. Feng's artillery bombards Tatung from ten every night to about three in the morning, and sends shells over spasmodically the rest of the time. What they must be suffering in the city won't bear thinking of: we just don't talk about it. The suspense of Dr. Bryan Brown is awful, and what his wife must be going through with those four children, having to spend most of the time in the cellar—not to mention the heat and the dirt, flies and smells of a Chinese city!"

When Etheldreda wrote of Feng's officers having 'requested' that the hospital generator be kept going to produce electricity night and day, giving the word its wry aura of innuendo with quotation marks, she could not have been aware of all the facts. If she had been, she surely would have been less reticent—unless, of course, she had deliberately committed herself to the policy of underplaying the actual events for the sake of her mother's peace of mind.

The day after the tunnels were begun, one of Feng's officers came to see Dr. Bryan Brown. He was a small, wiry man in blue-grey who seemed to gaze out from a previously prepared position at a world he half-expected to bite him. At his side was a scabbard; in it, a curved cavalry sabre.

"Well, and how are your tunnels coming along?" the Superintendent asked, trying to appear friendly.

The officer produced a suspicious little smile, then cut it short.

"That is why I have come," he said. "They are going well. They have gone so far the men have no light to dig by."

"Oh?"

"Therefore it is now necessary for you to supply us with electric lights and to wire the tunnels so the digging can proceed," the officer continued.

"But I am a doctor—I know nothing about electricity."

"No? But you do have your own generator in the compound. Somebody must run it."

The doctor hesitated. After a moment, he said deliberately: "We are not involved in this war. We are neutral and cannot take sides. If we were to help you. . . ." He let his voice trail away. Then he said hopefully: "You understand the difficulty?"

The officer's smile returned as a smile of suspicions confirmed. It was certainly not friendly.

"Up to now we have been very good to you," he said grimly. "We have given you food and we have hurt no one, killed no one from the hospital even though we are not sure that you do not spy here for the Shansi army. We would prefer to keep it that way if we can; but if you make things hard for us, how can we do it? Now we need electric lights and if you do not help us. . . ." Then he demanded sharply: "Who knows how to run the generator?"

The Superintendent saw that he was beaten; there was really nothing he could do but give in gracefully.

"Our engineer, Mr. Nikulin."

"The Russian?"

"Yes."

"Have him brought here."

When Nik was confronted with the officer's demands, he sucked in his breath. Though in his early thirties, he was a slender, boyish-looking man, who was never able to forget that, as a stateless White Russian, he lacked the privileges of his English colleagues with their legation and their extraterritorial rights. He had no one upon whom to fall back in an emergency for a last line of assistance and he was accustomed to thinking of the Shansi Government as the reigning authority.

He said: "But I can't do that—I can't help one side or the other!"

The little officer screwed up his face as if he were readying to spit. Then he shouted: "Enough!" With a flashing movement and the scrape of metal, he had his sabre out, holding it high over Nik. "You have a choice," he said between his teeth. "You wish to keep your head on your neck?"

Next day, the digging continued—under lights.

Nik had wired the tunnels, but the hundreds of troops involved in the digging used the most primitive of methods. Mary, out of curiosity, peered into one of the adits. She edged forward, down the slope, and no one stopped her. Surprised, she continued on, picking her way by the long string of lights wired overhead. Nik, sabre-minded, had done a good job.

"It's amazing how well they're built and how far they've gone," Mary reported to Etheldreda when she came out again, flushed by her adventure. "But you know, they're bound to be awfully slow. They dig into the earth by hand and shovel it into small sacks and pass them along a human chain for emptying."

Days passed. The diggers dug, burrowed, handed back the sacks of earth. Nik, muttering protests under his breath, lengthened his line of lights. The tunnels were fifty yards along the way; seventy-five. When the hundred yard mark was reached the air became bad. The officer in charge of digging decided to go to the surface for ventilation. On the way up, his men passed through a graveyard which had been in recent use, so that now the air was not only bad but putrid with decay. More ventilation holes were dug, back along the tunnel. The diggers, in shifts, were working the clock around.

What the officer had forgotten was that a hole which let the air in formed a two-way passage.

"Last night the soldiers perched on the city walls looked down and saw an extraordinary sight—a string of lighted holes in the ground below them," Mary put in her record. "They realized at once that the electricity which gave the light must be coming from the hospital."

From the moment of that realization, the hospital came under sporadic gunfire. Fortunately for the patients and the staff, the thick Manchu wall protected the ground floor, but even at that the convalescent cases now chose to lie on the corridor floors rather than in the beds of the ground floor ward; the coolies slept in the cellar and scurried down during the day whenever a shell burst near.

Hit after hit was scored on the higher floors from the point-blank range. In her report, which she hoped she could get off to S.P.G. headquarters in London, Mary said: "The repairs that will be wanted will be tremendous. There have been shell and mortar hits; the walls are absolutely pock-marked with bullet holes; few windows on the south and north sides on the top two storeys have any glass left in them."

Indeed, one day, when it was pouring with rain, they were hit no fewer than twenty times.

Mary and Dr. Bryan Brown decided that at any moment an incendiary shell might set the hospital alight, therefore they should prepare to evacuate. All the bathtubs were filled with water. The corridors were lined with full pails and jugs. Nik had the coolies leave stretchers in strategic places and instructed them to carry out the sick and wounded if the necessity arose. Dr. Li divided his bemused interest between staring out of the shattered windows at the rain and watching the preparations. When these were all completed, he again volunteered his views.

"You know, Miss Ball, all this is of no use whatsoever," he drawled. "If the hospital does catch fire, we'll have time only to save ourselves. If we do take the patients out and it is raining, they will all get pneumonia. You see? They will die either by fire or by water, and what is the difference?"

There were times, Mary told herself, that Francis could be irritating beyond words.

Now that the battle was raging over, around and even in the hospital, there were many casualties amongst Feng's attacking troops. The hospital took them in, but in the circumstances it was functioning only on a makeshift basis.

Mary reported to Dr. Bryan Brown that, quite apart from food, supplies were petering out.

The Superintendent ran harried hands through his hair.

"Well, what *have* we got enough of?" he asked wearily.

"Not much," Mary told him. "Castor oil, cod liver oil and soda-bicarb."

"What about dressings and bandages?"

"No new ones at all. We've been washing and sterilizing the old ones."

The doctor groaned.

"Carbolic?" he asked. "Alcohol?"

"None. No cotton-wool, either. We do have half a tin of Lysol."

"We'll just have to do the best we can, then," the Superintendent said, sounding utterly depressed.

That afternoon, during a short lull in the firing, Mary went out into the hospital garden. Off to the west a fresh storm was brewing: a range of grey thunderheads rode an eastward wind. She had not been out for days and she was pleased to see that the hollyhocks were blooming at last. She picked some of them and a few blossoming thistles and put them in vases in the one ward they were still able to use.

Etheldreda, seeing them, was delighted.

"But fancy waiting until the end of June for the first flowers," she said.

That night—as for many nights before it—Mary and Etheldreda fell into their beds without removing their clothes. There was no telling what emergency might rouse them at any hour. The storm had still not reached them and the air was heavy, brooding with heat. Exhausted, Mary tried to woo sleep, but whenever she was at the point of winning it a shell exploded nearby or a machine-gun stuttered deafeningly from the Manchu wall. Presently, from somewhere not too far, she could hear the sound of snoring over the steady gunfire.

She said irritably in the darkness to Etheldreda: "How *can* those men sleep in all this firing?"

There was no reply. Suddenly the tension her nerves had been building slipped away and she began to laugh softly to herself. The snoring had come from the next bed.

Etheldreda had indeed become battle-hardened.

By June the twenty-seventh, the rumour flew around the hospital that one of the tunnels had reached as far as the city wall. This was coupled with a rumour that the explosives with which it was intended to breach the wall had not yet arrived.

"It will be a very sad and dreadful day when Feng's men enter the city," Mary noted in her diary.

A field hospital set up near the station by Feng's medical officers had established the practice of sending their walking wounded to the Mosse Memorial for daily dressings ("Rather a tribute to us, don't you think?" Etheldreda had asked Mary), but now Mary put her foot down: she wanted to help, but how could she without bandages, cotton wool and disinfectants?

"Unless you supply the wherewithal," she said to a medical corps officer who had called to inspect their facilities, "we'll have to limit ourselves to first dressings—nothing more."

"I'll see what can be done," the officer said, looking embarrassed.

He had scarcely left the compound when a gun from the city began to pound Dr. Bryan Brown's house, now occupied by Feng soldiers.

Minutes later, no fewer than seventeen wounded men were brought round to the outpatients' department, now itself somewhat the worse for war. Fortunately, just then a messenger arrived from the station with a bundle of dressings, and the wounded were cared for as they could not have been only a short time before.

On the second day of July, the digging in both tunnels was discontinued: the officer in charge had decided they had gone far enough.

There was a great deal of excited talk amongst Feng's soldiers. In so far as Mary could draw conclusions from this chatter, a ton of explosives was now placed in readiness at the head of each tunnel. She confided her latest worry to Etheldreda.

"If they breach the wall this way, what hope will remain of our ever continuing our work here? We shall be 'the foreigners who allowed their hospital to be used to destroy our city'. As if we hadn't been having a difficult enough time, even before all this began!"

By the next day the explosives in the tunnels had still not been set off.

"The soldiers aren't sure what will happen and are afraid to start," Nik told Mary with a smug satisfaction.

At that moment there was a reverberating explosion: the building shuddered. Then two other explosions followed within minutes. Nik picked himself up, beating plaster dust from his clothes. The series of blasts had thrown Mary against the wall and then onto the floor, knocking the breath out of her. When she got it back, she asked: "Was that it?"

Nik gave her a frightened glance and disappeared. He came back a moment later.

"It wasn't the tunnels," he told her. "The outpatients' department was hit by shells."

Mary rushed off to check the damage. One of the shells had torn a hole through the wall, another had taken a corner off the building and the third had blasted away part of the entrance porch.

"We cannot think of any room now which can be considered safer than another," she wrote that evening. "A mortar bomb landed on the engine house this afternoon and the roof has a large hole in it."

She put down her pen with a little inward prayer of thanksgiving. Nik, who had been compelled to spend long hours each day in the engine house, tending the generator, had not been there when the mortar had hit.

The next day, a Sunday, Nik brought her gleeful tidings: a grenade, dropped from the city wall into one of the ventilation holes had severed an electric wire—one of *his* electric wires. Now, he chortled, the explosives could not be detonated until the wire was repaired.

"They haven't decided whether to mend it today or wait until tomorrow," he added. Every minute of delay seemed to aerate his spirits a little, as if to compensate him for the indignities he had suffered from the officer in charge of the tunnels.

But in the evening that same officer told Dr. Bryan Brown that the moment of truth was approaching.

"At eight o'clock tonight the wall will be blown up," he announced confidently.

Nik broke in excitedly.

"He wants *me* to pull the electric switch to start the explosion! I can't do it, Doctor! If the switch doesn't work, they'll shoot me: if it does, I'll never be able to live in Tatung again!"

The officer turned a jaundiced eye on him. No doubt, he felt he had put up with a great deal from Nik.

He said coldly: "You are the only electrician here and we do not understand these things."

Nik flushed. "It doesn't take much understanding to pull a switch."

"Oh, this is really too much," Dr. Bryan Brown told the officer firmly. "It is impossible for Mr. Nikulin to have anything to do with the pulling of the switch. Absolutely impossible, you understand. The hospital has taken no part in the fighting and we are willing only to help the wounded—no more than that. You seem to forget that I can report your actions to the British Legation when this is over. I promise you that I shall do so."

The mention of the British Legation appeared to take the officer aback. He tried to argue with the Superintendent but his argument now lacked force. Finally, and reluctantly, he agreed that one of his own men would throw the switch.

Just before eight o'clock, Mary observed that the soldiers in the compound, anticipating the breaching of the city wall and the assault which would follow, were wearing their steel helmets and sharpening their evil-looking curved swords on the hospital's stone steps. The sound of steel on stone made her shiver: the thought of what it presaged filled her with horror.

"One thing is certain," Nik said nervously. "If we're not blown up, we'll be blown down."

No one, not even Etheldreda, thought the remark funny. They all waited. Mary could hear the thudding of her own heart.

Eight o'clock came. There was no explosion.

At half-past eight, Mary said: "Well, at least we can have supper, can't we?"

They ate, but without much appetite. All the patients who

were well enough to move, and the male nurses with them, had gone down into the cellar where they were huddled in small, fidgetting groups, waiting for the explosion. By ten o'clock it still had not come.

Midnight, and there was no explosion.

The night had gone eerily silent, the guns and the rifles on both sides laid aside as if in anticipation of some greater outbreak. One o'clock struck.

Mary and Etheldreda decided to go to bed. Surely by this hour Feng's men had decided to put off the throwing of the switch until after dawn.

At three in the morning, Etheldreda, feeling thirsty, left their room for a glass of water. On the way back she looked in at the ward. None of the patients was asleep: whispers, like the rustlings of fear, criss-crossed the large room. She returned to her bed, resting on the blankets, still fully clothed. A machine-gun began to chatter on the city wall. Another, from somewhere in the compound, chattered in response.

"Are you all right? " Mary whispered to her.

"Yes."

"I do wish I could get some sleep."

Not long after that, the hospital seemed to move a little.

"Now, was that it?" Mary asked, sitting bolt upright in her bed.

"I don't know. Could it have been? There wasn't any bang."

"Maybe there was a bang," Mary said. "Maybe it was partly muffled by the tunnel and partly by the machine-gun fire."

They listened, concentrating their attention on the expected shouting and firing which would announce the all-out attack. Presently the machine-guns fell silent. The night was still.

There was no sound at all but their own breathing and, in a little while, a chorus of stridulating insects.

At first light, Mary peered out of a glassless window towards the city.

The end of the west tunnel had collapsed, she saw: but the officer must have stopped his men digging too soon for clearly it had ended not under the wall proper but under a large square buttress from which, now, all the brickwork had been blasted by the force of the explosion, leaving its earthen core standing like a partly collapsed sand castle. There was no breach in the wall itself: clearly operation tunnel had thus far been a fiasco.

Upset by the failure to blow up the wall at his first attempt, the officer in charge turned his spleen on the hospital's foreigners. He called them together—Mary, Dr. Bryan Brown, Etheldreda and Nik. He delivered an impassioned scolding which he finished off with an accusation that they had sent information to the city by a secret telephone.

"Otherwise, why did they know enough to drop a bomb into the tunnel at the right time—just when we were ready?" he demanded, implying that this explained and excused his failure.

"Oh, really!" the Superintendent said, exasperated. "You know we have no phone!"

"I know you say you have none," the officer curtly corrected. "We will find it. We will find it."

He put a squad of men at work to search the hospital. They poked into cupboards, peered under beds, removed stores of food from the kitchen pantries, even explored the darkest corners of the cellar. They went round tapping the walls and feeling for loose floorboards. But, of course, since there truly was no telephone, they could not find it.

When, finally, one enthusiastic searcher discovered a loose electric wire that had been cut by a piece of flying shrapnel, he reported it excitedly. The officer received the news with a grim smile, nodded an "I-told-you-so" to himself, and ordered a field telephone fastened to the wire. As a reward, the wire's finder was ordered to monitor the instrument. All that day and through the night the poor soldier sat, listening in to a dead phone, doubtless wishing heartily that he had kept his discovery to himself.

Nor did Nik—who had dared to refuse his orders—escape the officer's vengeance.

"The Russian engineer is having a horrible time," Etheldreda wrote. "The engine-room is in urgent need of cleaning, but the Chinese officer won't let him stop the generator to do so. Instead, he threatened him with a revolver if anything more went wrong. It is lucky the extraterritorial rights have not been abolished, or we might be in the same plight. As it is, the engineer can appeal to the Superintendent and the Superintendent can complain to the C.O. and point out that the engine cannot do impossibilities."

The tunnel officer decided to have his men dig the east tunnel a bit longer in order to be sure this time that it was under the wall itself and not merely under a buttress when the explosives were detonated. He was determined to take no chance of a second failure. One tin of explosives had gone off the first time: now he was planning to increase the charge tenfold.

Then, on the night of July seventh, a grenade was dropped into the second tunnel, again severing a power wire. The officer in charge was furious. He summoned all of the hospital's Chinese staff into his presence, then ranted threats of reprisal at them until they were certain they were destined for a firing squad. Having failed to discover a phone, the officer was still convinced that in some mysterious way information was being passed into the city.

Next day he curtly informed Dr. Bryan Brown that all the hospital staff and the patients would have to move out and into the railway station; but he avoided giving his actual reason for wanting this done.

"It is no longer safe for you here," he said, a fact which was certainly self-evident. No one had thought it safe for some time.

"Surely we all know his real reason for wanting us to move," Mary said. "They want to get rid of us so they can place machine-guns on the top floor and fire straight down onto the city wall."

"Oh, I agree," the Superintendent said.

"Well, as neutrals, would we be justified in evaculating the hospital then—I mean, knowing their intention?" she asked.

"There are certainly two sides to our responsibility," Dr. Bryan Brown admitted, tortured by doubts. "The assault must be very near; and with the assault near, what about our patients? Perhaps our first debt is to them. On the other hand, we do owe it to the S.P.G. to protect the building and equipment: if we go, will there be anything left when we come back? This is a decision for Solomon: I don't know what to do."

Mary nodded her sympathy.

"It has to be your decision," she said. "What bothers me most of all is this: if we pull out now, no Shansi man, woman or child will welcome us back again!"

And yet—the doctor pointed out—how much longer could the hospital stand up under point-blank shell fire? There were many gaping holes in the walls already and in several places even the ceilings were caving in. Nearly every member was now the host to one or more minor ailments—the result of insufficient sleep and general anxiety. Even the patients, needing rest in bed and freedom from extraneous fears, spent most of their time these days crouching from shell fire in the inner corridors.

The Superintendent sighed heavily.

"No," he said. "On balance, I'm afraid there is no doubt about it: we must all get out while they are still willing to let us go."

But where could they go? The besieged city was closed to them. Including patients and staff, the hospital inmates now numbered eighty-three—a Chinese inn, lacking sanitation and other facilities, was out of the question for so many with such varied needs. Then Mary had an idea. Half a mile beyond the station there was a Roman Catholic seminary: what about that?

Dr. Bryan Brown brightened. "All right. I'll ask permission to go and ask the Father in charge if he's willing, and indeed able, to take us in."

He returned bearing good news: they would all be welcomed at the Seminary. On his way back, the Superintendent had stopped at the railway station and telegraphed to the American consul at Kalgan, a Mr. Stanton, asking his help in getting Mrs. Bryan Brown and the children safely out of the city. The doctor had met him on more than one previous occasion and the nearest British consular official was at Peking, twice as far away. The Superintendent told Mary that he was sure Stanton would help if he were able.

On Thursday, then—July eighth—Mary organized a party to begin packing up for their departure.

Next morning the evacuation was begun along the zigzag communication trenches. The first to go, in Dr. Li's charge, were those patients able to walk, each man carrying with him a clean sheet, a padded quilt, a pillow, a suit of clothes, a teapot and a cup. The kitchen staff followed, taking the stove, boiler and tables.

"The laundry men went next," Mary said later. "They were grieved only that they could not move the fixed sinks and the water supply. All the staff packed their own things, but we three —Miss Fisher, Dr. Bryan Brown and myself—concentrated our efforts on hospital property. We were promised fifty soldiers to carry things and stretcher bearers for the seven patients who could not walk. By evening, all the staff and coolies, except for two who stayed to cook us food, had gone. About twenty soldiers came and took the lighter goods, but refused to take the heavy boxes. Then we heard rain spattering into the ground. We were told that the stretcher bearers wouldn't come because of it, so we settled down to wait the rain out."

It rained all through the night and halfway through the morning. A friendly officer came round to see if everyone had gone. Finding the two women still there with Dr. Bryan Brown, Nik, the two coolies and seven immobilized patients, he asked: "What about food? Have you any?"

Mary shook her head. "It's all been moved out."

He clacked his tongue in sympathy. Then he sent a man to the railway station to bring them supplies. The man returned presently with two smoked chickens, bread and several dozen eggs. Mary carved up the chickens and portioned them out. Food had been no serious problem for some days, but over the past months Mary had lost a great deal of weight. She had gone down from her normal nine stone three to seven stone.

At one o'clock on Sunday morning, the stretcher bearers finally returned. As Etheldreda described the scene: "We were suddenly galvanized into activity. Mary and Dr. Bryan Brown moved the patients onto the stretchers while Mr. Nikulin and

I took their beds to pieces and stored them away. Mary's final act before leaving was to haul down the hospital's flag."

At quarter to two in that starlit morning the procession set out: the stretcher bearers in the lead with their burdens, Etheldreda, Mary, Nik and Dr. Bryan Brown bringing up the rear. It had been exceptionally hot during the day, but now it was pleasantly cool. There was no moon, but the stars gave a faint glow to the night so that it was possible to discern the communications trench and use it as a direction line. Presently the hurrying stretcher bearers left quite a wide gap between themselves and the four foreigners in their wake.

For some time, brooding over the evacuation, Mary said nothing. To her it was a sad, if unavoidable admission of failure. Then Etheldreda's quiet chuckle caught her attention.

"Just what do you find funny in this?" she whispered.

"Have you paused to consider—" Etheldreda began, and broke off into an uncontrollable giggle. "H-have you paused to consider," she tried again, "what an extraordinary collection of oddments we've snatched up to carry at the last moment? I've got three candlesticks with nearly burnt out candles, matches, two fly swats, two packs of playing cards. . . . What about you?"

Now it was Mary's turn to chuckle.

She totted up her score: "Smallpox vaccine, about *fifty* keys, an umbrella, a bottle of ink, scissors and a Red Cross flag."

Dear Etheldreda: she always saw the funny side. Perhaps things weren't so completely black after all.

They felt their way through the cool night.

"Who goes there?" a voice rapped out of the darkness.

"The head of the Benevolent Place of Healing," Dr. Bryan Brown replied, giving the hospital's Chinese name.

"Where are you going?" the sentry demanded.

"To the Hall of the Lord of Heaven." That was what the Chinese called the Roman Catholic seminary.

"*Where?*"

The doctor sighed.

"My voice is not as big as all that," he said. "Come over here and talk."

"No—one of you come over here."

The doctor did so, and after a short exchange was given permission to proceed. Then they went through the lines.

At about half-past two they arrived at the seminary and were shown their beds. Back in the direction of the city, heavy firing had broken out again, but for once Mary could not bring herself to dwell upon it. She was very tired.

She checked to make sure that the evacuated patients were cared for, and then, for the first time in many weeks exercised the luxury of taking off all her clothes and getting into a nightgown.

She did not remember getting into bed. Sleep came upon her like the flicking of a switch.

She did not awaken until half-past ten the following morning, and then only because of voices outside the door of her room.

Coming wide awake, she heard Dr. Bryan Brown saying in Chinese: "Go and tell Miss Ball."

She was out of bed in an instant and because of an inner prompting she could not explain rushed to the window.

A motor car was parked at the seminary gate. It was flying an American flag. She had already begun to dress when a knock came at her door and a Chinese voice told her that Mr. Stanton, the American consul, had arrived from Kalgan: Dr. Bryan Brown had gone down to meet him.

She finished dressing and hurried to join them. Stanton was a pleasant man, anxious to help. He would write a note to the general in charge of the city and have it delivered to him, he promised; he hoped that, as a result, Mrs. Bryan Brown and the children would be allowed to join her husband.

He also tried to persuade Mary to return to Kalgan with him.

Mary thanked him for his concern.

"But I'm afraid I can't do it," she said. "I'm responsible for our patients, you understand, Mr. Stanton, and also for the nursing staff, who are far from home. I really couldn't leave them now."

It took two days for a reply to come to Stanton's note. The Shansi general regretted having to say that no foreigner could

Mary with Chinese girl, one of her Caesarean babies.
Soon after, she left China.

Main Street, Tatung, cluttered and dusty.

Above left.
Christmas, 1939, in the men's ward. "The Japanese made a shambles of our efficiency," Mary said.

Earth-emptying in sacks from the east tunnel by human chain. The aim : to blow up the city walls.

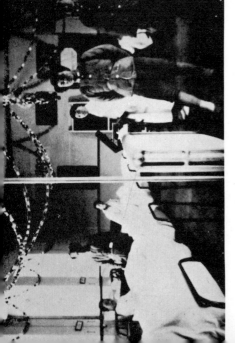

be permitted to leave the city as he had a special order from the Governor of the province to protect all foreigners: he feared for their safety if he were to let any of them go.

"That isn't his real reason," Mary commented. "I think they're being kept as hostages." The General had added gratuitously that food was plentiful in the city and that all the foreigners there were safe and well.

Next morning, Stanton sent in another note, no longer requesting but *demanding* the release of the Bryan Browns. At eight o'clock that night word was received that Mrs. Bryan Brown and the children had been given permission to leave the city.

By then, a representative of the Swedish Legation—a Mr. Larsen—had arrived on the scene to represent the Swedish nationals trapped in Tatung. He, Stanton and Dr. Bryan Brown decided to call on Feng's area commander to arrange an armistice so that those allowed to leave the city could do so in safety. A twelve hours' cease-fire was granted. It was to extend from noon until midnight.

"The arrangements were that we should be at the hospital by three that afternoon," Mary explained afterwards. "The ones to be let out would be on the wall by then. First a Chinese was to go with a white flag and say we had come for the city folk. Then five coolies with hospital arm bands should go to receive their goods and chattels, then Mr. Larsen and Dr. Bryan Brown should go with the coolies for Mrs. Bryan Brown and the children."

Mary went with the others as far as the hospital. She examined it fearfully for further damage but found none. This was her first chance to take a good look at the shell holes in the roof: somehow they appeared larger than she had expected: It made her heart sick to see them and to realize that now the building was open to the weather and that it would likely be a long time before any repairs could be effected.

They waited for Mrs. Bryan Brown and the children to appear on the city wall. When they did, they were more than an hour late. Under a flag of truce, Dr. Bryan Brown, Mr. Larsen and—

deciding to go at the last minute—Mary crossed the field to the foot of the wall. For some reason of their own, never explained, the troops on the wall had shouted down that the American consul was to remain behind.

"I had linen laundry bags for travelling," Mrs. Bryan Brown said later, describing the lowering. "Big canvas ones. I tied the children in them, the bigger children with their heads out, and the soldiers lowered them down on a rope. When my turn came, the bag only came to my knees, but I was tied in somehow. Mr. Scott, who had come to see me off, said: 'Look at the sky and you won't be giddy.' Somehow, we all made it. We were nearly in rags, our stockings clumsily patched, as there had been no darning wool in the city."

Lowered down with the Bryan Browns was the widow of a Swedish missionary—a Mrs. Hoagland—and her small son. When they were all safely down, they walked the three miles to the seminary.

By now, the railway line was open to Peking, controlled by Feng's army. Mrs. Hoagland wasted no time, but left at once. A couple of days later an Australian Salvation Army woman, Major Gilliam, stopped at the seminary. She had come from a city up the line.

"I am going to Peking," she said. "Would anyone care to come with me?"

Etheldreda looked at Mary. Surely the worst was now over.

"Well, yes," she said. "I think it would be all right for me to go now." She had come to Tatung for a holiday of one week and had been caught up between the battle lines for twelve.

"It had been very hard on her," Mary said later, "but I don't know what I should have done without her to bolster my courage."

As for the explosives in the second tunnel, they never were set off. Soon after Etheldreda left, the city paid a ransom to Feng and the siege was lifted.

When Mary moved back into the hospital, she was shocked by what she saw. Nearly everything that was movable had been looted; mattresses had been slit and emptied of straw, and it was strewn through the wards. The dispensary floor was a mess of broken bottles.

At once she went to work to set things straight, though there was little she could do beyond tidying up the worst of the mess. The girl nurses returned from the city, but the hospital could no longer accommodate them. By the end of September, the last one had left for Peking. Then Dr. Bryan Brown went down to report to the Bishop that they would have to begin again almost from scratch.

Hearing this, the Bishop wired for Nik and Mary to take the first train to Peking. Isabel Garnett, the matron Mary had relieved, was now back from England. While she had been in Tatung, she had adopted a small Chinese girl named Hung Yin, now eight years of age, and she asked Mary to bring her along to Peking to attend school there.

However, the railway and its rolling stock had suffered greatly during the fighting. It was no longer easy to find travelling space, even in goods wagons. Nik said to Mary on the station platform: "You wait here—I'll see what I can do."

He came back to announce proudly that he had wangled space —he didn't say how—in a covered carriage. They climbed into it and found it nearly full of soldiers and civilians. Two elderly Chinese women nodded at Mary, smiling knowingly.

While they arranged their luggage to sit on, Mary saw the two women take a second surprised look at them. They looked first at Hung Yin, then at Nik and finally at Mary, increasingly puzzled. They stared at Mary's red hair.

One of the soldiers asked: "Is that *your* little girl?"

"Oh, no," Mary said.

One of the women asked the same thing. Then the other woman spoke directly at Hung Yin.

"Is *that* your mother?"

The child shook her head.

Nik nudged Mary. "I hope you don't mind," he said. "I hope you don't mind but I got these places by saying you were my wife and child."

Mary looked first at Hung Yin, so obviously Chinese, then at Nik, so obviously not, and bit her lip. But she could not keep the laughter in: it came out in a rippling cascade, loosening the tensions of the past weeks.

And Mary thought: If only Etheldreda were here!

*   *   *

CHAPTER VIII

IN Peking, Mary had a down-to-earth talk with the Bishop concerning the future of the hospital. Clearly, with all the repairs needed for the building, it would not be functioning properly for some time. In addition—the Bishop told her—Dr. Bryan Brown had come to a reluctant decision: to return to England with his family.

"All of you went through a very hard time during the siege," the Bishop said sympathetically. "Was it too much for you, Miss Ball? Are you fed up with Tatung? Would you like to be sent somewhere else?"

"Somewhere *else?*" Mary said, surprising herself with her own vehemence. "Oh, no! The job there—it's only begun."

"You mean you actually still like the city, after all this?" the Bishop asked curiously.

"Yes—I feel quite at home in Tatung."

The Bishop twisted his episcopal ring, the amethyst gleaming under the room lights. "That's very odd, you know—very odd, and very satisfactory. It's been difficult to get people to go there to work. They've been reluctant because of the town's reputation as the wickedest in China."

"Then they must have been the wrong sort of people."

He laughed, and his laughter made him sound younger than his years. "You are an outspoken young woman, aren't you? Not that it's always such a bad idea."

The Bishop fell silent. From behind his large desk he seemed to be journeying far into the future; then he focussed back on Mary.

"I wonder—" he began, and shook his head as if clearing his thoughts. "Miss Ball, you may recall a conversation we had some time ago. I said that one day we intend to have the hospital run by the Chinese themselves—that it is S.P.G. policy to teach them to do so and eventually to hand over to them."

"I remember our talk very well," Mary said with a faint smile.

"Ah—yes," the Bishop said, his own lips twitching. "Now I wonder if the time hasn't come to take another firm step in that direction. . . . Would you be willing to go back to Tatung—after you've had a good rest, of course—and work there under a Chinese superintendent?"

Without hesitation, Mary said: "Certainly. Aside from anything else, I feel it would be the best way to break down the local resistance against us."

Mary could be decisive when the need arose ("She was very firm with her nurses and the doctors," Mrs. Bryan Brown said of her, "but they all loved her"); yet now she hesitated. Somehow, in the Bishop's presence she always seemed to feel rather like a very junior schoolgirl being brought before the head.

Then she blurted out: "Can you tell me if the man you have in mind is anyone I know?"

"Certainly. It's Dr. Li."

"Francis?"

"Yes." The Bishop's eyebrows shot up. "How do you feel about him?"

"I get along with him very well," Mary said carefully. She was, indeed, fond of the Chinese doctor; and though she had some small, lingering doubts about certain facets of his character, she did not wish to hurt his chances.

She could tell by the way the Bishop looked at her that he sensed her reservations; but he did not pursue her about them.

He said: "Of course, you'll find his methods are different from ours—you must make all allowances for that: he thinks like a Chinese, not a European. Yet I do feel this is the right step to take."

But the times were still unsettled in China. As Isabel Garnett has put it: "After the trouble between the war lords, we started all over again—late in 1926. Then, in the spring of 1927, Mary and I were ordered to evacuate the hospital and return to Peking when a wave of anti-foreign feeling spread through the country, accompanied by some violence. It was not considered safe to allow foreign women to remain in isolated stations.

"We were both quite rebellious at the area of having to run away from our posts, but of course we had to do as we were told. I used to envy Mary the beautiful simplicity of her outlook; and I often thought how well the description of St. Barnabas fitted her, for she was certainly a good woman and full of the Holy Ghost; but she was no plaster saint. We began, sadly, to wind up our work and pack our trunks and presently Mary came upon a box of chocolates we had been planning to keep for Easter. It was then the beginning of Lent.

"'Let's open it now and eat them up,' Mary said. 'How can we be expected to keep Lent rules under these circumstances?'

"We sat down, in the midst of the confusion of packing, and opened the box. By the time we reached Peking next evening, there wasn't a chocolate left. Mary was a very human person."

They had, by then, scarcely begun to get the hospital back in running order, but Dr. Li, Nik and a skeleton Chinese staff remained to finish the job. The two women did not get back again until August, 1928.

They arrived at the Tatung station at four o'clock one afternoon—not aboard a scheduled train, for none was running then, but in a cattle car. Dr. Li and Nik, who had met every incoming train for days, were waiting on the platform.

Dr. Li hurried forward, smiling, with Nik's gangling form at his heels.

"We're very pleased to see you back again," the doctor said. "Nikulin, if you'll look after the luggage, I'll arrange for rickshaws."

Francis has become accustomed to authority, Mary thought. She also noticed that during her absence he had become friendly with the railway officials and the military personnel who occupied the station. Indeed, a smile from him was enough to take them straight through, without the customary examination of their luggage.

Mary found her heart beating more quickly as they came to the hospital compound.

"I'm afraid you won't find things as they used to be," Dr. Li said, as they got out of their rickshaws, "but I've done my best to keep the hospital together. I hadn't realized how much you ladies did—" he chuckled wryly,"—nor how often you must have been awakened from a sound sleep to fasten the banging windows the nurses always open without fastening. I've had plenty of *that*."

When they had unpacked, Mary and Miss Garnett went on an inspection tour of the hospital. The building had been repaired and much of the equipment had been restored, but not enough new linen had yet arrived. Mary noticed that much now in use had been torn during the siege and had been clumsily mended.

When she spoke to Dr. Li about it, he appeared to be embarrassed.

"I'm responsible for that, I fear," he said. "I did the mending and I'm no expert at such things. It's not the same as stitching up a wound. Did you notice that the white cotton mending thread gave out halfway through? I had to finish up with black."

"I noticed," Mary said gently. She was both amused and touched. How contradictory Francis was: once not seeming to care whether patients lived or died and now himself mending the sheets for their beds. Had he really changed? Had his new position as superintendent given him a radically altered view of his responsibilities?

One newcomer to Tatung during Mary's absence had been an elderly S.P.G. priest named Griffiths who had plans to start a mission to the Mongols. Tatung was to be his stepping-off place after all his preparations were complete.

One evening, Mr. Griffiths came to call at the hospital and to volunteer a report on Dr. Li's behaviour in the past few months. The priest was frankly puzzled. "Your Dr. Li seems almost to be two separate persons," he told Mary, frowning. "I must say I don't understand him at all."

"Why, what do you mean?" Mary asked.

"First let me say that I have only the highest praise for one thing he did after all the foreigners were evacuated. He called together all the Chinese members of the S.P.G. and the China Inland Mission and had them form a Christian alliance, drawing up a declaration of their common belief in God. Considering how high the anti-foreign feeling was then, this was extraordinarily courageous of Li.

"But at the same time, do you know what else he was doing? Consorting with the military leaders of the city—certainly not fit company for the doctor in charge of a mission hospital, with their drinking, gambling and carousing. Your Dr. Li has fallen into evil ways. He has succumbed to the temptations of the city."

Mary thanked the priest—though not effusively—for his information. Privately she was inclined to belittle his criticism. After all, she thought, Francis is a Christian. And although they still lived in their village near Peking—far from Dr. Li's post in Tatung—he did have a wife and children. Besides, she had known him now for some time. He certainly had inscrutable ways and ideas foreign to her own, but she had always thought of him as basically good and kind. Still, she could see that it would not do for the superintendent of an S.P.G. hospital to be smeared by scandal. She would keep her eyes and ears open and try to help Francis if he needed it.

Mary settled in again at the hospital very quickly. In a week, it seemed to her that she had never been away; and yet it was not the same as it had been before the siege. The attitude of the people had changed radically: for now they seemed to look upon the hospital and its staff without their former doubting rancour. The fact that a Chinese doctor had been made superintendent undoubtedly had made a difference, but the change was due to more than that.

It had to no small extent come about *because* of the siege; because Mary and Dr. Li, Nik and all the other staff members who had remained at their posts had gone through the same hard and dangerous times the Tatung people had experienced when, had they so desired, they could easily in the beginning have cut and run. As an indication of their newly-acquired respect for Mary, the Chinese of the area took to calling her *Po hsien sheng*: Teacher Ball. She was accepted by them at last, and she was glad.

However, it still troubled her greatly that the people in the rural districts around Tatung did not make use of the hospital. She volunteered to go villaging with a mission team in order to spread the word of their return. This began with short forays every Tuesday, setting out in carts, taking a picnic lunch, and returning before sunset. The carts were drawn by mules, with bells round their necks.

When the village children, playing in the earthen streets, heard the tinkling of the bells, they stopped their games to shout: "Look! Look! The foreign devils have come!"

The mules would pull the carts into the village, through the gate and behind the mud wall that protected it from bandits.

Mary's helper, a male nurse, would tell the children: "If you have anyone at home sick or who needs medicine, the doctor is here now. You can come and have free treatment." Mary, of course, was the 'doctor'.

On one occasion, a small boy said to the male nurse: "My granny can't see. Will you come and look at her eyes?"

"Can't your granny come here to the doctor?"

"Oh, yes—she can come; I will go and fetch her." After a couple of steps he turned back anxiously and said to Mary: "You'll be sure to wait, won't you, doctor?"

"I'll be here."

Presently he returned along the village street. A bent old woman hobbled along beside him, one hand clutching a heavy stick, the other leaning heavily on the boy's shoulder.

Mary looked at her eyes and saw that they were covered with a white film; turned back her eyelids and saw the granular growth characteristic of trachoma. Still, Mary knew, it was possible that the old woman might have some very slight vision out of the sides of her eyes, in which case possibly an operation could help her.

"Can you see the sun?" Mary asked her gently.

The old woman looked towards the sky, feeling for the warmth with her blind eyes.

"No," she said. "I can't see the sun."

Mary held up two fingers, close to the side of one of her eyes and asked if she could see them.

"No: I can't see anything."

Mary sighed within herself and gave the old woman a caressing pat on the shoulder. It was very hard to deny all hope to her.

"Honourable old lady," Mary said, "I can do nothing for your eyes. You are blind."

Expecting tears, Mary waited for her reaction; but when it came, she was stunned.

For the old lady's face lit up with joy. She groped for Mary's hand and squeezed it with bony fingers.

"What a wonderful doctor you are!" she chortled. "You are quite right—of course, I cannot see!"

And the people of the village, who had gathered round Mary's cart, nodded their heads knowingly to one another and to Mary and said in a happy, ragged chorus: "Oh, you're quite right! She hasn't been able to see for years!"

As a result of her villaging, many old ladies brought to Tatung for a week's Bible school by the Chinese Inland Mission would come to pay a social call on their friend, *Po hsien sheng*.

These old ladies were delighted when they saw the hospital stairs. While they laughed and giggled, Mary would try to help them up and into the building, one at a time.

"This must be like going to Heaven," one remarked. "I've never seen things like these before."

But most of these old peasant women could not bring themselves to *walk* up the stairs which were like a new plaything to them; instead they would crawl on hands and knees, attacked by a fresh fit of giggling at every step. And when their visit to Po *hsien sheng* was over, they came down again—these old and wrinkled ladies—sitting on each step like children and lowering themselves down with great caution to the next.

"I can picture them yet," Mary recalled with pleasure, years later. "Twenty old ladies with bound feet crawling on all fours up the stairs, with me tending behind them like a shepherd dog, giving each one a great heave at the top to get her on to her unsteady feet—then leading the way to the ward to show them the doctor's hand basin. I would turn on the water.

" 'Where does it come from?' they would exclaim in wonder.

"I would point and say: 'From the pipes.'

"They could scarcely believe it. I would then invite them, in turn, to wash their hands which they did with noisy glee. But the greatest moment of excitement came when I pulled the plug and the water disappeared. In a chorus, they all flopped onto the floor to try and find out where it went.

"They were less joyous but even more astounded at the lavatory. They found the rush of water terrifying and considered the open fields far better; besides, since they had to buy water by the pail or else walk some distance to their wells, they thought our system an unnecessary waste. Their feeling seemed to be: 'This is the way the foreigners live, but it would *never* do for us.'

"They were like children, full of curiosity and joy and scarcely able to wait for their return to their village so that they might tell of the wonders they had seen."

When Mary began to extend her villaging to more distant regions and for periods of a week or more at a time, she was joined by Agnes Elisson, a fair-haired Swedish evangelical missionary with large and solemn blue eyes. She was very young to be stationed in an outpost like Tatung, in her early twenties, and she suffered from perpetual self-doubts. She was never confident of her ability to cope with the Chinese people.

But while Mary continued to use a mule cart for these long back country visits, Agnes forced herself to ride on donkey-back. It was her way of flailing out at her self doubting.

Mary had known her since before the siege, at a time when a Miss Fredericksson used to do the village work for her mission, which was run with Teutonic thoroughness—and strictness—by a Miss Beschmidt and a Miss Lochman, both well over seventy.

When Miss Fredericksson left for home, Agnes was ordered to take over her village work. She had not long since completed her Chinese language course, had never before spoken the language in public, and now, on her first villaging trip with Mary—to a hamlet in the hills about forty miles east of Tatung she knew that she would have to address the local inhabitants. She was almost beside herself with worry. She could not contain her fears.

"They'll never understand a word I say!" she told Mary. "What ever shall I do?"

Mary tried to bolster her confidence, but nothing she could say appeared to help. By the time they came to their destination, the young missionary seemed on the verge of hysteria.

"Now pull yourself together, Agnes," Mary told her firmly. "Your Chinese is very good indeed: you've really no cause to get yourself into a state."

Pale and trembling, the young woman addressed the villagers. As soon as she finished, she sat down and burst into tears.

"They d-didn't understand a word!" she sobbed. "N-not a single word!"

But her Chinese Bible woman had already stood up to speak to the small crowd.

"I hope you village people will do everything Miss Elisson has said," she began, and then—to Agnes' amazement repeated her address almost word for word, showing in her tactful Oriental way that the young foreign woman had been completely understood. Agnes, drying her eyes, brightened; but then the Bible woman continued speaking on her own.

"If you wish to thank God for anything—if the harvest has been good or there has been a son in the family—what do you do? Make a feast? Offer a money gift at the temple? Or just kneel down and thank God for it?"

Her audience of Chinese villagers looked blank. She bent forward and shook a fierce finger at them.

"No," she said, "I know what you do: you gather up large stones in the field and build an altar and kill a lamb from the flock and offer it as a burnt sacrifice."

At that the villagers smiled and nodded to one another, saying: "Yes, yes—that's what we do."

Agnes leaned towards Mary, whispering: "Why, they sound as if they came straight out of the Old Testament!"

Mary smiled. "Yes, and it's your job to lead them straight into the New—and in Chinese."

"Oh, Mary—do you really think I can?"

"Of *course* you can," Mary told her confidently. "See how well they understood you today!"

One great stumbling block at the hospital now was in the recruitment of dependable young Chinese men and women to study nursing; for the trained and partly-trained nursing staff had been dispersed after the siege, most of them to take posts or continue their education in hospitals far from Tatung. To replace the lost women trainees, Miss Garnett decided to try out several orphan girls from a home run by the China Inland Mission.

"I had a busy time cleaning them before I dared put them to work in the wards," Mary told a friend. "Lysol baths, head compresses and fumigated clothing were the first order of the day. But, as it turned out, they were very slow, physically and mentally, and hadn't the slightest idea of what nursing meant."

In fact, one of these girls, on night duty, was discovered asleep in bed with a patient suffering from acute tuberculosis. Shocked, Mary gave her a severe dressing down which reduced the culprit to tears. Two nights later, she was again found asleep in bed with another patient. The experiment was dropped forthwith. Thus the finding of replacement staff was again a high priority problem.

One evening that autumn, a young man of about twenty walked wearily through the hospital gate, carrying over a shoulder his bedroll of padded quilts. Since Mary was on duty, he was brought to see her.

His name was Luke Hsieh, he told her, and he wanted to become a nurse at the hospital.

"Where have you come from?" she asked, having noted the signs of travel.

"A town near Hung Tung," he said. Hung Tung was a good three hundred miles to the south.

"That's a very great distance," Mary said appreciatively. "How did you get here?"

The youth hesitated.

"By foot," he said at last. "Sleeping in the open, living off the land."

"But why did you walk? Why did you not come by train when it was such a great distance?"

The boy appeared flustered, obviously not wishing to admit that he was penniless; but finally he looked into her eyes. "There was no way out," he said. "I *had* to walk."

"*Ni hao?*" Mary asked him then. "*Chih la fen mei?* Are you well? Have you eaten?"

"*Chi la.* I have eaten."

But he looked to Mary as if he had not; his hesitant manner gave him away.

"Well, come along and have a little with me, just to keep me company. I'm having my dinner now."

She gave him hot water and he washed his hands and face.

As they sat down, Mary said: "You look very tired, Luke. How many days has it taken you to come?"

"Very many," the boy said.

She could see that she had presumed correctly: he was bravely trying to restrain his hungry haste, but there was no doubt that he had been half starved. She let him attack his food in concentrated silence until it seemed it would serve him better to slow him down. Then she plied him with further questions and he answered them between mouthfuls.

Why had he come so far to study nursing? Was there another reason?

Yes, he admitted: he had come to satisfy his desire to continue the Christian studies he had begun some time before, under the tutelage of the Salvation Army missionary in Tatung.

"Here?" Mary said, surprised. "Right here in Tatung?"

The youth nodded. He had worked as a telegraphist in Tatung; he had been there a little before, and all through the siege; but after the siege was over he had been sent by the Shansi Government to the town near Hung Tung where he had not been able to find anyone who could continue to teach him about Christianity.

He said: "We in the city during the siege heard a great deal of talk about the First Benevolence Hospital, and about the Christian foreigners who stayed to care for the Chinese patients without minding that they risked their lives to do it. It seemed to me that it would be a very fine thing to learn to become a nurse from such Christians—who could also help me go on with my religious studies." He looked anxiously at Mary for approval. "Is it not a good idea?"

The boy was intelligent and his attitude could hardly be more suitable for a mission hospital, Mary reflected. He certainly did not fear the foreign devils.

"Yes; indeed it is a very good idea," she said.

It was little short of a miracle, she thought, the way the attitude of the local people had changed towards the hospital. Yet she could not help wondering what the attitude would now be if Feng had assaulted the city from the hospital grounds—and had succeeded.

By now, Mary's command of the language—and especially of the local 'earth talk' made her feel even more thoroughly at home in Tatung; instead of her nurse's uniform, she had taken to wearing a Chinese gown; she had even begun to *think* in Chinese, and there were times when, with a wry turn of inner amusement, she caught herself listening to English spoken by others as if that were the foreign tongue.

But Nik, who had been in China ever since he had escaped from the destroyed White Russian Army by crossing Siberia and over the North China frontier hanging onto the rods of a passenger train, had no ear for the language at all.

At about this time—in the autumn of 1928—he decided to keep white rabbits in order to be less mindful of his loneliness.

He bought several pairs and built a hutch for them behind the engine house. He poured a great deal of his attention on these rabbits and took great pride in them.

Once Mary and Dr. Francis Li, relaxing after a difficult Cæsarean, found him trying to feed them and looking worried over their unprecedented lack of interest in food.

Dr. Li waved to him.

"And how are your rabbits today, Nik?" he asked in Chinese. The word for rabbit in the northern dialect is *tu tze*.

Unfortunately for Nik—who found it difficult to master such subtle distinctions—the word for stomach is *tu tzu* so that his reply came out as: "My stomach is rotten."

The Superintendent burst into spontaneous laughter.

Nik, secretly puzzled, joined in. But when Dr. Li left them, he turned to Mary, scratching his head.

"What was he laughing at?"

Mary explained and added: "You can't blame Francis—you must admit it was very funny."

Crestfallen, Nik said: "I don't blame him—only myself. Oh, this Chinese! If I'm here for a hundred years I'll still never know it!"

Indeed, the difficulty he found in speaking Chinese was no joke to him: it sorely limited his social life, and he was a gregarious man by nature.

Like many of his countrymen, his moods reached out to both extremes, the high peaks of exuberance and the deep valleys of despond—the latter usually forced upon him by the special awareness of being alone that came from complete separation from his own kind. There was no other Russian living in Tatung.

Even if a stranger from his own land had come to be his neighbour in exile, Nik, certainly at first, would have viewed him with suspicion. As a White Russian, he lived in constant terror of the Reds. Once, Mary recalled, not long after her own arrival in Tatung, an itinerant Russian salesman had knocked on Mrs. Bryan Brown's door. Nik happened to be away for a few days, but when he returned Mrs. B.B. told him about her caller, thinking that he might take some vicarious pleasure out of the fact that a fellow countryman had passed through the district. Mary remembered how pale Nik had turned. "Maybe they're after me!" he had muttered, hurrying for cover to his engine room as if the Russian secret police were only a step behind.

When Isabel Garnett remarked that what Nik really needed was a wife—preferably White Russian—Mary felt compelled to agree. Nik was not the sort who lived happily alone.

The longer Mary worked alongside Francis Li, the more she realized that the Superintendent was a many-sided person. Doubtless as an inheritance of his farm upbringing, he was fond of gardening and took a keen special interest in the vegetable plot in the hospital grounds. Whenever it needed hoeing or weeding he would call for volunteers amongst the men and women nurses. Since they were fond of him, they responded magnificently, and under his overlordship the vegetables prospered as they never had before.

But he was especially fond of flowers. Once, on a visit to Peking, he bought a hundred chrysanthemum plants and brought them back to Tatung with him. These, with loving care, he potted and placed along the windows of the hospital's corridors. Every day, when he had a spare half hour, his tall form could be seen, bent over them, watering the pots and picking off the small buds so that in the end he nurtured one exquisite bloom on each plant. Then, every morning, in a mild ecstasy of appreciation, he would take Mary with him, stopping at each blossom to bask in the very special beauty it appeared to radiate for him.

"We'd better see these patients first," he would say, smiling happily. He would pause. "Now, this one I expected to be pink, but you see it turned out to be one of the much rarer lemon-coloured ones. I'm very happy about that."

On occasion, members of the nursing staff who were on duty would leave their patients for long enough to trail after him, enjoying his enthusiasms. He would turn round to them and say almost passionately: "Now, remember! No one is to touch or water these plants but myself!"

He was also keenly interested in collecting small antique

bronze or stone Chinese statues, enormous china vases and exquisitely carved bits of jade. He spent much of his spare time in Tatung's curio shops looking for such treasures, and from his private patients was always happy to accept, in lieu of a cash fee, any *objet d'art* which would add lustre to his collection.

Now that he had entered his forties, Francis decided·that he was getting old. In keeping with his advanced years he took to taking snuff out of an ancient, golden-brown bottle; and he replaced his former pipe with one he considered more dignified— a long one with a bamboo stem, tiny silver bowl and jade mouth-piece. He had previously always gone bareheaded while on duty, but now he affected a round Mandarin hat of black satin with a black button on the top, even when he wore a white uniform coat over his black Chinese robe. How was Mary to know that, far from settling down as he had seemed to, into sedate middle age, Francis had in fact entered his dangerous years.

As the months passed, Mary almost forgot Mr. Griffiths' warn-ing that Francis had succumbed to the evil ways of Tatung. She had become satisfied in her own mind that there was no real basis for his accusation that the Chinese superintendent had taken up with bad company, though on the face of it there did seem to be some evidence which might be construed to indicate this. The simple truth was that, liking Francis, Mary was reluctant to believe that he was being led astray.

It was now true that he was the only qualified doctor in Tatung. Therefore—she told herself—was it not natural that the military governor and his lieutenants should come to him and bring their families for medical treatment? It was certainly true that the military clique lived to the corrupt limit which Tatung offered: they drank and gambled to excess and consorted with the women of the streets. But they did control the city. Mary was convinced that it was Francis's desire to make them understand the work of the hospital and not hinder it, as they certainly could if they wished, that made him befriend them.

Eventually, it became clear that the city's military governor, General Chao Ch'eng Shou, who also commanded the garrison and the area around Tatung, had gone out of his way to court

Francis's friendship. It was this discovery that first made Mary wonder if, after all, there might have been a real basis for Mr. Griffiths' criticisms.

Chao, a tall and heavy-set man in his late thirties, was all-powerful in Tatung. A man of many moods, he could be devastatingly charming or utterly ruthless. Whenever he walked through the town he was followed by three fierce-looking bodyguards.

Not until much later did Mary learn how ambitious the general was, or that, in the name of the Governor of Shansi, he held the deeds to the land on which the hospital was built; nor could she possibly have guessed at this time that he was already laying his plans for the day when he hoped to take over the hospital for his private financial gain.

Neither was she aware that he had already made approaches of surface friendliness to Nik, suggesting that he might one day become his technical advisor in connection with his grandiose but indefinite plans to modernise the city.

Chao had six wives: the first he had pensioned off as past her prime; the second, who had already given him nine girls and a boy, was reserved for the production of children; the third was kept for the pleasure her beauty gave him; the fourth and fifth acted as nursemaids for the children of the second; and the sixth was merely an afterthought.

Originally it was because of his wives—to minister to their ailments—that Chao often called Francis to military headquarters. Then, doubtless thinking that he might be of use to him in other ways, he began inviting the Superintendent for social visits.

Out of the city's miasmal flow of gossip, Mary was able to guess that there were no boundaries to the general's amorality, but gambling was his favourite vice. He would play for high stakes all day and through the night with his cronies, held in a kind of quiet frenzy by the lure of Mah Jongg, a game which in a certain stratum of Chinese society made slaves of more men than opium.

What Mary had no way then of knowing was that Francis had already succumbed to the general's sly invitation to 'take a hand'—though she soon enough learned of it; and that this was the true source of his eventual downfall. For, though he began in a small way with stakes he could afford, the Superintendent soon lost all restraint.

As yet unaware of the reason, Mary nevertheless could hardly fail to observe how Francis's habits had changed. Where, previously, he had seldom left the hospital, now he began to stay out in the evenings, returning at first before midnight but staying gradually later and later until he would not re-appear until after eight in the morning, barely in time to take breakfast and start on his morning rounds.

He made no excuse or comment. If there were operations to be performed, he would operate at ten as usual; if not, he would hurry to his room and sleep the morning through.

His mild, cheerfully languid manner was replaced by an unaccustomed surliness, especially with the outpatients, so that many times Mary cringed with embarrassed shame over his behaviour.

Late each afternoon, after his last outpatients' round, he would disappear into the wicked city. By the time this frenetic routine had continued for some weeks, Dr. Li had begun to look pale and drawn, like a man suffering under great strain.

Sometimes he would leave an address with the dispenser at the outpatients' department, in case of an emergency. Eventually, by these addresses and an increasing flow of rumours, Mary was able to trace his activities. She learned of his daily rendezvous with the general and, remembering back to her arrival at the station she knew at last why the military personnel there had shown him such respect. Later she heard that he had become involved with a small gambling den where the stakes were perilously high.

This was a time of inner trial for her. She was desperately anxious for Francis—whom by now she considered to be a dear friend—to extricate himself from his follies, equally anxious lest he suffer because of them; but at this time the responsibility was not hers.

"I know that Miss Garnett frequently wrote to the Bishop that

Francis had not been present for emergencies," she said in an unhappy recollection of the times. "Garnie was a great worrier, and Francis's extra-curricular activities were becoming increasingly bandied about by the foreign members of other missions in Tatung—a very strait-laced lot. 'Do you know,' they would say primly to Garnie and to me, 'do you know that your Dr. Li is gambling in the city now—and goodness knows what else?'"

By then, not the least upset over the Superintendent's waywardness, was his sponsor, the Bishop, who from distant Peking tried to puzzle out a way of stopping the rot. At last he decided on drastic measures: to send the doctor's wife and children up to Tatung from their village and to give the Li family Dr. Bryan Brown's former house to live in.

His hope was that a renewal of family life would pull the Superintendent together. At the time, neither the Bishop nor Mary knew the full story of his marriage.

When the Bishop wrote to Francis, announcing that he was sending his family to join him, he also sent a note to Mary advising her of his action. She spoke to the doctor about it, expecting some small sign of pleasure from him at the news, but he did not commit himself one way or the other.

But when Mary suggested that they join forces in preparing the house for his wife's coming, he refused to participate.

"It's no use your doing anything for Mrs. Li," he said sourly. "She must fix her house the way she likes it when she gets here."

At six o'clock one morning, Mrs. Li arrived at the hospital with her five small children, the eldest eight years of age, the youngest a babe in arms. She had been travelling more or less continuously on the still disordered railway for four days and was tired to the point of exhaustion. Her husband had neither gone to the train himself nor sent anyone to meet her.

The small, prematurely aged woman—at thirty-eight she looked a good fifty—herded four of her weary brood up the stairs, carrying the youngest, a boy nurse leading the way to the doctor's bedroom on the second floor.

Dr. Li had come home earlier than usual that morning. When the knock came at his door, he answered.

"I thought I told you not to come," was all he said in an icy voice; and he slammed the door shut in her face.

Mary, sleeping at the women's end of the same floor, was awakened by the sudden clap of sound. The children, frightened, had begun to cry, and she listened to their wailing for a moment in half-sleepy puzzlement. Then the crying stopped. Still dopey with sleep, she turned over in bed to win it back.

A moment later, just as she was slipping off again, a hurried knock sounded on her door. She slipped into a robe and answered it, surprised into full wakefulness at the sight of Mrs. Li, whom she had once met in Peking, still holding her youngest child in her arms.

Without preliminary, the unhappy woman poured out her troubles.

"Oh, Miss Ball," she concluded, verging on tears, "what are we going to do?"

"Why, Mrs. Li, I'm so pleased to see you!" Mary exclaimed, searching her mind frantically for the best thing to do. "Won't you come up to the next floor with me?" The small flat Mary shared with Miss Garnett was located there—a dining room, sitting room and spare bedroom.

When mother and children were made comfortable, Mary awakened Miss Garnett and brought her into the picture. By now the hospital coolies were carrying up bulky bundles of bedding. Mrs. Li kept repeating nervously: "If you'll just give the children a drink of water, we can wait here until Dr. Li gets up."

"Oh, we can do better than that," Mary said. "Now, you wait here with Miss Garnett."

Excusing herself, she hurried down to the kitchen where she arranged for the cook to send up breakfast to Mrs. Li and her children. At sight of the millet gruel, the youngsters brightened. They finished it and curled up on the floor to sleep with no cares on their consciences.

Satisfied that they had all dropped off, Mrs. Li again sought out her husband. When she returned, her cheeks were wet with tears and later that morning, Dr. Li sent the coolies up to collect the children and luggage for removal to the house in the compound. He sent a note to Mary asking if there were any pieces of furniture which could be spared for them.

But he made it quite clear that he himself had no intention of moving with them. He would engage a cook and a coolie to help his wife, but he would sleep at the hospital as before. Since she had come against his specific orders, he felt no need to change his way of life now that she was here.

"For Mrs. Li, this was a dreadful situation," Mary commented at a later date. "There she was in a foreign house, far too large for her needs and in comparison to anything she had known before, with ceilings much too high for her taste—and nobody to talk to but her own children. She had had bound feet when she was younger, so it was difficult for her to walk to the hospital more than once a day to make friends with the nurses. She was really quite isolated."

Yet Mary, knowing Francis, was convinced that from his viewpoint he was not altogether in the wrong. In a rare burst of confidence, he substantiated her belief when he told her that his parents and his wife's had arranged a betrothal between them when they were children and unknown to one another. She was a simple country girl with no desire to improve herself, and when he became educated, had his conscience been clear to follow his own desire, he never would have married her. But, according to Chinese custom, if he had turned her down then she would have been unlikely to find another man willing to marry a rejected woman. That was why he had gone through with the wedding.

Knowing the Chinese people by now, Mary could assume the rest. Since his marriage, Francis had been put in a place of high trust by the Bishop and was looked up to by most of Tatung's men of influence. His drab and countrified wife must have seemed to him far from adequate to embellish his present position in life. Years later, a relative of Francis's told Mary: "Mrs. Li never tried to improve herself and could not entertain the new friends he made."

Who then was basically responsible, Mary wondered, for what had taken place? Francis himself? Mrs. Li? Or, indeed, the missionary society that had taken him out of his environment and made an educated man of him?

* * *

CHAPTER IX

THE months carried the seasons past, and yet no day seemed like another to Mary, nor long enough to contain its own absorbing offering of events. Often and again she tried to reveal to her sisters at home what her life in the mission hospital now meant to her, but always felt that in her letters she had somehow failed. It was much more than time and space that separated her from them.

How was it possible to convey to anyone in England the incredible variety of experience in this North China outpost— the poignant and capricious, tragic and cynical, comforting and comic, barbaric and beguiling and utterly fascinating moments of insight into the hearts of a backward people?

Could Margaret or Annie Elizabeth or Emily Helen from their far civilization ever understand why—instead of condemning poor Mrs. Liu—her heart felt like breaking for that poor woman? Two months before she had helped Dr. Li deliver a baby son to the Chinese woman by Cæsarean section; and today had admitted her back into the hospital, suffering from pneumonia.

"And how is your little son?" Mary had asked her, hoping to cheer her up.

"Oh, I gave him away," Mrs. Liu had said, with a casualness concealing torment.

Mary, shocked, repeated: "Gave him away, Mrs. Liu?"

"I was given a bolt of material in exchange for him. We must have winter clothes or freeze to death; and I could not nurse him; so I thought it best to exchange."

What was more tragic than this depth of poverty, Mary thought—again feeling the inner hurt; and yet, could poverty of any degree in Tatung be understood a full half world away as reason for such complete surrender to life's pressures?

122

But surely she could reach her sisters with *some* of the flavours that made her work precious to her.

"Sometimes I feel like recommending that all nurses who come out in the future are first given veterinarian courses," she wrote. "I was called out to deliver a kid the other day and had no idea how such an animal ought to be born; and later I was asked to diagnose if another nanny was pregnant, so I must have made a satisfactory goatherd's substitute. In my work, one simply cannot specialize!

"We have three charming children in hospital. One poor mite had her feet bound when she was eleven and both have gone gangrenous. It wasn't until the smell compelled the parents to bring her to hospital that she had any medical help.

"I deliberately say things to these children in English for the delight in hearing them mimic me. I tried to teach one little girl, suffering from TB, to say, 'Popsy, wopsy, pudding and pie,' while putting her splint on this evening, hoping to take her attention from crying. It proved wondrously successful. For an hour after, all three children were still trying to get their tongues around 'popsy, wopsy,' but they made no attempt at 'pudding and pie'. They said they had no idea what it meant, but it had a very pleasant sound and they felt sure I meant I loved them. Life is so full of good and tender things, even in the midst of sadness!"

Could Mary tell her sisters (in a way they would understand, and yet not be shocked) of the blind bondage in which gambling held the Shansi men?

Not more than a few miles from Tatung there were so many outcrops of coal that the villagers often had their own private mines. They would come into the city to buy dynamite to loosen the coal seams, and—was it only last month?—two of the villagers had come in to make just such a purchase.

On the way back home they had met a friend and were soon hotly discussing the best way to detonate the explosives. One man insisted that his method—using a simple hempen fuse—was not only the cheapest but most convenient. If he changed his mind even after the fuse was lit, he said, all he had to do was pinch the fuse with his fingers and stop the spark from travelling to the charge.

"I'll bet *that* won't work," snorted one of the others.

"Bet you fifty cents it will," said the fuse's champion. At the then rate of exchange, fifty Chinese cents were worth less than an English penny.

"Done!"

There and then, by the roadside, the first man fixed a fuse to a stick of dynamite. Lighting it, he pinched it half-way down with all the force he could muster in his fingers. Unfortunately, the spark had never heard of his argument. It travelled along the core, between his pinched fingers, and ignited the dynamite.

All three, seriously injured, were brought into the hospital where one later died. The other two were permanently maimed— all for the love of gambling.

There was so *much* to tell. Should she write of Mrs. Cheng's curious complaint—an uncontrolled craving to eat the plaster off the wall of her room and sometimes the gravel from her garden? Should she describe the treatment, partly suggestive, partly by dosage of Kaolin—the fine white clay used for making porcelain —which eventually cured her? Or her husband's satisfied comment?

"I am glad you have made her well," he had said, completely serious. "It was too expensive to have the walls of our room so often repaired."

Would they be shocked to the point of nagging for her return if she told her sisters of the time she was asked to go into the city to attend a woman who—the messenger said—had fallen down and badly cut her head? For she had found the place to be a brothel and discovered the woman to be not merely injured but stone dead.

Enquiries had revealed that she had been a good woman. Her husband, an opium addict, had gone greatly into debt to satisfy his craving; and one day, taking his wife out in a rickshaw, had left her at the brothel with strict instructions to earn money with which he could pay off his impatient debtors.

When he had called round to collect her first earnings, she

had thrown herself on him, weeping; protesting at the foul life he had forced on her; demanding that he take her home. In a blind fury, he had grabbed for the first thing at hand, striking her with it. The weapon was a heavy iron bar and the unhappy woman had never recovered consciousness.

What, indeed, should she tell her sisters and what leave out? And yet, she thought, acting as she felt she must as her own censor, how would they even guess at the life she had led in Tatung or why she found it utterly compelling?

CHAPTER X

SINCE Mary was captivated by every aspect of her work, it was certainly not for a pleasant change from hospital routine that she went out on her tours of the remote villages with Agnes Elisson. "I felt that God would use the things I could do with my hands in helping the ill, the poor and the physically dirty," she once explained.

Indeed, far from being romantic adventures, her villaging often wrought hardships no one could have relished for their own sake.

Once, for example, she and Agnes set out at half-past ten of a sunny morning in late autumn with two Chinese helpers—a man and a woman in their middle years.

"The jolly little Chinese woman shared the cart with me," Mary said, describing this tour. "She sat inside and I sat on the shafts. Agnes rode Nesa, her tough little donkey, and the men walked.

"I was well packed up with medicines and dressings, a writing pad; books, bedding and food, fresh and tinned: a smoked chicken, flour and rice. From the flour I used to make Alfred-like scones in the k'ang fire, putting them in on a shovel as we had no stove, only a cooking bowl. Potatoes were the only vegetables we could buy. We knew that after our meats ran out we could get eggs in the villages."

The day began well enough. They came to the river that flowed past Tatung, the Jade, and—as .they had done before—quite enjoyed the crossing; for the river was wide here but not deep. Ten miles from the city they stopped for lunch at an inn; but, setting out again, they found the sun had been swallowed up in a bank of clouds which was quickly filling the sky. By mid-afternoon, Mary could see in the distance that a dust storm was bearing down upon them.

She called Agnes, and the young woman, slapping her knees against Nesa's sides, came up to the cart.

"Have you noticed that?" Mary said, pointing towards the storm.

Agnes nodded. "Do you think it's going to be a bad one?"

"It looks as if it might be—and we're a long way from our usual stopping place. We'd better stay the night at the first village we come to."

She flicked the reins against her mules. Sensing the storm, they trotted quickly forward. Fortunately, Mary sighted a village just as the first gritty gusts slashed into their small caravan.

As they drove through the village gate, the blinding dust was joined by snow and sleet.

"It was a terrible storm," Mary said afterwards. "Thankfully, we turned in at an inn and made a hot drink and food. After that, fully dressed—even keeping our hats on to protect our heads from the icy storm beating through the broken paper windows—we went to bed."

They were up early next morning and on their way along what was locally known as 'The Big Road'—("Although few at home would recognize it as a road at all," Mary commented). The passing of the storm seemed to have brought out many travellers, for they met dozens of carts, loaded with vegetables and pulled by oxen, mules and donkeys. At each village they came to, Mary would ask about the harvest. Some villages had done well, others had fared very badly. Late in the afternoon, the party reached Ling Yi, the hamlet of about a hundred homes where Mary planned to begin work.

She and Agnes rented a compound from which to base their temporary operations.

"We started by cleaning the three small rooms and making fires, both to warm the mud beds and to heat food on," Mary recounted. "It was a very small compound: in fact, when I opened my consulting-dressing-dining-kitchen-bedroom, I had to be careful that Nesa, whose stall was opposite, was not too frisky. It could have been embarrassing.

"People soon came to call on us and we were kept very busy. Fortunately, since we were tired after the journey, night was not far off and when it became dark everyone went home. A meeting was held next morning—Saturday—and I saw any sick people who came; quite a large number of people came to the two Sunday meetings. On Monday morning, I called on those sick folk who had not been able to come and see me.

"That afternoon, a man rushed in, making a terrible fuss over a badly-cut hand. I took him into the surgery and washed and dressed it for him. He came for fresh dressing every day we were there and was nearly healed when we left—quite astonished that his hand had not swollen or become infected. Some of my patients brought produce in gratitude for treatment: we had quite a collection of eggs, salted vegetables and a kind of haricot beans.

"On the Tuesday, we walked to another village two miles away where Agnes preached and I looked after more patients. We got back in time to attend a feast we had been invited to by one of the mandarins.

"After much ceremony (each of us nudging and gently pushing one another and saying we were not worthy to sit on the beautiful fur-covered mud bed, nor were we worthy to eat the splendid food, nor were our manners fit to match the occasion) we sat down to the feast. We ate *garlic* and fat pork, *garlic* and scrambled eggs, *garlic* and salt beans, *garlic* with other vegetables and then rice. Fortunately, vinegar was served which helped considerably.

"Our host and his family all ate in the kitchen, leaving Agnes and me alone, except when they brought in more food. We were asked to another feast on Thursday but I said we were leaving that day. No excuse was allowed! They had prepared all the food and the bread had been steamed—we would simply have to have our feast first thing, before our hour of departure. And that was to be at dawn!

"To our horror—for we had hardly recovered from the previous overdosing of garlic, we were given *garlic* and pork, *garlic* and scrambled eggs and so on and on, as the time before; but steamed bread was served instead of the rice."

Superintendent Philip Li . . .
was still suffering from prison
camp malnutrition.

Romantic Nik. Mary thought he
looked like Lindbergh.

Mary and Agnes called at this village.

The hospital.

The sand-bagged machine-gun nest at the hospital's main gate during the siege of 1926.

On the Wednesday, it had snowed very heavily, so that when they started home after their devastating breakfast the road was hidden under drifts and a bitter wind cut into their faces, making their eyes water badly. They came to a mountain river they had forded on their way out but now the banks were choked with several feet of snow. As a result, they had to cross a bridge made of tree boughs lashed together with rope and suspended across the river's gorge.

"It was very wobbly and had no handrails," Mary said. "To get across, it was best to trot quickly while men stood at intervals with their legs well parted, trying to keep the bridge in balance. That was bad enough, but I could hardly look when the mules and cart were being brought across. And, of course, after we all made it to the other side we had to go back again to bring the things that had been unloaded from the cart! A little forethought would have saved at least one dangerous passage!"

When they were still many miles from Tatung, they were met by a messenger who said that Dr. Li, worrying about their welfare because of the storm, had sent a cart out to meet them, but that it had become stuck in a snowdrift down the line. He also had a special message for Mary: Isabel Garnett had taken ill.

"Then we must get back as soon as we can," Mary told him.

"But Teacher Ball," the messenger pleaded, "I am tired after my troubles. Can't we rest the night and go back tomorrow?"

"I must get back to Miss Garnett," Mary said, single-mindedly, and they travelled on into a bitterly cold wind for twenty more miles before putting up at an inn for the night. At daybreak, they were on the road again, stopping only for some warming tea at the same inn that had sheltered them on their first night out, when the dust storm had overtaken them.

This time, however, the landlord greeted them unenthusiastically.

"I thought his reluctance was the result of a death in the family," Mary recounted later. "I could hear loud crying coming from the room his family occupied. But I was shown into the room and found that there had been no death. Sitting on the k'ang was the grandmother of the household, a pitiable sight in patched and padded clothes, rocking to and fro and crying: 'I am seventy-six and not dead yet. My husband has been dead eight years and everyone asks me why I don't die.'

"The unexpected entrance of a foreigner caused a lull in her cries. I enquired about her family and asked for some boiling water to make tea. We each had a bowl of it. After this, she took a good look at me.

" 'Why, you're the one who came last week!'

" 'Yes,' I admitted.

" 'And did you go to the villages and teach your faith and help the sick?'

" 'We did what we could,' I said.

" 'And how many sick people did you see?'

" 'Over a hundred,' I told her.

" 'Over a hundred,' she repeated. She thought about that admiringly. 'Now,' she said, after a while, 'please tell me about your God and your faith.'

"So the woman catechist and I told her of Christ and of the hope we have in the future life. She asked many questions, and when we left came to wave us off and asked me to come again and tell her more.

"I arrived at the hospital at six-thirty that evening. It was quite a thrill to get back after so long in the wilds. I had seen twenty-six people suffering from eye diseases, four of whom were completely blind; seventeen suffering from chest troubles and coughs; and sixty-five with other complaints."

Of course, the reason Mary had driven herself so hard to return to the hospital was her concern over Isabel Garnett, who recently added a revealing postscript to the above from the Philippines, where, as Sister Isabel Mary she now serves in the Convent of St. Anne at Upi, Cotabato.

"I remember another occasion when I had reason to be very grateful to Mary Ball," she wrote. "When she was away on one of her tours of the villages, I contracted a severe eye infection and had great pain, so that I could not sleep for three nights, nor could I open my eyes. The evening she came back I was almost in despair. She rushed up the stairs and straight into my room, gave one look at me and—regardless of her own exhaustion, hunger and need for a bath and change of clothes—set to work at once with efficient treatment. After she had made me comfortable, she began to attend to the needs of the patients I had been unable to look after because of my illness.

"She was like that; single-minded in her sight of duty; reticent about religious matters, but deeply religious. I never knew her to make an uncharitable remark about anyone, nor try to impress anyone with her own good qualities."

With the winter season, villaging had to be put aside; but as soon as the roads became passable that following spring, Mary went with Agnes to an area many miles from Tatung where cloudbursts had earlier brought disaster—causing the banks of the mountain torrents to gush over and the wild floods to scour away the thin layer of earth from the terraced hills. As a result, there was now insufficient grain to feed the inhabitants of Ta Wang. Upon their arrival, the two women were visited by the Mandarin. He had, he said, a very special problem. Could they help him to solve it?

"Just what is the problem?" Mary asked practically.

"It is very hard to solve," the Mandarin admitted, shaking his head. "In the village we have eighteen unmarried girls, all of them engaged to young men in another village not far away; and when the famine came upon us their own families did not have enough to feed them and sent them to the families into which they would marry.

"But *these* families did not have enough to eat, either, and after a while sent them back hungry. Yet the first families insisted that it was the responsibility of the in-laws to feed the girls and sent them there again; and the in-laws, growing angry, said that they could not and again sent them back.

"Now," he said, sighing, "all the girls are in poor health, not having had enough to eat, and having to travel many times over the winter passes, until their bound feet bled scarlet in the snow."

The Mandarin turned hopefully to Agnes Elisson.

"Can you not take them and care for them at your Chinese Girls' School in Tatung?"

The hands of her young Swedish friend fluttered nervously, telegraphing her thoughts to Mary. She knew then that the girl was filled with a private terror of Miss Beschmidt and Miss Lochman, the two old women who ran their mission strictly to rule and seldom allowed her the initiative of taking a decision.

"Oh, Mary," she said, already surrendering to her fears. "I'm sure we can find accommodation for them; but what *they'll* say is that we haven't enough money to keep them."

The Mandarin shrugged off a sigh, his dark eyes sharply observant.

"Ah, well," he said, "if you can't take them, there is only one way out. We will have to sell them to the wandering actors."

The two European women exchanged a look of horror, for both knew that this was tantamount to being sold into prostitution.

"I think I can guarantee the money to feed them," Mary said quickly. "Provided, that is, the school could guarantee them accommodation and their families could provide clothes and bedding."

"*They* can't possibly object to that," Agnes said, with a nervous twitch of a smile.

And so it was arranged.

When their work at Ta Wang was done, Mary hired a large open cart. It was loaded with the bedding provided for the girls by their relieved parents; and then all eighteen piled aboard for the forty-mile journey over rough country roads, chattering excitedly about their first visit to the 'great city'. On the way, more than half became quite ill from the bumpy passage, but because of their feet—still raw from the mountain trails— they could not seek even the temporary relief of getting out to walk.

Nevertheless, they all reached Tatung safely in the end, were tided over the time of famine and—eventually—returned to their mountain homes.

Events had carried time along so swiftly it came almost as a rude shock to Mary to be told that, as more than four years had passed since her arrival in China, she was due for leave back in England. She decided to set out in January of 1930.

Some weeks before her scheduled departure, Nik stopped her in a corridor. He seemed to her to be wrought up by an inner excitement, for his manner was animated and his eyes bright, but after he had kept her listening to inconsequential tit-bits for some moments she felt that she must have been mistaken.

Then he blurted out in a rush: "Mary, I've been writing to a White Russian girl in Harbin and we've become engaged!"

"Why, Nik, that's splendid—really splendid! I do congratulate you. When do you plan to be married?"

He laughed self-consciously. "Well, early in the new year. I'm going to ask for time off and go up to Harbin for the wedding. Do you think there'll be any difficulty?"

"You mean about getting the time off? Of course not; none at all, Nik. Would you like me to discuss it with Miss Garnett and Dr. Li?"

"Would you?"

"I'd be very pleased," Mary said. She knew that Isabel Garnett would be as delighted as she was to hear that Nik was to be married, for Garnie had often mentioned her distress at his loneliness. It was arranged for him to go in January.

As the trains were running very irregularly still, and as Mary herself planned to travel home overland via Siberia, she and Nik decided to keep one another company as far as Peking. At last the day—or night—of departure came, for the train was to leave the Tatung station at two o'clock in the morning.

While Mary waited on the platform in a bitter night that was ten degrees below zero, Nik arranged for two seats, facing one another. He called to her from the carriage doorway and she hurried into the warmth, gratefully. They sank back into their seats.

Soon, with a wild beginning jerk, the train puffed out of the station and settled down to its clackety-clack rhythm over the rough road-bed.

"Going-off-to-London, going-off-to-London," the wheels seemed to say to her against the soundbox of the rails. It had been a long time since she was home.

Then she stubbed into a sudden awareness. Home? Could any place be more home to her than Tatung had become? And though she had scarcely left it, she now ached to be back in the hospital amongst the Shansi people she wanted so to serve, and whom she had grown to love despite their wicked ways. Nik was breathing deeply and regularly, already sound asleep.

He seemed so young and oddly innocent, awkwardly hunched in the carriage seat; tall and slender, even then. He looked, she thought, rather like the photos she had seen of that young flyer Lindbergh in the copies of *The Times* Emily Helen had posted from London. She was very glad for Nik that his long years of loneliness were coming to an end. Garnie had been quite right: marriage would be the answer for him—poor, lost, stateless, emotional Nik. . . .

She awakened suddenly at the changed rhythm of the train. Yes: it was travelling much more slowly now. And dawn had come. She scraped at the thick, gritty, frost-pattern on the window beside her. She breathed on the place and rubbed again and, putting her eye to the peephole, peered out. They were approaching the Nano Kow Pass. She heard Nik groan slightly, and then he stirred. He rubbed sleepily at his eyes with both his knuckled hands. Then he smiled at her.

"Mary—"

"Yes, Nik."

"Do you really want to go home?"

"Of course I do. Why?"

"Well, I've been thinking," he said. He still didn't seem fully awake. "Don't you think you'd like to marry me instead? It would save you going home and save me going to Harbin. The Bishop could marry us in Peking and we could go back again to Tatung."

"You're joking, of course."

He shook his head. "I mean it, Mary."

She sighed. "Oh, really, Nik!"

"Well? Will you marry me?"

"I don't think I could do that," Mary told him gently. "After all, you are on your way to marry a Russian girl, and that would be far better for you."

"Oh," he said, nothing more, and dropped the subject with a shrug.

When they reached Peking, Mary stopped over for a rendez-vous with Etheldreda Fisher, while Nik proceeded onward to his own rendezvous in Harbin. It was heart-warming to see Ethel-dreda again, and especially so since she, too, was going home on leave and they planned to travel together the long, long journey across two continents. Some days later, the two friends stopped off at Harbin to change trains. There, on the platform was Nik, standing forlornly, pinched with cold.

"Why, Nik!" Mary exclaimed. "What on earth have you done with your overcoat in this bitter weather?"

"I've lost it," he said guiltily. Even in Tatung Nik had made himself a reputation for mislaying his belongings. "I've been wondering if you could lend me the money to buy a new one."

"Of course: we can't have you freezing to death," Mary told him.

Their trans-Siberian train was not due to pull out for some hours. Nik invited them up to his hotel.

"Well, Nik," Mary said cheerfully, after she had thawed out a little, "how's your wife?"

Colour flushed over his cheeks. "I—I'm afraid I haven't got one!"

"You haven't—" Mary began in amazement, and then caught herself. "I'm so sorry, Nik! What on earth happened?"

He shrugged. It was the same inconsequential shrug with which he had dismissed her own refusal of him.

"Oh, nothing much," he said. "She just changed her mind. I'm going right back to Tatung tomorrow."

She hardly knew what to say that might comfort him. And then she decided not to say anything, for if Nik's change of plans had seriously broken him up, it did not show on the surface; and past experience had caused her to think that he was not a man who liked to gloss over an emotional upheaval.

Mary remained in England for nearly a year, visiting with her sisters and speaking on behalf of the S.P.G.

She was sincerely happy to see her friends and family, but her thoughts kept returning to Tatung—to Isabel Garnett and Nik and Francis Li, and to the full and fascinating existence she had left there.

When, in mid-January of 1931, the time came to sail again for China, it was none too soon.

And yet, when she was newly back at the hospital again, it seemed to her as if she had never been away. Even Nik's amorous saga had picked up almost at the point where it had left off the year before.

This time, he was visiting not Harbin but Tientsin; but his purpose was the same. While he was gone, a letter came from A. J. Britland, the S.P.G. official who had discovered and hired Nik in the first instance, asking Mary to prepare a home for the Russian engineer and the bride he was bringing back from Tientsin's White Russian colony. How wonderful that Nik had proven himself resilient enough, Mary thought amusedly, to try again after that other failure! She had the hospital coolies clean out and whitewash a small, unused house in the compound. She rummaged around for odd pieces of furniture which could be spared and added them to Nik's meagre belongings to make his new home comfortable.

Meanwhile, the news had spread through the hospital. Everyone was pleased for Nik, for despite his Quixotic ways he was liked by all. The nursing staff pooled together to buy him a set of china as a wedding gift. And then all was ready for his happy home-coming.

At seven o'clock, a couple of mornings later, the cook rushed up to see Mary, flushed with news of Nik's early and un-announced arrival.

"He's brought his wife," the Chinese lad burbled joyfully. "Wait till you see her: she's very good-looking."

Mary rushed down the stairs. In the entrance hall was the prodigal: beside him, a tall, slender girl, fair-haired and hand-some, but—the thought passed through Mary's mind—looking a little lost.

"Oh, Nik!" she cried, smiling a welcome at the girl. "You've brought her home! We have a house all ready for you. But, really, first you must both come and have breakfast with Garnie and me: you must be starved!"

Nik coughed uneasily, not at all the picture of a joyous newly-wed. Had they quarrelled already?

"Now, wait, you mustn't be so quick," he said. "She—she isn't my wife."

"She isn't?" Mary said blankly. "Oh, Nik! What went wrong?"

"Well, the girl I was to marry decided not to marry me," he admitted sheepishly. "This is her friend who has come up to see what Tatung is like and—" he swallowed "—and to see if she would like to marry me instead. I'd like to take another three days off duty to show her around. Do you think you could find a place for her to sleep in the hospital?"

"Why—why, yes of course," Mary said, a little stunned by the turn of events.

In the next few hours, she picked up further details. The girl spoke neither English nor Chinese, and before her arrival had somehow formed the impression that Tatung had a Russian colony—people of her own kind to whom she could talk and eventually befriend. Disabused of this, she made up her mind at once, demanding that Nik take her back to Tientsin, not in three days time, but by the first train out. Glumly, he did as she asked.

Poor Nik!

In his absence, the furniture was redistributed and the nursing staff returned the set of gift china for a refund. It looked as if the engineer would never find a wife.

And Mary wrote in an interim report to S.P.G. headquarters: "No village work has been done this year on account of wandering soldiers and bandits, or because the wards have been busy and it was impossible for me to leave. I still hope to go before Christmas."

Indeed, she was looking forward to going that autumn because by then Agnes Elisson, her villaging companion, was expected back from an eighteen months furlough in Sweden.

But when Agnes returned to Tatung, it was with instructions to take over the running of the Chinese Girls' School, as the two elderly German women, the Misses Beschmidt and Lochman, were due for retirement. If she had been unsure of herself before when faced with comparatively minor undertakings, this time she had worked herself up to a state bordering on collapse.

She came round to see Mary at the hospital with her news, literally shaking with terror and inner doubts.

"I don't see how I can cope with the job," she confided despairingly.

"Now, Agnes, I've seen you worried before," Mary said, seeking to calm her. "You've always managed to win over yourself in the end."

"B-but, Mary, don't you see? This is quite different! I-I've never before had to take charge of the whole school."

"Indeed I do see. You'll be responsible to no one but yourself. You won't have *them* to worry about."

The younger woman, distraught as she was, had to smile— if weakly—at Mary's usage of the emphasized *them*, which she recognized as her own.

But she had seemed greatly upset, Mary thought, after her friend had gone; and wondered if she had been too brusque in dismissing the fears which, to Agnes, were very real. Two days later, she called round at the school, but Agnes was not there. She had broken a tooth and had left that morning for Peking where she could get dental treatment.

One morning in the following week, Mary had a totally unexpected caller at the hospital: Miss Beschmidt.

"Miss Ball, I am here to see you because Miss Elisson is not well," the elderly woman said in heavily accented English. "She has a hot fever. Is it that you can come?"

Typhus at that time was not raging in the area in epidemic proportions, but there were a number of cases in Tatung.

"Yes, of course," Mary said, worried about her friend. She put some slides in her bag on which to take blood smears. But when she arrived at Agnes's bedside, she found her delirious.

"Is she bad?" Miss Beschmidt asked.

"She is seriously ill," Mary told her. "She must be taken to the hospital at once."

She wrapped her friend up warmly in blankets and had her transported by rickshaw to the hospital where her worst suspicion was confirmed. Agnes had typhus.

During the next few days, Mary hurried through her other duties so that she could sit at her friend's side, soothing her in her delirium.

"What shall I do with this big pile of cotton?" Agnes would cry, burning with fever. And, with Mary trying to puzzle out what she meant, she would burst out again, amplifying the problem that was nagging at her bewildered mind: "How can I get all the padded clothes made for the school?"

"Never mind, dear; I'll help you," Mary would reassure her; and then the beleaguered woman would rest—until some freshly imagined task gripped her in a new bout of sweating terror.

Presently, the delirium passed. When it did, Dr. Li took Mary aside to tell her that, because of the raging fever, her friend was left with a gravely weakened heart.

Agnes was put on a light liquid diet. Then, as she slowly regained strength, she was given solid foods.

One afternoon, when she seemed well on her way to recovery, Miss Beschmidt came to the hospital to see her. Suddenly, Agnes began to weep.

"P-please can't I have someone to help me in the school?" she pleaded with the stern old woman. "I—I can't possibly take on all the responsibility by myself."

But Miss Beschmidt was quite firm.

"No. You do not need someone to help. You can do it your own self."

"But—but Miss Beschmidt—however can I be expected to look after all those children when you and Miss Lochman always had your hands full? And there were *two* of you!" There were thirty boarders and seventy day students at the school.

When Miss Beschmidt merely shrugged stolidly, Mary could restrain herself no longer.

"Now, look here: couldn't you both put off your retirement for a while?" she said to the older woman. "Miss Elisson certainly shouldn't take on the school for some time after her illness. At least you can—"

"We have made our plans already," came the stiff interruption. Rising, Miss Beschmidt announced: "Now, I go." She swept out.

For the rest of that day, Agnes cried almost continuously. "I can't possibly take it on," she kept repeating weakly.

That night she had a massive heart attack, and with Mary beside her fought for her life through the hours of darkness. But when dawn came, in the middle of a sigh, she died.

Mary had lost a dear friend. She was never to go villaging again.

*   *   *

CHAPTER XI

THE departure of Isabel Garnett from the hospital in the spring of 1933 ushered in what must remain, even today, a largely secret chapter in Mary's life at Tatung.

It was made secret by her omission of any reference to the unofficial activities she embarked on, in her reports to S.P.G. headquarters; made secret in that she revealed no word of what she was doing or why she was doing it to her most intimate friends in the mission field; made secret, indeed, in the care she took to tiptoe around that veiled experience when, years later, in week upon week of intensive interviewing, she yielded to the author the bulk of the material narrated in these pages.

Only once, on a visit home to England, did she breathe a word of it—and then to her sister Margaret when, doubtless in an unguarded moment, she mentioned that she had sometimes performed operations on Chinese patients. She told specifically of having successfully amputated the gangrenous leg of a miner who had been injured in an accident.

A leg amputation! And performed by one who, as a child, had cowered away from the world under the kitchen table!

But *why* had she dared to cross the forbidden frontier that separated the work of nurse and matron from that of doctor and surgeon?

The answer was an illumination of Mary's brave simplicity of character, once accurately measured by Etheldreda Fisher. "She would go through anything if she saw the thing was right," Etheldreda said.

For, as Mary now saw it, in the only way she knew she was reaching out as far as she dared to protect a friend while, at the same time, she was saving others from suffering from the consequences of his lapses.

In truth, Francis Li was still enmeshed in the tentacles of the wicked city and upon occasion neglected his duty as both surgeon and superintendent. Yet Mary could not betray him. She could not snuff out the desperate hope that he would come to see how mistaken were his ways.

But, even more than to Francis, Mary owed a loyalty to the Shansi men and women who, after their early misgivings, at last had come to put their faith in the hospital. She scraped down to the quick of her conscience—there in the remote outpost, with hers as the final decision—and acted according to her lights.

A very few may have suspected the course she had taken, but only Mary knew in fact how deeply she had committed herself.

"Some desperate cases came to the hospital," observed Dorothy Mitchell, an S.P.G. evangelical missionary who lived for a while in Tatung during these months. "The doctor was a clever surgeon, but often not available. At times, Mary had to go ahead in an emergency without him. I do know that she even trained a boy nurse to help her."

Yet she must surely have known that neither discretion nor raw courage were enough indefinitely to sustain her compromise with events. Nor, even then, did she realize how utterly Francis had succumbed to the city's temptations.

Thus Mary's responsibilities piled up far beyond the load imposed on any matron. Yet, she now entered into a curious battle of wills with the corrupt and ruthless military governor of the area.

General Chao, who held complete dictatorial power over Tatung, appeared to feed on showing it off. He had certainly succeeded in making both Nik and Francis afraid of him, watchful and jumpy. Now he went to work on Mary, thinking that in having possession of the deeds to the hospital land he held all the trumps he needed against her. For a while, he seemed inclined to toy with her, teasing and tormenting. Time and again he summoned her to his headquarters and hinted that he really must get around to taking over the hospital.

Mary stood her ground.

"The hospital is a spiritual expression," she told him firmly. "We will not allow you to make it into a commercial enterprise." For, of course, what the General had in mind was personal profit for himself.

Mary gradually perceived that this was all part of an intrigue on the General's part—first to get Francis Li and Nikulin under his power, and then to take over the hospital and run it as a private business to line his pockets.

She knew that Nik, in particular, feared him. As a displaced person, without passport or papers, he was afraid of anyone in authority.

And she also knew the General wanted Dr. Li under his thumb because he was the only qualified doctor for many miles around. In his cruelly subtle way the General must have given Francis a very bad time.

But Chao had never met anyone like Mary before.

"You could say that she shone with a kind of inner radiance," Lieut-Col. George Lancashire, a Salvation Army officer with Tatung then as his headquarters, said about her. "But she was also very straight up and down, and she could be just as straight with a Chinese general as anyone."

However, after these many summonses to military head-quarters, Mary must have thought the General was about to take the hospital away.

There came a showdown at a last dramatic meeting when the General delivered his expected ultimatum. Mary stood, red-haired and fiery, as straight as a ramrod, and threatened him right back. She would stand no more nonsense!

"I will take the case directly to the British Legation in Peking!" she declared.

Incredibly, the General backed down. Even Mary could not have suspected in advance that this outpost tyrant secretly feared the British lion.

All that mattered to her was that the hospital was saved.

Francis Li was still not sleeping in the house in the compound with his family, but in the hospital, apart.

One noon, in the late summer of that year, Mrs. Li stopped Mary as, relaxing after a particularly difficult morning, she was strolling amongst the fruit trees.

"Miss Ball," she said tentatively, "have you seen those blue vases that Dr. Li had? Do you know if he's got them in his room at the hospital?"

"I did see them there some time ago," Mary said, caught unawares, "but not recently. I thought he must have taken them to your home."

The Chinese woman turned her head away, hiding the face that was old before her time.

"Ah, but they've gone now," she said with a sigh.

Mary suspected nothing at that moment; but later she reflected that Mrs. Li must somehow already have learned how inextricably her husband had become involved.

A few days later, George Lancashire called round at the hospital to see her.

"Have you seen the notice in the Tatung papers?" he asked. "I mean the one about Francis Li."

"No, I haven't—what does it say?"

"That a man is suing Dr. Li for having stolen his wife."

Mary stiffened with shock. Only that morning she had noticed that Mrs. Li had been crying again; but when she asked her why, the Superintendent's wife murmured that she had been lonely. Of course she had known!

There was nothing more she could do, Mary realized, to protect Francis from his own folly. He had gone too far for that and his misdeeds were now public knowledge. Yet, even then, she could not bring herself to write to the Bishop without first giving Francis a chance to explain.

Next morning, heart pounding, she knocked at his door.

"Come in," Francis said. When she opened the door he smiled. "Ah, yes, Miss Ball?"

To cover her nervousness, she spoke formally to him.

"Dr. Li, I hear that there is a report in the local newspaper of a probable court case against you."

"Oh," Francis said, not turning a hair. "Well, I don't think that will come to anything. I have spoken to my friend, the General, and he will see the judge and arrange that the case never comes up."

Mary saw that she would have to be blunt.

"I'm afraid you don't understand. Some of the foreign missionaries know of your gambling and of—of the cause of the lawsuit. I may be forced to write to the Bishop about this, but I wanted to speak to you first. Is there anything you would like to say?"

Francis shrugged.

"Only that I don't feel that my private life—and what I do when I'm off duty—has anything to do with the hospital," he said coldly.

"But it *has* affected the hospital!" she said. "Oh, Francis, don't you see? Apart from anything else, as superintendent of a mission hospital you are expected to set a good example for the staff. . . . Couldn't you possibly change your attitude so I can assure the Bishop it won't happen again? I—I don't feel justified in letting this talk continue. It's ruining our reputation in the city, and you know what trouble we've had in becoming accepted here."

"Do as you think best," he said curtly, turning away. Then he turned back and, looking full at her, said with sudden gentleness: "I'm truly sorry, Mary. I shouldn't take it out on you—but I'm afraid this business has gone past recall."

Later, she learned what he had meant. He had already bought a compound in the city and established in it as his wife the woman he was accused of stealing. It was to this new household that he had taken the missing blue vases.

Reluctantly, Mary at last wrote to the Bishop: "The enclosed newspaper cutting will tell you why I feel I must report Dr. Li to you. You will, of course, act as you see fit."

The Bishop replied at once.

"Instruct Francis to come to Peking for an interview," he ordered.

Later, the Bishop told her that he had tried his best to get Francis to give up his dissolute life.

"I have done wrong according to the church ruling," Francis had replied, "but I have done it, and now I have to stand by my actions."

He then told the Bishop that he had very carefully taken everything into account and had decided that it would be best if he resigned his post. The Bishop could only accept.

Not long after this, Francis took charge of a small emergency hospital, run by the Tatung Coal Mining Company in the hills twenty miles south of the city. He did not forget his friends.

"From time to time he would send us the serious cases he was not equipped to handle," Mary later reported. "From these men we learned that the miners thought that our loss was very much their gain. 'We have never had such a doctor,' they said, expressing astonishment that we had let him go.

"The city people were surprised, too. When they asked me why Dr. Li had left, I quoted an old Chinese saying. 'He's gone to change his breath for a while.'

"They would nod understandingly and remark: 'Ah! Well, we all need a rest at times.'

"We didn't hear from him directly for a long time. But somehow, Mr. Liu, the catechist, who was very fond of him, managed to maintain contact with Francis. He told me that Francis was very lonely. He hadn't been able to take either wife to the mines —there was no accommodation for women there."

At times, Mary must have wondered if General Chao had not, in the end, taken his revenge for the way she had blocked his bid to take over the hospital. He was a major shareholder in the Tatung Coal Mining Company.

CHAPTER XII

A FTER Francis resigned, a series of doctors were sent to serve in the hospital; but, largely because of low pay and the life of enforced isolation, for the most part these tours of duty were brief.

Mary worked efficiently and well with one newcomer after the other; but, somehow, with Francis gone, the atmosphere was not the same. He had been her closest Chinese friend and had supplied a valuable link of understanding between her and the north Shansi people; between her and the wicked city.

As months slipped by, she became used to the idea of working without him but, from time to time, she would prod Mr. Liu for news. Presently, in that way, she learned that Francis had left the coal mine hospital in the hills. He had bought a compound in Tatung and set up a chemist's shop with a small back room he used as a private clinic.

Mary hastened to call on him. Francis did not look as clean and smart as he had been when he was superintendent. He was wearing a dirty white coat; he had started to grow a beard that came out in untidy tufts; and his hands—his surgeon's hands— were ill-kept, the nails long and not altogether clean.

"I'd heard he was taking opium," Mary said, "but I saw no evidence of it."

When Francis showed her round his back-room clinic, she sensed his intention: to demonstrate there was nothing in it stolen from the hospital. It was meagrely stocked indeed—a wooden table which he used for operating on and for examining his patients, and a few instruments in glass cases. It was obvious, considering how little he had to work with, that the most he could do was remove a small cyst, open an abscess or remove teeth.

Mary asked him if he would be going back to his own village.

"No," he said. "I can't go back there. Anyway, my little wife wouldn't be content to leave Tatung."

His 'little wife' was his second, a tall woman with a clear complexion and a loud, penetrating voice. She was the one for whom he had resigned from the hospital, a woman of Tatung's *demi monde*, who still wore the garish clothes of that class— loose, flapping, wide-legged trousers—and still kept her face glossily lacquered and maintained two-inch nails on her little fingers.

She invited Mary to have a cup of tea, talking like a fish-wife in her raucous voice, gabbling on and on while her husband took no notice of her. He and Mary continued to converse in low tones while she said:

"Oh, you've come to see us! Our house is very dirty. I didn't really like to ask you in, but if you can spare a moment I'll soon have the kettle boiling."

At the same time she raked vigorously at the fire and called a servant girl to wash the dirty tea cups which were strewn around the room.

"Why haven't you washed these cups before?" she screeched at the girl, as if they had just come to her notice.

She squatted down on a small stool and began to pump a bellows into the fire.

"Why those are the cups we had last night!" she cried in a false note of discovery. She jumped to her feet. "Now you work the bellows," she said to the confused maid servant, "and I'll wash the cups."

She dug some money out of a bag at her wrist and gave it to the, by now, open-mouthed girl, asking her to go and buy some cakes.

Mary tried to stop her.

"Don't spend any money on me," she protested. "I'm not staying."

But the second Mrs. Li shrugged her off.

"If I spend a little money it doesn't matter a bit," she said, airily petulant. "You just have a cup of tea and a biscuit."

In spite of her clothes and paint, Mary conceded to herself that she was a handsome woman. By now she had achieved several gold teeth—an indication that Dr. Li was keeping her well. But Mary had the distinct impression that Francis was far from ideally happy. His 'little wife' was much too overwhelming for him and he had gone to seed.

"I was sorry to think that such an able surgeon had sunk to this," Mary recalled. "But he would not let me go without asking about Nik and his other friends at the hospital."

And Nik had been following what by now had become a predictable course. One day, he told Mary: "This time I really *am* going to get married."

After so many of Nik's truncated romances, Mary found it hard to stir up a show of enthusiasm, but she said: "Are you, Nik? Who is the lucky girl?"

When he said that it was the same one he had been originally engaged to in Harbin (but who was now working in Shanghai), Mary wished him luck once again.

However, when she and other members of the staff talked it over, they decided it would save embarrassment all round if they did not this time prepare a home or buy gifts—until, and indeed, unless, he actually did return with a wife.

The wedding was to take place in the Russian church in Tientsin. Mary was amongst those invited, but the only S.P.G. representative who turned up was A. J. Britland, who had a comparatively short train journey from his headquarters in Peking. Britland later told Mary that he arrived in Tientsin on a Saturday and went to stay at the home of a friend. That night the front door-bell rang and Nik was shown in.

"Sit down, Nikulin," Britland said heartily, "though I must say I'm surprised to see you. I thought you'd be far too busy with your preparations for social calls this evening."

Nik sat down, but on the edge of his chair, leaning forward.

"I'm very sorry, Mr. Britland."

"Sorry? What for?"

"To have brought you down from Peking."

Britland, in a sharp voice, said: "Why, what do you mean, eh?"

"I mean I'm *not* going to get married tomorrow."

"Oh, no!" Britland exhaled heavily. "Really, Nikulin, what's happened now?"

Nik said: "You see, I'd been at the Russian club here and met a friend who had come from Harbin.

"'What are you doing here in Tientsin?' we both asked at the same time.

"And, can you imagine it? We found we had both come to marry the same girl. She had written to us both. After talking it over, I said: 'You can have her.'

"But he said: 'No, *you* can have her.'

"So—you see?—we decided that neither one of us would marry her. That was all there was to it."

On a spring day in 1935, Nik came to Mary as an emissary from the General, who had just returned from the fighting against the Japanese in Manchuria. One of the General's Russian aides, Nik said, had a motion-picture camera with which he had taken a film of the General in action at the front.

"He wants to know if he can use the outpatients' department waiting room to screen it," Nik told her. "Shall I say it's all right?"

Mary had not entirely forgiven Chao, but she could hardly afford to put his back up over so trifling a request. She told Nik that she had no objection.

On the afternoon of the screening, General Chao arrived with his armed bodyguard, a short, arrogant, squarely-built man, strutting with insolent pride. Presently the film was shown.

Nik, seated next to Mary, nudged her.

"Can you see anything funny about this film?" he whispered.

"What can *you* see?" Mary whispered back.

"It isn't what I see, but what I don't see that's so funny. This is supposed to be the film of a battle, but there's no firing from either side. In fact, there isn't any other side!"

"Why, that's so!" Mary said, her eyes now glued to the screen. "Nor are there any wounded or dead."

The film flickered on, showing men in trenches. Then, finally, they leaped up over the edge of a trench and fired their rifles and ducked down again. There was a cut to a machine-gun in action. At the end, there was a scene—how peaceful it looked! —showing General Chao sweeping the horizon with field glasses.

Nik leaned over, putting his lips to her ear: "It's just a fake battle, Mary: no battle at all. My Russian friend told me so."

But the Chinese nurses, who had never before seen a motion picture, had hardly noticed that this one purported to show actual fighting.

"Oh, look!" one cried. "There's General Chao!"

The General preened.

And another nurse cried: "Yes! One leg's moving!"

"Now *another* leg is moving!" the first nurse shot back in a transport of delight.

And the General, strutting around after the showing, appeared to think that, on any level, the film had been a huge success.

In the heat of that summer, Mary took some days off to go to the seaside near Tientsin. While there, she received a printed invitation from Nik to attend his wedding—the fourth time such an event had been announced. Mary dismissed it with an indulgent smile, thinking: "Oh, Nik's just having another try."

But when she got back to Tatung a pleasant shock awaited her in the persons of a grinning and triumphant Nik and—it seemed incredible!—his bride. Helen Nikulin was a tall and lovely dark-haired girl, easy-going, quick to smile; and, best of all, Mary thought, she obviously doted on Nik. He would not be lonely now.

Yet, wasn't it just like him? Wasn't it just like the unpredictable Russian to make them feel absolutely sure that he would never win a wife, and then to fool them all?

Garnie would be perfectly delighted to hear the news: Mary resolved to write to her without delay.

And soon, again, five years had flown since the last time, so that it was turn for her second furlough to England. Mary left Tatung in August, 1936.

While she was still away, the incident at the Marco Polo Bridge occurred, outside Peking—the incident that, in July of 1937, marked the beginning of the Sino-Japanese war within China's borders.

Soon Peking fell to the invaders and, shortly after, Tatung. One of the first to flee the wicked city before the arrival of the enemy was General Chao—a wise decision, without doubt; for his reputation as a Chinese militarist, surpassing his valour, would certainly have earned for him a Japanese firing squad had he been caught.

Indeed, the news of the fall of Tatung might have given almost any woman second thoughts about returning. On Mary, as might have been expected, it had exactly the opposite effect; for although she was certainly no trouble seeker, she never sought to avoid it when she saw that trouble stood before her and the straight line to her duty. She set sail for China.

For most of that autumn, Mary chafed to get back to her post in Tatung, but was prevented by the Japanese from leaving Peking. For months—so the Bishop had told her—there had been no word from the hospital; and this vacuum of news caused her to suffer an acute agony of doubts.

Was the staff safe and well? Was the hospital still functioning? Had the invading troops taken it over? She knew that the Japanese controlled the railway, but she also knew that Chinese guerilla bands were constantly nipping and prodding at them from behind their own lines, keeping them trigger-happy and on edge. In an outpost like Tatung, these would be hazardous days.

At length, through sheer persistence of effort, Mary won from the Japanese reluctant permission to try to make her way there. They warned her of the dangers of the journey and in fact would sell her rail tickets only as far as Kalgan. From there—if she could—she would have to get fresh travel visas to proceed onward.

In a chill early November dawn, clad in sheepskin-lined cloak and woollen bonnet, she waited at Peking's *Shi chi men* station for her train. With her was Claire Abbiss, a young S.P.G. missionary. The station was jammed with a milling mass of Chinese civilians and uniformed Japanese who, like the two European women, were waiting to travel west. Eventually, the train chugged into the station. There was a concerted and chaotic rush to get aboard, with fanatical jostling and angry outcries.

"Remaining serenely calm, Mary somehow managed to squeeze us into a carriage, leaving disappointed hundreds behind on the platform," Miss Abbiss later recalled.

When they reached Kalgan, Japanese guards searched through their luggage and said they could travel no further. From that point, all trains were being used only for troop movements.

Mary snorted her scepticism and besieged Japanese headquarters, demanding permission to continue onward to Tatung.

"Impossible!" she was told; but each morning she went to try again. Eventually, the Japanese must have decided that anything was preferable to being harried day after day.

On the sixth morning, Mary and Miss Abbiss were summoned to appear at Japanese headquarters. They were ushered into a large room. Facing them, from behind a table, were half-a-dozen grim-faced military officials. The senior officer spoke to Mary in Chinese, some of which Claire Abbiss was able to follow.

She heard him use the word meaning 'kill' and threw a startled, questioning look at Mary.

"Do you understand, Claire?" Mary said quietly, in English. "They want to know if you are prepared to risk being shot if we go on. They say that their soldiers are young and that they hate the 'arrogant' British; and they say they cannot be responsible for their actions."

"I'll do whatever you do," Miss Abbiss said, benumbed.

If Mary was worried, she did not reveal it. "In fact, she seemed to me to be a tower of strength," Miss Abbiss said not long ago.

"I recall feeling better when I noticed that all the officers kept staring at her lovely red hair as if they could not resist its attraction."

When the two women arrived at the Kalgan railway station next morning they found a great contrast to the chaos of *Shi chi men*; and they observed that the Japanese had lied to them about onward trains being reserved for troop movements only; for a long, orderly queue of Chinese civilians were awaiting tickets.

"You'd better sit here and keep an eye on our luggage," Mary said, and took her place at the end of the queue.

It was cold in the station, at or below the freezing point, and a harsh wind moaned through it, scudding dust and bits of paper on its moving breath. Mary steeled herself for a long and miserable wait. She shuffled ahead once or twice, beating her hands together against the cold, as the queue edged slowly on; and then she saw a short and rotund Japanese officer bearing down upon her.

"Are you a missionary woman?" he asked in Chinese.

Mary acknowledged that she was, wondering what was in store for her.

But the officer flashed his teeth in a brief smile.

"Yes, yes," he said, suddenly friendly, his breath congealing into mist which was torn from him by the wind. "A missionary was once very kind to my family in Japan. Come!"

Leading the way to the ticket office at the head of the queue, he arranged for her tickets and then took the two women to a first-class carriage, reserved for Japanese officers, and found seats for them. Presently, they were again on their way; but twenty miles from Tatung the train pulled to a stop: guerillas had blown up the line.

After some hours of delay, they completed their journey, pulling into the Tatung station after dusk.

"There were no porters and no conveyances," Mary recalled later, "so I sent Claire on to the hospital on foot for help and stayed on the platform to mind the luggage. The station was like an army camp. There were piles of ammunition and hundreds of soldiers marching past and the great din caused by motor lorries racing about.

"It was fiercely cold, but I felt very bucked at the thought that we were the first foreigners to come in since July. After a long wait, when almost everyone came over to ask me who I was and my age—simply out of curiosity—I saw a motor lorry draw up and out hopped Mr. Nikulin."

Nik rushed over, grinning from ear to ear, his gangling form endearingly familiar. Shaking his big and bony hand, Mary felt at home again, despite the hubbub of troop movements.

"My, but it's good to see you, Nik!" she told him. "Helen is well, I hope?"

Nik's wide grin seemed to expand even further. "Oh, yes, she is quite well again."

"*Again?* Was she ill?"

"Not ill, exactly," Nik said, full of joyous mystery, like a small boy bursting with good news yet reluctant to release it all at once. Then he was able to hold it in no longer.

"Mary—we have a baby boy!" he said, and accepted her congratulations with unconcealed pride.

On the way to the hospital, he became gravely anxious.

"I don't know how to tell this—please don't be sad about it. The Japanese have taken over part of the hospital."

"Oh, Nik: no!"

He nodded. Then he made a great show of peering ahead through the windscreen at the path the headlamps threw over the bumpy dirt road.

"This lorry is one of theirs—they let me use it to meet you."

But Mary could not be put off.

"What have they taken it over *for?* and how *much* of the hospital?" In her anxiety, the questions tumbled over one another.

"The whole second floor—for their wounded," Nik said. "You must be prepared for this: they are a very dirty people."

"But what about Dr. Hansen: couldn't he stop them?" Mary asked. "Or is he no longer with us?" Dr. Adolph Hansen, a

156

German who had been expelled from his own country for anti-Nazi sympathies, had been brought in as hospital superintendent just before she had gone on furlough.

"He is still here," Nik said, and swung the wheel around to turn in the hospital gate. He was silent for a moment. Then he applied the brakes and switched off the ignition. A stillness settled over the night. Nik sighed softly and added in a low voice: "He is a lonely man and very afraid of the Japanese, I think."

"Part of the hospital has been taken over by the wounded of the conquering race," Mary wrote to a friend in S.P.G. headquarters in London. "Absolute bedlam prevails and I sometimes feel that I'm living in a nightmare.

"Our outpatients have dwindled away almost to nil now that our 'guests' share the building, but we keep some in-patients going. The R.C. school has had a bout of typhus and we are caring for some of the girls. In the men's ward we have ten patients who were left behind by the retreating Chinese army.

"The day before yesterday we had patients come in with very bad burns, a mother and her three children. Poor things—they had been trying to collect coal out of the train cinders, not realizing they were still glowing! I do pray to be given wisdom and patience during these trying days. The Japanese officers keep making demands on us and hours and hours are spent haggling over trivialities. The language difficulty is a great barrier.

"The other day, two officers came and wanted us to fill in an application form for a local passport. This resulted in two sessions of three hours each, although there were only ten questions in all.

"What caused the delay, you ask? Well, Japanese officer number one would tell number two what to say in his own language, number two would tell me in Chinese, I would explain to Dr. Hansen in simple English, he would mutter to himself in German and then come back to me in broken English. Thereupon, I would put my best Chinese to number two who would explain to number one in Japanese—and so on and exhaustingly on.

Under such circumstances, it's all too easy for a misunderstanding to arise and *they* are terribly suspicious.

"Just a week ago, twenty-four Japanese Red Cross women nurses arrived. They work very hard, and we hope things will soon be easier for us all. But they are not a clean race. There will be a great deal of tidying up needed when they depart."

It was not long before the Japanese decided that they wanted not merely a single floor but the entire hospital; yet, because they were not then at war with Great Britain, they could not simply take it by force. When they began to scheme, their first attentions lit on Dr. Hansen who—as superintendent—they thought to be the ultimate controller of the hospital's destiny.

They knew his passport had expired. Early in December, he had travelled to Peking to call on the German Embassy and had been told that a temporary renewal would be forwarded to him at Tatung; but when he got back he waited in vain. Unable to leave the city except by special permission of the conquerors, he must have felt singularly vulnerable. And the Japanese must have known it.

For, one night, they invited him to a banquet in the city and made sure his glass was never empty. Presently, when he was befuddled, they reminded him of his lack of papers.

"Unless you get the hospital for us, we will have to deport you back to Germany," he was told with simulated regret.

Terrified, hardly knowing what he was doing, he signed a document promising to help his hosts. But when they discovered that there was actually no way he could put the hospital into their hands, they applied pressure on him to resign as superintendent. He announced to Mary one morning that he was taking a half day off duty and never returned.

For a while—so Mary heard—they still made use of him in the Tatung area as a medical officer; but soon he was sent off to another post. Later, through roundabout sources, the news reached her that he had contracted typhus and died.

This still left the hospital with a doctor—a Chinese named

Yang who had been Hansen's assistant for about a year—but he was ill-equipped as an administrator and dumped all his burdens on Mary's lap. Thus, once again, she found herself in complete charge.

"Dr. Yang seemed unable to make decisions and refused to interview anyone who came to deal with the hospital," she had to report. At this time, Claire Abbiss had been recalled temporarily to Peking, leaving Mary as the only Englishwoman in the district. Her responsibilities were sometimes terrifying.

Though she was reticent of her experiences at this time, Mary's laconic account of one emergency reveals the courage she could draw upon when it was needed.

"The presence of the Japanese made a shambles of our efficiency," she said, "especially since the doctors persisted in getting horribly drunk and, when in that state, tried to go upstairs to molest our girl nurses.

"As their matron, I had to protect them. I stood on guard at the top of the stairs when I heard the Japanese roistering. Soon they began to lurch up; and as the first one reached the top I lunged forward suddenly with a push. He toppled back against his friends and they fell drunkenly down the stairs."

Superbly understating her case, Mary added: "It was very trying for me. But I managed to keep them off time after time."

Soon after her heroic stand at the head of the stairs, at the end of January, 1938, the Japanese pulled out of the hospital. Her strong-mindedness surely had something to do with their withdrawal. Her courage must have persuaded them that it would take more than browbeating or skulduggery to win the premises over for their use just then.

By the time Claire Abbiss returned, Mary again had the hospital in full running order; but the coming of the Japanese had brought other than political problems.

"The number of patients keep up well," she reported to the S.P.G. "Besides the usual outpatient clinics, there is a special one now for V.D. With the mixing of the nations, this trouble continues to increase.

"Our problems with the coolie staff have increased immeasurably, for, with the great influx of Japanese, wages have gone up where it is impossible for us to compete. As a result, there have been nights when I wondered if there would be any one on duty in the morning. Frequent changes of staff do not promote good work and, indeed, the kind of help we can get now is far from efficient and not even clean.

"As for reliability—well, recently a coolie came for me at midnight, very upset, with the report that one of the boys was possessed of a devil and that two others had fainted out of fear. I took them all into the men's ward and by morning they declared they were much better. But an unforeseen result was that the other patients were terrified. More than twenty went out in the following two days.

"We now have a hospital baby, named Ann. Her mother was a very deformed woman who came for the operation of Cæsarean section, and when she discovered that she had a small daughter said she did not dare take her home as, being an illegitimate child, she would have to have her strangled. She was delighted when I told her I would take the child. Ann has many ailments, mostly inherited, but she is improving now. When she laughs, it brings infectious smiles to us all.

"One of her little friends, in hospital suffering from extensive syphilitic ulcers, is a girl of thirteen! She has been sold and re-sold three times. On the last occasion, she told me proudly, she commanded a price of twenty-four Chinese dollars—about one pound sterling.

"A short time ago, we had a man admitted with gunshot wounds in both legs. He had been held up and robbed. He was put to bed in the men's ward and, about a week later, another man with gunshot wounds was admitted and put in the bed next to his. I noticed that this seemed to have an extraordinarily depressing effect on the first man. I asked him what was wrong.

" 'He is the bandit who held me up and shot me,' I was told.

"Of course, I moved the second man away. His victim cheered up at once, quite remarkably."

And, later that year, she wrote home: "How I wish you could

be here for September 11th—the date the Bishop has fixed for the opening of the new hospital chapel. I intend to send a notice to all the priests-in-charge in the diocese to remember the new church and all it will stand for in this wicked city. The cross on the church is golden (cement covered with gold paper and varnished). It stands high and shining in the sun. I do hope that we soon start a new era here.

"About two weeks ago, we had a small child admitted in desperate condition. A wolf had tried to eat it, poor mite, and only three miles from the city walls. Today we have another one, not so badly eaten, from the same village. It seems curious to me how things come in batches: we have had no other wolf bites for years."

A few weeks later, Mary wrote again: "What a marvellous week-end we had for the dedication of the new chapel! The Chinese staff collected money enough to buy a big family Bible for the lectern, ten Bibles for use, ten hymn books, ten prayer books. Mr. and Mrs. Nikulin gave the bell, an iron one cast in the city, engraved in Chinese with the words: 'Blessed is he who hears the bell and comes to worship God'. The Bishop gave us a silver Communion set, Claire and I gave a lectern, two prayer desks, two chairs and a credence table; and there were many other gifts.

"We were thrilled at the number of guests, among them the Bishop, Priest Ting from Ankuo Hsien, Priest Chao from Peking, Mr. Britland and Dr. Mosse. What a putting up! Friday night, when most of them came, it poured with rain, but Saturday was a lovely day and that afternoon Mrs. Nikulin had a tea party. In the evening, we had a Chinese feast in the Outpatients' Department Hall.

"Then, on Sunday, the chapel looked like a beautiful jewel, filled with a wonderful sense of prayer. The Bishop asked me what hymn I would like at the dedication, and I chose 'We love the place, O God' as it was Father's favourite. We had it as the first hymn of the festival, as well as in the afternoon. Our little TB girl, who is a communicant, said afterwards she felt that Heaven could not be better!

"With all the festivities, we did have one problem, I think amusingly solved. It was to have tables big enough to entertain on with so many guests in so many places. Nik has a large one, so I borrowed it: on Saturday it was at our house for breakfast and lunch. For tea it went back to Nik, supper to the Outpatients' Department for the Chinese feast, back to us for Sunday breakfast, and so on. One kept meeting coolies with pieces of the table dashing from place to place. To their credit, it was always in the right place at the right time."

In June of 1939, after many months of comparative tranquillity at the hospital, the Japanese made another move to take over control with an offer to buy it. The Bishop came up from Peking to explain to them that they would have to deal with the S.P.G. Headquarters in London.

After several meetings over a period of some weeks, he told Mary how bewildered he was by their apparent inability to appreciate that the hospital did not belong personally to him, and that he could not sell it.

"I really don't know how I'm going to make them understand," he confessed.

One night, he was having supper with Mary when a group of Japanese officials drove up to the hospital and demanded to see him.

"Excuse me, Miss Ball," the Bishop said, laying down his knife and fork with a resigned sigh. "I expect I had better deal with them."

He went to meet his callers in the next room.

Presently, Mary heard the Japanese shouting and thumping on the table with the butts of their pistols.

"Will you sell or will you not sell?" one shouted angrily.

"But I've already told you that I cannot," she heard the Bishop reply.

"You lie! Why do you lie to us?"

"I am telling you the simple truth," the Bishop said.

This one-sided discussion continued for more than an hour, with Mary praying on the other side of the wall that the Bishop could keep a firm rein on his temper. If he did not, she feared he might be shot. Mercifully, despite great provocation, he managed to restrain himself. When he came out of the room to rejoin Mary, he looked very tired and—she noticed with a sense of shock—older than his years, which must have been nearly seventy. Shaking his head, he murmured wearily to her: "I cannot understand them, Miss Ball. If they shout at me all night, I am still in the same position. I cannot sell the hospital."

After some moments of thought, he told her that he had decided to return to Peking in the morning and go to the British Legation for advice.

He looked at her with old eyes, full of concern.

"If you are worried at any time," he added, "telegraph me and I shall come."

Mary was greatly touched.

Shortly after this visit, the Bishop recalled Claire Abbiss from Tatung, so that, again, Mary was the only British national there. Then the staff nurses, terrified by Japanese pressures and the unsubtle whispering campaign against Mary, began one by one to leave.

"Quite a number of the patients left as well," Mary said later. "Remaining with me were eighteen probationers, the coolies, Dr. Yang, Mr. Liu and Nik."

Yet she hung on; and at the end of that year she was able to report: "The first time that our Bishop came here about all this trouble, in June, he reminded us that our work was dedicated to the glory of God and that we were to wait and see what God's will was: whether we were to stay or to go. It has been astonishing how one bubble of difficulty after another has been pricked since then, often just when the situation seemed unbearable. Six months ago we were thinking we were to go, now we hope we shall be able to stay—though that is not quite clear even yet.

"Naturally all this has affected our work, and many patients, terrified by the Japanese, have stayed away. Insofar as the nursing staff and coolies are concerned, many were given a bad time from behind the scenes and had to leave, but no one left without permission, and that says a lot for their loyalty. At the present time, our 'friends' seem to have sent us to Coventry, a change, I confess, I am enjoying. It is not enviable to be the target of their whisperings and newspaper notices and out-and-out threats.

"Miss Abbiss came to help me before Christmas and we hope to carry on, though all our best nurses have left. We have not turned anyone away because of shortage of staff.

"Our 'friends' have stopped us getting coal, so that the inside walls and ceilings are glistening with frost—a remarkable sight, but the cold does not make it any easier for us to function.

"Because of general difficulties in the country, there have been many destitute people knocking at our door, and we have had a large number of beggars who, poor dears, nearly all come when the only thing we can do for them is make them as comfortable as we can and then bury them when they die."

But Mary's optimism about her chances of keeping the hospital running was short-lived. The Japanese, keeping the pressure on, brought the Bishop up from Peking time and again for consultations aimed at having the buildings—as they slyly put it—'transferred'. Not only that, due to their corroding influence on the economy of the district, food was in short supply and the hospital suffered along with the Chinese civilians.

"Food is now a terrible problem," she wrote to a friend in England. "But if we can save the hospital for the poor and the suffering, we will, if it means sticking like leeches and just managing from day to day. If we have flour, millet, rice and oatmeal in hand for two weeks we consider ourselves lucky. Many times we have doled out our last grain and wondered where the next meal was coming from.

"One day, I remember, the last bit of food was handed out at noon—even the kitchen floor was swept for small particles—and that evening a former patient came to call on me, one I hadn't seen for years. He said: 'Teacher Ball, I have some rice for sale and heard that you were in short supply. Do you want any?' It is wonderful to have such proof that we have friends in the city, especially since the conquerors have made it clear that they frown on anyone willing to help us."

The time had come, the Bishop decided sadly, to remove the apse of the chapel, the memorial stones and the cross. He sent appropriate instructions to Mary.

"You can imagine how I felt," she said, remembering. "I decided we would have a last beautiful service in the chapel, so we decorated it as on its dedication day: flowers in the chancel and on every window sill. It looked so beautiful!

"Next day we had a choral celebration with hymns as on dedication day, too: 'We love the place, O God', at the beginning and 'Jesus shall reign' at the end. I think we all cried a bit.

"The apse was taken away, the memorial stones sent to Peking, the cross given to Mr. Nikulin for his little boy's grave. I remember thinking that if we had to leave, Tatung would always hold much of my heart: and that I had loved the people there and my work amongst them since the very day I arrived."

One cold morning towards the end of 1940, the hospital cook knocked at Mary's bedroom door, rousing her from sleep. She saw that it was barely past five o'clock. She climbed wearily from her bed, felt the freezing draught from her open window and shut it with a bang. Slipping into her robe, she opened the door.

"A man from the Chinese Inland Mission would like to see you," the cook said.

"Oh? Is one of the ladies at the Mission ill?"

"Ill? No one is ill. He wants to sell you a pig."

"But I don't want a pig," Mary said, rubbing the sleep from her eyes.

The cook coughed gently.

"I think you better get it, Teacher Ball. He wants to sell it very cheaply and if you don't buy it the Japanese are going to take it."

"I'll get dressed and be right down," Mary said.

When she arrived at the front door of the hospital, a grubby, middle-aged Chinese was awaiting her. In his hand was a length of rope; at the other end of the rope was an enormous black sow.

The man's eyes lit up.

"Teacher Ball, do buy this pig from me—the Japanese are confiscating all the pigs in the city." He leaned towards her and whispered confidentially: "This is my favourite sow and should have a litter in about a month's time." He perceived that Mary was not particularly impressed. To encourage her, he added: "She usually has seventeen or eighteen piglets."

"Oh, well," Mary muttered, and after some dickering agreed to take the animal for twenty-seven silver dollars, while the cook, who had come to witness the transaction, kept hopping about in anger, shouting: "Too much! Far too much!"

Despite him, the pig was taken to the pigsty.

In due course, there were eighteen piglets, one of which died. Early in the next spring the cook came to Mary and reported gravely that the wolves were foraging very close to the city, attacking not only children but the farmers' pigs as well.

"Then you'd better sell some of our piglets," Mary told him.

His eyes lit up.

"Good!" he cried, bound to regain face. "Now I can make back all that money you paid for the sow!"

He sold all but four of the piglets at ten dollars each and brought the money to her with his round face wreathed in smiles. Then he persuaded Mary to hire the services of a boar for $2.50. As a result, that July, they had a second litter of sixteen piglets; but, by autumn, with the wolves again on the prowl, the cook became fiercely protective and, each day at sunset, wearing a white apron, he would go to the pigsty and open the gate.

Shaking his apron before him, he would shout a sing-song "La-la-la-la-la", and, walked backwards in the hope that he would be followed.

The sow, to Mary's great amusement, seldom obliged; and she would watch, convulsed with inner laughter, while Cook screamed for the coolies to come and they would all shoo the sow and her litter away to her night-time quarters.

But, after this had gone on for several days, she discovered to her horror that they were housing the family of pigs in the empty mortuary. The joke had gone too far.

She bought a roll of wire netting in the city and had it spread over the top of the sty as protection against the wolves, hoping that it would be more effective than the method of the villagers on the outskirts of Tatung who whitewashed large 'O's on the village walls, simulating openings. A wolf was supposed to crash into an 'opening' and beat a puzzled, pained retreat.

At long last, in February of 1941, the S.P.G. in England decided that the position of the hospital in Tatung was no longer tenable. They agreed to accept three thousand pounds compensation from the Japanese Government—a ridiculously inadequate amount—and hand the hospital over to them.

One morning, after helping the doctor with a Cæsarean section, Mary received the following telegram from the Bishop:

"EXPECT SURVEYOR MEASURING LAND AND BUILDINGS MYSELF GOING KALGAN SIXTH SIGNING AGREEMENT BRITLAND GOING TATUNG TENTH FOR VALUING EQUIPMENT THIRTY DAYS GRACE FROM SIXTH WRITING".

She was heartbroken.

"I told the patients to inform their relatives that they must be taken home. Two women, both of whom had had Cæsarean sections a few days before, were carried out on stretchers. One little boy was carried out, too. He had been badly burned and was just beginning to take an interest in life. I didn't dare think what his people would do about the complicated dressings I gave them.

"Mr. Britland arrived, and I was glad to hear that, at least, we could move anything we needed. We packed our chapel furniture to go into the city. The Japanese representatives came and inventories were counted over and estimates made. Then the hospital was swept and polished: there was no cubbyhole left in disorder. I gave the old sow back to the man who had sold her to me. Nik took his family to one of the houses in the Church compound in the city, where The Holiness Mission used to be many years before. Mr. Liu moved out, and Dr. Yang and none of the staff was left.

"Our compensation from the Japanese Government did not include payment for the small quantities of dressings, drugs and other supplies that still remained in the hospital—and, thinking of Francis Li and his ill-equipped clinic, I sent him a note advising him that if he wanted anything from the hospital he had better send around for it within the next two days. With the note, I sent as a gift a large striking wall clock that belonged to me, personally, which I certainly had no intention of passing along to the Japanese. It was quite an unusual timepiece for Tatung, and I thought it might attract patients for him.

"That same day, I had a note from Francis in reply: he would call round to see me.

"He came after dark the following evening: it had become very unhealthy to be seen associating with foreigners. He seemed glad to see me again and he had obviously gone to some trouble to tidy himself up. He made a selection of dressings and drugs, paying what he could afford, but refused the more expensive equipment.

"Then, clearing his throat, he said: 'Thank you very much for the clock. I have always admired it, you know. But I will keep it for you and let you have it back when you need it again.'

" 'I don't suppose we'll ever get back *here* again,' I said with a sigh.

"Francis shook his head.

" 'These people aren't going to be here forever, Mary. You'll be coming back. Perhaps I'll even be able to help you do it.'

"Then he went quietly out into the night, carrying his bundle of supplies.

"More than two weeks of our month of grace was still left, but a completely empty hospital was too sad a place to stay in any longer. I left it on February 18th, moving into the Church compound in Tatung."

In the city, without the facilities of the hospital at her disposal, Mary turned to evangelical work, devoting much of her time to teaching the Chinese children who came to attend Bible class at the church school.

Even then, the Japanese would not leave her in peace. At first, she heard at second hand that they were making peripheral enquiries about the mission compound—the one the S.P.G. had taken over from Anna Holt. They let it leak out that they wanted it for a special school of their own; then changed their story and said they needed the quarters for a military training centre.

Then they moved in to engage Mary more directly, calling on her with their arguments and pressures two or three times a week.

Unable to move her, they forbade any Chinese to cook her food: she simply added cooking to her many chores. The shop-keepers of Tatung were then instructed not to allow their clerks to serve her. At last, even the children in her Bible classes were ordered to stay away, until the point was nearly reached when life for Mary had become intolerable.

One day, Helen Nikulin told her that she had seen a Japanese dogging Mary's footsteps in the street and was sure that the Englishwoman was suspected of being a spy. Then, early in July, when the heat of summer was beginning to build up, a notice was posted on the city walls.

It read: "Anyone found serving any British person or taking him in a rickshaw will be liable to punishment."

At whom was it directed?

Mary was the only British national left in Tatung.

Late one night towards the end of that month, Mary was sitting, quite alone, in her room at the compound. It had been raining earlier, but now it had stopped, and a damp silence seemed to hang over the city.

Mary heard a dog barking at the compound gate, then the gateman fumbling with the bolts after a nervous, "Who's there?"

She heard no reply to the challenge; but then the gate opened, squeaking on its hinges.

From her window, she saw the dark figure of a man, hurricane lamp in hand, hurrying up the path towards her.

"It's the Japs again!" was her first anxious thought, but as the figure approached she saw that the man was too tall for a Japanese.

When he tapped on the door, she hurried to open it. There stood Francis Li.

"Francis! Come in quickly," she said in a hushed voice.

His cape was wet with the recent rain, and he came in, standing on the mat inside the door, looking troubled and drawn.

"I won't take my raincoat off," he said.

"No, you'd better not," Mary agreed, for she knew that he had taken a great risk in coming to see her in defiance of Japanese orders.

He said: "Mary—I could not rest until I could come to urge you to leave this place for Peking as soon as possible. Believe me, this is no place for you now. Don't ask me why, but please go." He was silent for a moment. Then he added with special emphasis: "And don't come back while they are here!"

She questioned him about conditions in the city and learned that he had been advised by his friends against coming to warn her.

"But I had to come," he said.

"Thank you, Francis. But, please, don't do it again. It could bring you serious trouble."

He shrugged his agreement.

"But as long as you're here," he added, "send your coolie to me any time you need food. I'll see that you get some."

He nodded, unsmiling, and slipped into the unfriendly night.

*   *   *

CHAPTER XIII

AFTER Francis' warning, Mary left Tatung in August for Peking. Then, when war was declared by the western allies in December, the Japanese confined all enemy nationals in that city within its own boundaries. Surprisingly, they were not then imprisoned, though the men were made to wear red arm bands and the women to carry scarlet passes which they had to produce for scrutiny when patrolling soldiers demanded.

The system of arm band identification seemed to fascinate the Japanese, for they issued others of green to neutrals and—ironically—yellow for their German allies, the same colour *they* had forced upon the Jews in their distant homeland. Out of shame or pride or arrogance or secret guilt, the Germans refused to wear them. As a result, they were constantly being picked up for questioning, which, Mary admitted later, "gave the rest of us much pleasure".

During this uneasy time of limited freedom, Mary and her friends were under constant surveillance, a great annoyance to them, so that it came almost as a relief when she was taken to a concentration camp at Wei Hsien, Shantung Province, south of Peking. The camp had formerly been an American Presbyterian Mission compound—a large one, as it had to be to house even cheek to jowl the two thousand American, British and other nationals the Japanese sent there.

"For me, it was actually a holiday in the beginning," Mary was to recall of this experience. "There were so many people to talk to now, in contrast to my last months at Tatung where I had been cut off and alone. We were reasonably comfortable. At first I shared a room with seventeen other women, giving each of us a space two feet longer than our beds and the width of a bed plus a small table."

Indeed, at the Wei Hsien Civil Internment Centre, Mary was reunited with many old friends—Etheldreda Fisher, Claire Abbiss, the Bishop, A. J. Britland, and dozens of others she had met in her nearly twenty years of living in China. However, fighting had made a mess of the former mission and Britland recently recalled "how wonderful Mary Ball had been in getting the place straight—cleaning out the filthy latrines herself and doing the work of two. During all our time there, Mary not only did her job, but did it splendidly, and was a mainstay to those whose nerves had broken."

Yet, according to Etheldreda, "Wei Hsien seems to have been quite the best of all the Japanese internment camps," and, indeed, their captors must have made a special effort to treat the inmates reasonably well, for they were allowed within certain limits to run their own camp. They did have to attend roll-call punctually twice each day but otherwise were given only one order concerning the behaviour expected of them towards their guards. Tactfully translated, it read: "When meeting a Japanese guard, step to port or starboard: avoid a head-on collision."

Thus, the prisoners set up their own committees and distributed daily tasks to every inmate. Mary was appointed theatre sister in the hospital's operating room.

"She was a great favourite," Claire Abbiss affirmed. "By the time I arrived, she had started nursing lectures to a group of the young girls in camp. I became quite used to seeing her with her collection of youngsters gathered under a catalpa tree, part of a fine avenue the American missionaries had planted. It was through the keen interest she aroused that some of these girls later became nurses.

"I was married in the camp in borrowed clothes, with Mary as matron of honour. She managed to wheedle some extra bread and sardines from the Japanese guards for a wedding feast."

Though the Japanese did conscientiously try to make this camp better than most, life was far from easy as time went on at Wei Hsien.

"Every kind of labour became more difficult, owing to lack of equipment," Etheldreda Fisher said. "There was only one brush for scrubbing vegetables; eight knives and three pails were provided for a kitchen feeding five hundred. The pails had to be used in rotation for washing vegetables, fetching drinking water and washing up. Endless delays occurred, and queues were long and slow moving. Waves of depression attacked us from time to time; but the people who really suffered were those who could not or would not adapt themselves to living in crowded quarters and were continually trying to get an extra foot of room in the dormitory or trying to find some excuse for avoiding community work."

Moreover, the stubborn Chinese guerilla forces grew stronger and more active, until, after some months they were able seriously to harass Japanese supply columns. As a result—though the Chinese had not aimed it at the European inmates—the inflow of food to the camp was reduced to a trickle.

"At first we were fed quite well," Mary said. "For instance, Christmas dinner in 1943 was roast pork and fruit pudding; but Christmas a year later found us banqueting on watery soup and sour bread. Like everyone else there, I lost weight rapidly."

Mary was lecturing her neophyte nurses on the morning of August 17, 1945, when she heard the deep drone of an aircraft flying overhead.

"That's not a Nippy!" she heard a man cry.

Presently, she saw it: a Superfortress, circling low over the camp. The men and women all around her began to shout and to wave their hands hysterically.

"Look!" one of the girls she had been lecturing to screamed with joy. "Look! That's an American flag painted on its side!"

The Superfortress circled the camp again and leaflets began to drop lazily in its wake. Mary raced across the compound and picked one up. Its message, in English, French and Russian, read: "Prisoners of War—you are free. In two hours we will return to drop food, clothing and medicines. Don't over-eat and don't over-medicate." Excitement was a wild thing, boiling and bubbling through the camp, Mary's mingled with it.

At ten o'clock, a flight of six aircraft flew over, dropping parachutes which, in their yellows, blues and reds seemed to Mary to be lovelier than orchids. Most of them fell outside the camp area. The last aircraft circled the camp and then out of it dropped seven parachutists.

Exultant, Mary surged with the mass of her fellow prisoners towards the barbed-wire gates of the camp that had penned them in for so long. Two Japanese sentries looked at one another uncertainly and crossed their bayonets in the path of the prisoners.

An Englishman walked boldly over and slapped one of the sentries on the back.

"All right, Johnny," he said, "your day is over. Don't try to stop us now."

The sentries exchanged another glance and stepped hurriedly back. The prisoners streamed out through the gate, the first time in two and a half years any of them had left the camp. All around Mary her companions were sobbing, laughing, chortling and babbling their joy. She was carried along in a river of humanity until they came to a grain field and saw the parachutists in American khaki uniforms crawling on their hands and knees out of the tall grasses, rushed to them and lifted them to their shoulders. They carried the American airmen into the camp.

Trotting beside one of them, Mary called up to him.

"Wherever did you come from?"

"Okinawa," was the laconic reply.

At that moment, it seemed as if out of nowhere, the camp's tattered Salvation Army band joined the triumphant hotchpotch and broke into what Mary later described as "the most stirring march I have ever heard".

Soon after her release, Mary was taken by American troopship to Hong Kong. One of her travelling companions was Etheldreda Fisher.

In Hong Kong, the two old friends spent all of one morning and much of the afternoon in sightseeing—exploring the waterfront, the street markets, the shopping district: still revelling in their freedom. The day was hot and damp and the humidity at last began to have an effect on their enthusiasm. They were not strong; the last hungry year in prison camp had sapped their reserves of energy; and they had both lost much weight. Mary, always slender, was now gaunt, her bones bowing outward against taut skin, her clothes flapping on her pitiably scrawny frame, threadbare and roughly patched. On her feet, and much too large for them, she wore a pair of heavy American army boots.

Etheldreda, wiping at her forehead, said: "Let's sit down a while. I'm exhausted!"

Mary was glad to agree.

"But where?" she asked.

Etheldreda looked around. "There doesn't seem to be anything better than the curb."

Without needing further discussion, they sank down at the street's edge.

"My poor feet," Mary said, sighing her relief.

"Yes—what I wouldn't give for a cup of tea," Etheldreda breathed.

At that moment, a woman crossed purposefully towards them from the opposite pavement. She was well-fed and prosperous, the kind of woman who tended to look upon herself as a pillar of society.

Mary nudged Etheldreda.

"It looks like you're going to get your wish," she whispered. "I think we're going to be asked for tea."

"Oh, splendid," Etheldreda whispered back, licking her dry lips.

The woman came to a stop before them, standing in the road-way. Her eyes travelled over them expressionlessly, from big army boots to sweating faces, innocent of cosmetics. After a moment, she asked: "Are you by any chance just out of an internment camp?"

"Yes, we are," Mary said, thinking of the tea.

"Well," the woman breathed out from what seemed a great height. "So *that* accounts for it!"—and walked away.

Etheldreda said later: "Then we looked at one another, really *saw* one another for the first time in months. We did look

like scarecrows but, until that instant, had been blissfully unaware of it.

"Suddenly, we both roared with laughter. We laughed until
our sides ached, and even then we couldn't stop—laughing out of
all control as we sat on the stone curb in the roadway. We kept
reminding one another of the incident, giggling over it afresh, all
the way home to England."

Mary arrived in England to learn that her second sister, Emily
Helen, had died while she had been in Wei Hsien. Britain was
still short of food and many items were rationed.

"But to my eyes, there seemed plenty of everything," she
said. "The fruit shops seemed marvellous to me and the meat
ration enough for a banquet. Yet I felt that anything that had
happened to me was minor, compared to what the people had
suffered from doodlebugs and bombings at home.

"For a while I rested; then I went on deputation work around
Britain and spoke a great deal; and after that I took a refresher
course on the new drugs and treatments, at St. Thomas's Hospital,
Westminster.

"The first time I came home from Tatung, in 1930, wireless
had become immensely popular and Emily had bought a new
portable set; the second time, in 1936, I remember my sister
Maggie's husband Bill showing me the traffic lights and the
covered-in double-decker buses; then, early in 1947, a shop was
advertising TV and I went to see it. In all this time, in material
things, China had almost stood still."

*　　*　　*

CHAPTER XIV

A T that wretched time of the Japanese takeover, when Francis Li had predicted to Mary that he might help the S.P.G. one day to win back the hospital, it must have seemed even to him a singularly improbable dream; but he did not forget it. As soon as the Japanese were gone from the city, he set to work to make his prophecy come true.

His first move, during the time of anarchy between governments, was to visit the deserted hospital and snatch from it such few worthwhile pieces of equipment as had survived wartime vandalism. He moved these into an old granary in the city for safe-keeping just in time; for early in 1946 the Communist Eighth Route Army, a guerilla force then, besieged the new Kuomintang garrison. This attack proved premature, and they withdrew after two months of living off the land beyond the city's walls.

In the treacherously shifting sands of recent history, Francis had become a past master in the art of personal survival: in particular, he had learned how to ingratiate himself with whom-ever was temporarily in power. Now he made a twenty-bed hospital out of the granary compound—a square of one-storey buildings around an open yard—and sold the idea of financing it to the Nationalists. The compound was primitive to begin with, mud-floored and dark, but Francis had large windows cut into the walls facing the courtyard and set about making other basic improvements. Soon he had won the admiration of his Nationalist sponsors (who now also held the unused Mosse Memorial Hospital compound by right of possession), and he attacked them with arguments to return it to the S.P.G. At length he won them round, but on condition that the Society pass along the three thousand pounds they had been given as indemnity by the Japanese.

At once, Francis carried his triumph to the Bishop in Peking. As a result of that meeting, the Mosse Memorial at Tatung again became S.P.G. property—the only one of their four hospitals in China they were ever to repossess. The formalities of transfer were completed by mid-December.

Mary was paying a Christmas and New Year's visit to her younger sister, Margaret, in Derby when, on the last day of 1946, she was thrilled to receive a cable from the Bishop in Peking. It read: "SPG REPOSSESSED MOSSE MEMORIAL RETURN TATUNG AS MATRON SOONEST." Mary had no idea her old friend Francis was responsible.

In her eagerness, she took the next train down to London, on New Year's Day, but was told at S.P.G. Headquarters that no immediate passage to China was available.

The earliest she could get—via Hong Kong—sailed from Southampton on March 4th, and she did not reach Peking until April's end. There the Bishop introduced her to a Dr. Philip Li, who had run a small private hospital during the Japanese occupation, but had now agreed to give it up in favour of taking on the position of superintendent of the Mosse Memorial in Tatung.

Li was a common name in China, but Mary, thinking she detected a family resemblance, asked him if he were related to Francis.

"Oh, yes: we're cousins," Philip Li said.

"Philip is a little worried about Francis," the Bishop said mildly.

"Oh?" Mary said. "In what way, Dr. Li?"

The Chinese doctor shrugged. He was a smaller man than his cousin, but not small for a Chinese. His mannerisms were quite western.

"Not so much about Francis," he said hesitantly, "but more about what the people in Tatung will think. Francis is well known there and he is, of course, a very good surgeon. He is a favourite of the local government—and he is running the Government hospital. Aren't the people likely to think that I am taking on the job of his competitor?"

"Oh, I should hardly think so," Mary told him. Turning to the Bishop, she said: "Francis would hardly help us to get the hospital back and then look on us as competition or resent our coming. Don't you agree?"

The Bishop did not commit himself.

He said: "You'll both be able to judge for yourselves soon enough. I'd like you to go up to Tatung on Monday to reconnoitre the situation there—see what work is wanted on the hospital and what supplies you'll need to get started."

Travel conditions had not much improved, Mary thought as they boarded the train early on Monday morning. They had been able, once again, to get tickets only as far as Kalgan, and the carriages were overcrowded, mostly with Kuomintang troops. When they came into the mountains they were stopped at Tien Chen—The Heavenly Needle—named for a high peak overshadowing the town, and told that there would be a delay because a bridge had been blown up earlier by the Communist guerillas. They were held up all that night. There was no restaurant car, and most of the windows on the train were broken, but Mary as an experienced campaigner had brought with her a basket of food and a bed-roll. In the morning, the train was able to edge its cautious way over the temporarily repaired bridge. Soon after, it pulled into the Kalgan station.

The train had been stopped in such a way that the carriage they were in was just beyond the end of the platform. Swinging from one car to the other in order to reach it, Mary lost her footing suddenly. Falling, she caught her leg on the rough-sawn edge of a plank and felt the rending shock of injury. She saw that she had cut her shin down to white bone. Feeling faint, she sat down on her roll of bedding on the platform.

Dr. Philip Li, mouth agape, seemed more stunned by her accident than she was herself. He ran off and presently returned with a drink of water, but he had lost his facade of western manners.

"It doesn't matter," he kept murmuring in the typical Chinese way of belittling misfortune. "It's of no consequence."

Mary gritted her teeth. The pain was now almost unbearable, seeming to flood upwards from her shin in an overpowering wave. She feared the disgrace of being violently ill in front of the Chinese doctor, and under almost any other circumstance would have been amused at having herself acquired a consciousness of 'face'. Neither she nor the doctor had brought any dressings, so she bound her small white pocket handkerchief across the grinning wound and her large khaki one over it to hold it securely in place.

She had no further treatment during the rest of that day or night, which they spent waiting in the station. By morning, her leg was badly swollen from ankle to knee and Mary began to fear infection. There had been very little Philip Li could do to help, beyond piling her suitcases to keep her leg parallel to the ground.

"I felt so stupidly helpless and hated to be making extra trouble," Mary once said in recalling the incident. "When Chinese accompany foreigners, it normally attracts attention, which the Chinese are not fond of getting. But anything like my accident is bound to draw a crowd. All the time we were there I was the centre of attraction, with people remarking: 'Oh, look at the blood!' or 'She's bleeding, isn't she?'—as if I were on exhibition."

By early Wednesday afternoon, Mary's leg felt quite numb and in her eagerness at approaching Tatung she temporarily forgot her injury. As they had stopped along the way they had picked up new passengers, and the sound of the Tatung dialect—more clipped than the speech of Peking—seemed warm in its familiarity.

Then the train crossed the high bridge across the Jade River and she could see the city walls below her in the distance, but the hospital compound which she was most anxious to glimpse was screened from view by the north suburb which had sprung up around the station. She sensed the rising excitement of returning to a home she loved after five years absence, even though it had not always been kind to her. And she thought: What has happened to the hospital? What needs to be done to put it in working order again?

She and Philip Li took rickshaws directly there, bowling along
the macadamized road the Japanese had made, and which had
been merely a cart-track the last time she had seen it.

When they came to the parade ground adjoining the hospital
property, Mary saw that the Japanese had built as barracks
hundreds of red brick huts with corrugated tin roofs. The mud
walls around the parade ground were broken in many places. She
was filled with fresh fears. Would the hospital itself also be in
ruins?

Entering the gate, she saw at once that the Japanese had shut
in the two porches, had built a large garage, two large store-
houses, a new wing and a nurses' residence; but the residence had
been partly demolished by the shells of some guerilla attack and
every window in the main building was broken, while the garden
was despoiled by trenches and dugouts.

Limping around the hospital with Philip Li at her side, Mary
was appalled by what she saw. The Japanese had redesigned the
two large wards on the first floor, making them smaller than
they had been. The operating room and scrubbing-out room had
been used as lavatories; holes had been burned in the floors by
open fires; the walls had been pierced by shells; and Mary was
dismayed at the filth and rubble in every room.

At length, she turned to her companion.

"It's pretty bad," she admitted with an involuntary grimace,
"but with a great deal of hard work we can use the first floor
and the outpatients' department, at least. The rest will take much
longer."

Sighing, the doctor shook his head.

He said: "Believe me, Miss Ball, I would never take this work
on if you weren't here to help me." He appeared to be greatly
depressed by what he had seen.

With the hospital in such derelict condition, there was no
question of sleeping there that night. Mary decided to stop at
the Swedish Mission, but now that their survey was completed,
she again noticed the dull throbbing of pain in her leg. Her
companion suggested that they take rickshaws to his cousin's
hospital in the city where the wound could be dressed.

When they arrived, Francis—who had already heard of their arrival in Tatung—shook them both by the hand.

"I'm glad to see you home again, Miss Ball," he said, bowing his head. "I hope we can work together for the people of the district."

She remembered the last time she had seen him, when he had come in the darkness to warn her of the Japanese, and regretted that in his oriental way he had reverted to punctilious formality.

"I'm very pleased to be back, Francis," she told him. "I'm sure I wouldn't be here if it hadn't been for your goodness in putting forward the case of the S.P.G. for the return of the hospital." The throbbing in her leg was becoming more insistent.

They chatted for a while, and clearly Dr. Philip Li was becoming impatient about her wound which had gone for so long without attention.

He burst into the conversation apologetically: "Francis, Miss Ball has had an accident to her leg. I didn't have any dressings and wasn't able to tend it properly."

Francis nodded without surprise.

"Well, I did notice she was walking badly," he said. "Let's have a look at it."

But Mary was sure that he had been quite anxious about her from the moment of their meeting, yet too inhibited to be first to mention her wound. ("I sometimes believed that if you were dying he wouldn't be so impolite as to mention it unless you did first," she once said of him.)

By now the wound had stopped bleeding. It was inflamed at its edges and extremely painful, but there seemed to be no infection. The leg was still very badly swollen.

"When will you be going back to Peking?" Francis asked as he wound on the bandages. He pursed his lips and frowned as he tied the final knot. "You should get anti-tetanus serum injected as soon as possible, and I'm afraid I have none."

Mary returned to Peking next day with Philip Li to report to the Bishop. She had her anti-tetanus injection and spent a week in bed recovering not only from her leg injury but also from a cold she had picked up on the journey. By then, she was seething with eagerness to return to Tatung for CNRRA (UNRRA in China) was planning to close down their operations and, to be eligible for aid from the United Nations Relief Organization the hospital had to be functioning by June. They would need all the medical supplies, bed linen, instruments and general hospital equipment they could get, and there still remained the problem of rounding up a hospital staff.

Since Dr. Philip Li, the new superintendent, had shut down his own nursing home in Peking, Mary suggested that he offer jobs in Tatung to his former employees. As a result, they were able to recruit one trained male nurse, three girl student nurses, two men for office work and a cook. A friend of Mary's recommended three other male nurses. It was also agreed that the S.P.G. would buy the equipment from Superintendent Li's nursing home and send it up to Tatung.

Because his eldest son was about to be married in Peking, Superintendent Li was unable to return with Mary. She went on ahead with Mr. Mei, the male nurse, his wife and two children, and two of the three girl students. The third girl nurse, a Miss Chao, was engaged to marry the Superintendent's second son and because she already considered herself to be a member of the Li family had remained behind to be a bridesmaid at the wedding, intending to follow with her father-in-law to be.

On the way, Mary learned that the Meis were also part of the Li clan: Mrs. Mei was—it hardly seemed possible!—Francis's grown-up daughter. But, yes, her two small sons *did* have something of the look of their grandfather.

Arriving at The Heavenly Needle, the travellers found that guerillas had again blown up the bridge, which had suffered considerably more than it had the last time. As a result, they were five long days in getting to Tatung—and they arrived at three o'clock in the morning.

"There were no rickshaws at that time of night," Mary was to recall, "so the rest of us walked, carrying our bundles, while

Mr. Mei remained behind to look after the heavier luggage until he could hire a cart to take it on to the hospital.

"A watchman had been sent up from Peking, Li Wen Kuei, Francis's eldest brother, but considered in the Chinese fashion to be the eldest brother of Philip's branch of the family as well. We arrived at the hospital and knocked at the small side door used at that time of night.

"No one came.

"We took turns pounding on the door with our fists. After a great deal of fruitless banging, Mrs. Mei called out in a shrill voice, quavering from exhaustion: 'Mr. Li: open the door, open the door.'

"No answer.

"'We have come—we have come from Peking,' she cried out for her uncle to hear.

"Then we picked up some stones the size of a man's fist and threw them against the door while the children joined in an anxious chorus: 'Kai men, kai men. Open the door, open the door.'

"At last, a full half hour after we had begun to knock, we heard an inside door squealing on rusty hinges, and Mr. Li called: 'Lai-la, lai-la. Coming, coming.' He had a deep voice, and sounded overjoyed, for he was a Peking man amongst strangers and must have been delighted at the prospect of seeing people from home.

"He opened the door—a man as tall as Francis, with a very wrinkled face and glistening, bright eyes, like a spaniel's, seeking interest in everything that went on round him.

"When he saw me, he clasped his hands over his stomach and, bowing deeply, said: 'Po hsien sheng yeh lai-la. Teacher Ball has also come.'

"Then he helped carry in the bundles and the remains of the food and Mrs. Mei's pottery basin and chop sticks and led the way into his room, a long narrow one the Japanese had built onto the outpatients' department. He had pushed two wooden beds together to sleep on, since there was no k'ang and had covered them with his padded mattress, no thicker than a comforter, with his padded quilts neatly folded on one side. I guessed then that he had heard us almost from the first but had tidied up before letting us in.

"The children were given water and we washed their hands and faces and made them comfortable on Mr. Li's bed, covering them with the quilts. They fell asleep immediately, poor exhausted mites. But the two girl nurses, weary as they were, insisted on setting right out on an inspection tour of the hospital.

"Mr. Li said to me: 'I will show you the room I have prepared for you.'

"He took me into one of the private patient's rooms on the first floor and with considerable pride explained how he had scraped the walls with the top of a tin can, then white-washed them and the ceiling.

"He apologized because he had only been able to give the floor a cursory scrubbing.

"'I have no cleaning rags,' he explained with a shrug. 'I hope you have brought some up with you.'

"'I did leave some mops at the station with Mr. Mei,' I told him.

"In fact, he had done wonders with the room: it was quite spotless. But there was not a stick in it, nothing at all. I bowed to him in Chinese fashion, my hands clasped to my left side, and said: 'Mr. Li, it is wonderful of you to have done so much. I will have my bedding brought up when it comes.'

"By the time it came, it was close to six o'clock, with the pink rim of the sun nosing the horizon. I spread the blankets on the floor, collected the two girl nurses, and we all laid down on the bedding. I fell asleep at once."

Next day Mary began to set the hospital in order. The June deadline for getting it on the active list was ever on her mind, prodding her on to greater efforts. There was scrubbing and cleaning up and whitewashing. There was the gathering together of odds and ends of furniture so that the outpatients' department and the first floor ward could be skimpily outfitted; the assignment of staff members to their duties, the supervision of meals, and—for a while—the hard facts of day-to-day living when there was never enough of everything to go round.

The only time Mary took off from this donkey work at the hospital was to call on Francis Li in order to report that her leg was much better. When she arrived at his city hospital, in the former granary, she was effusively greeted by Mr. Fan, one of her former nurses who was now Francis's assistant.

"He showed me into the Doctor's office and insisted on examining my leg," Mary recounted. "He said that Francis was out on a case but would be back shortly. In fact, I think Mr. Fan must have sent a coolie runner dashing out after him, for Francis arrived by rickshaw in a few minutes and after greeting me asked with some concern: 'And how is your leg now, Miss Ball?'

"Mr. Fan interjected importantly: 'Oh, I've dressed it and it's getting on very nicely.'

"Francis nodded, returning quickly to apparent impassivity. He thanked me politely for my small share in bringing his two small grandchildren up from Peking, but made no mention of his daughter's simultaneous arrival. After all, she was a woman and not of much account in China then. He led the conversation along very general lines for a while, as if gradually feeling his way back into the fringes of our former friendship, testing it through the barrier of years.

"Then he said with a small, deprecating smile: 'You know, I do not have the proper anæsthetics or the right instruments or any qualified assistants—all these years I have not been able to operate on a single Cæsarean!' He paused, gave a hesitant little cough, and added: 'There's a little woman in the side ward who badly needs a Cæsarean. Would you like to see her?'

"He would not, of course, ask outright, but this was as close as Francis ever came to saying that he needed help. He was sorely out of practice in this special branch of surgery and, because we had worked together for so many years on just such cases, he probably felt that it would reassure him to have me to support him now that he was ready to begin again. But I had to be very careful, in offering my help, not to cause him the slightest loss of face.

" 'I'd like to see her,' I said, and when I looked at the woman, I offered, as casually as I could : 'If you think it would be of any help to your nurses, Francis, I could choose the instruments and ligatures. . . .'

"His face lit up with a relieved smile.

" ' If you would be kind enough to instruct them what to prepare—and help me to operate—I would thank you very much, Mary,' he said.

"We were right back on our former friendly footing. The Mosse Memorial Hospital had a big name in the district, and now he knew for sure that we were anxious, not to swamp him out of existence by competition, but to co-operate in any way we could."

After Dr. Philip Li, the new superintendent, came back from Peking (bringing Miss Chao, his future daughter-in-law, with him) it was decided that his first duty would be to open diplomatic channels with the civic and military leaders of Tatung. Mary approached Francis to see if he would introduce his cousin to the local authorities. Francis said that he would be happy to perform the service.

"There is one thing that worries me," Mary confided to her old friend. "I imagine the officials will expect us to have a big reception for them all, together with a grand formal opening, but we don't have enough money for that. Even worse, the hospital is in no condition just now for them to see it."

Francis nodded. Then, with a smile, he said : "But this is no great problem. Philip should say to each official : 'We are opening the hospital temporarily, but we hope to ask you to a formal opening later in the year.' Then they will not be insulted."

When the two cousins made the rounds of the city fathers, the gambit Francis had suggested was used by Philip—and it satisfied everyone.

There were still a few last chores to be done before the hospital could begin to function, even on an emergency basis. Mary had managed to scrape together seventeen wooden beds, and now she borrowed a small, hand-operated sewing machine from a Salvation Army friend and made seventeen large sheets for them— one for each. In-patients, for a while, would have to bring their own blankets. The June deadline was drawing uncomfortably close.

Then, at last, Mary composed a notice and had in inserted in the Tatung newspaper. Literally translated, it read: "Outside the north gate of the city the Mosse Memorial Hospital hopes to re-open on June 9th. The entire staff bows to the public. Outpatients to be seen between ten and twelve each morning."

Mary was all too aware of the hospital's inadequacies, made unavoidable by the pressure of time. However, on leaving London the S.P.G. had supplied her with a wooden crate filled with instruments, basins, gloves and operating gowns; and the equipment from Dr. Philip Li's erstwhile nursing home had arrived— an operating table, more instruments and medicines, including sulpha drugs; so that she felt they were at least equipped for an emergency. Besides, knowing that the hospital had built up a reputation for specializing in Cæsarean cases, she had brought up a complete sterilizing unit from Peking: towels, gloves, gowns, gauze, swabs, caps and masks—enough for one abdominal operation.

It was just as well. Hardly had the hospital opened its doors on June 9 when a tiny woman, less than four feet tall, hobbled in with the aid of a stick. She was in the final stages of pregnancy and was obviously suffering from the local complaint, ostramalicia. With her was a ten-year-old boy and her husband. The woman registered. Then Mary went forward to welcome her with a smile.

The woman said: "I am glad you people have come back to the hospital. I have only this one child—" she indicated her son with a nod "—and I have lost four in difficult labour. I hope you can save the one I am now carrying." Then she added, almost casually: "And, after that, may I please be sterilized?"

This was by no means an unusual request at the hospital, but according to Chinese law it could be fulfilled only with the consent of the husband; and very often a husband made a point of stipulating that if the pregnancy resulted in a girl-child the sterilization should be postponed until he could either gratify his wish to father a son or bury his wife. But, even in the event of the husband's consent, the hospital had long since established its own policy on such requests to sterilize, doing so only if the mother's life were likely to be endangered by another pregnancy. And in the case of the tiny woman, the Superintendent decided after examining her that he would not be justified in granting her wish.

Since the operating room was not ready for use, he performed the Cæsarean section in the outpatients' department with Mary assisting. The baby was a boy. Now, Mary came face to face with a minor emergency: there were no infant's diapers amongst the hospital's all too meagre stores. In desperation, she made four nappies out of an American flour bag.

The following morning, she heard shouting from outside the hospital gate. Hurrying to the window, she saw the gate being opened by Mr. Li, and a large CNRRA lorry drove into the compound to unload a hundred blankets addressed to the hospital.

The blankets, of course, were most welcome on their own account; but, more important, the gift was a tacit indication that the hospital had opened in time to be considered eligible for further CNRRA assistance. To confirm this, a Canadian CNRRA official named Lewis called that afternoon—and mentioned in passing that Dr. Francis Li had recommended the Mosse Memorial as worthy of aid.

"Dr. Francis Li?" Mary repeated, puzzled.

"Yes—do you know him?" Lewis said. "He's head medical officer for this part of Shansi Province and we have been asking his advice regarding where our grants should go."

"I see," Mary murmured. And Francis had mentioned no word of this to her!

She showed the Canadian round the hospital. When they came to the baby she had helped deliver the day before, she picked him up.

"Our first male patient since the opening, Mr. Lewis," she said, smiling.

Lewis stared incredulously. Then his lips twitched into a grin. "Well, now, just look at that diaper, will you?" he said, pointing to it. Across the baby's bottom in red capital letters was the word FLOUR. The grin, fading, was exchanged for a look of concern. "Haven't you anything better than that for the purpose?"

Mary shook her head. "Just now we seem to be in short supply of everything but willingness to work."

"It must be very hard on the child," Lewis muttered. He brightened, and said to Mary: "I'll try to send you some flannelette, if you'd like."

The Canadian was every bit as good as his word. Two days later, a vast bolt of flannelette arrived, and was followed by several more, out of which Mary was able to have made a plentiful supply of diapers as well as twelve dozen sheets. Still later, Lewis sent an operating table, instrument tables for the theatre, three years' supply of gauze, absorbent cotton, bandages, operating-room gowns, masks, caps, gloves, instruments and great quantities of medicines.

By the end of that year, the hospital was no longer suffering from a shortage of supplies. The word had spread into the outlying villages: the Mosse Memorial was back on the job again —and so was Teacher Ball.

As for Mary herself, again she was experiencing the satisfaction of finding complete fulfilment in her work.

"It was," she told a friend, "like a shower after a dry time."

*   *   *

CHAPTER XV

THE next many months seemed like a time of soothing peace to Mary, when the hospital in Tatung was able to re-establish itself; but in other parts of China, the Communists were stepping up the pace of their civil war against the Nationalists.

"There were, of course, rumours of advancing Communist armies," she said, in explaining her own detachment. "But nobody in Tatung gave much heed to them."

Indeed, when in mid-March, 1948, Superintendent Li took his wife to Peking on a short holiday, it had not occurred either to him or to Mary that a time of crisis was approaching. But he had been gone for only a few days when, on a Saturday morning, a delegation of Kuomintang officers came to tell Mary that they would be needing the hospital premises as part of a defence line round the city for, they said, the Communist forces were coming close.

Hardly had the delegation gone when a runner came to bring her a letter from Francis Li. In it, he advised her to send all stores and moveable equipment inside the city's walls. Francis, having resigned from the city hospital as a result of a disagreement with the provincial government, was now a freelance doctor again.

By that afternoon, their relatives had begun to take hospital patients inside the gates. Mary had recently been given, as assistants, two S.P.G. nurses, Miss Eunice Preece and Miss Kathleen Porter, and now she asked them to start packing, with Mr. Mei's help, in readiness for the move into the city. She assigned Mr. Tung, from the hospital office, to arrange for carts while she went herself to her friends in the China Inland Mission to ask for space to store hospital equipment.

By the time she got back, a contingent of Nationalist troops was already in the hospital compound, trying to prod Mr. Mei and Mr. Li out of the small houses they and their families occupied. Mary had observed, on her way back from the city, that the inhabitants of the north suburb, around the station, had begun moving to safety inside the walls: the road had been almost blocked with their carts and wheelbarrows, together with the military lorries loaded with the grain the soldiers had collected in surrounding villages.

Gunfire could now be heard rumbling like low-pitched thunder in the distance. With the honking horns of the lorries, the babel of voices, the cracking of whips and the squealing of cartwheels, the din had become urgent and frightening, even hysterical. Presently Mr. Tung arrived with ten carts and just about then Francis Li appeared on the scene, quite unruffled, as a voluntary helper.

The carts were loaded, Mary assigning two men to each to ensure that nothing was stolen and that each cart would end up at the assigned destination. By nightfall, the hospital was emptied of such supplies and equipment as could be moved. Only Mr. Tung, Mr. Mei, Mr. Cecil Fox, an S.P.G. priest recently assigned to the hospital, Miss Porter, Miss Preece and Mary remained when a messenger from Tatung's military commander arrived bearing orders for "all foreigners and others still in the hospital to hurry into the city. It is surrounded and we are defending it. You cannot expect help from outside the city walls."

They hurried to the North Gate, but found it shut. However, the officer guarding the gate had received no orders from Headquarters to let them, or anyone else, in, a typical example of the lack of liaison in China in those days, and the weary party returned to the hospital for the night. They were soon joined there by about a hundred refugees, men, women, and children, who slept on the floor of the outpatients' department.

When the city's North Gate was opened at ten o'clock next morning, it was at once choked with fresh hordes of refugees. To Mary, the air—with its odours of unwashed bodies and petrol fumes and the sweat of oxen, mules and camels—seemed to be in a state of evil ferment.

"Yet, directly we got through the awful crush at the gate, the city appeared to be almost calm," she said. "The shops—low, one-storey brick stalls—were all closed and shuttered. There were very few people in the streets, only a few shopkeepers hanging round for fear their places would be looted.

"When we reached the centre of the city—a small square with four arches, each in the direction of the four city gates— we came upon several hundred soldiers marching towards the East Gate, each one bent almost double with his arms awkwardly and blindly supporting a huge stone on his back. They were going to barricade the gate, for the attack was expected from the north and east. We reached the China Inland Mission at about eleven o'clock and settled in to wait for the attack."

Next day, the military commander ordered every man in the city to help dig trenches beyond the North Gate. Even schoolboys were drafted for the job. An order also went out for each household to make five slabs of dried mud, two feet square by six inches thick. These were put out to dry in the sun and later collected in small carts by the troops, who used them to fill in the North Gate, leaving only a narrow passage down one side. The date was March 28th. The rumble of gunfire, now considerably more insistent, seemed pitched in a higher key, but there was still no sign of an attack.

It had not come by April 2nd. Mary, warming herself before an open fire in the China Inland Mission compound, glanced out of the window and recognized Father Devleecheum, a middle-aged Belgian Roman Catholic priest as he approached on a, bicycle. He turned in at the Mission and dismounted. Mary went to the door to greet him.

"Ah, Miss Ball—and are you well?" he asked in sing-song English. He had been in China for about thirty years. He wore a short, grey-salted beard.

"Very well, Father; but sad that we are not able to work as usual."

The priest nodded his sympathy.

"I have been delegated to bring a special message from the

other fathers," he said. "You realize of course that the situation is very serious and dangerous?"

"I suppose it is," Mary admitted.

"I believe the Reds will be in the city in two days," he declared, "and I believe that all the Christians in the city will be massacred. Can you send a telegram to your bishop asking for an aeroplane to evacuate all foreigners?"

Mary stared at the priest, astounded by the extreme pessimism of his assessment.

"Have you spoken to the China Inland Mission people?" she asked him. "Are they willing to be included in such a telegram?"

"I haven't spoken to them," Father Devleecheum said. "Would you speak to them for me?"

"If you wish it," Mary said. When she spoke to them, she was told that the Chinese Inland Mission staff would indeed like to get out of the city, given the opportunity to do so. Mary then discussed the situation with her S.P.G. companions, none of whom had previously thought seriously of leaving. They were horrified by Father Devleecheum's prediction of a massacre.

"I can hardly believe that would happen," said Mr. Fox, the tall S.P.G. priest, pale and almost emaciated in appearance, who had lost his left arm in the First World War. "I really doubt if there would be a wholesale massacre—but perhaps its just as well to send the telegram." Miss Preece and Miss Porter agreed with him.

"Very well, then," Mary said. "But there's just one point I'd like to make—I certainly won't go unless we can take the girl nurses with us. After all, they are Peking girls with no homes in Tatung. I feel responsible for them."

"I quite agree, Mary," Eunice Preece said. "It would be wrong for us to go without the girls." Kathleen Porter nodded.

Then they composed a short telegram to the Bishop. EVACUATION URGENT CAN YOU SEND PLANE. Mary arranged to have it transmitted through military channels. But when the reply came, it read: REGRET NO PLANES AVAILABLE.

The entire city waited edgily for the expected attack, which did not come. Instead, the Communists chose to by-pass Tatung, leaving companies of troops in the out-lying villages. By then, the hospital, under the shadow of the city's walls, seemed reasonably safe again. It was re-opened.

From the moment they met—many months ago—Chao Tsun Lan had captivated Mary's interest: she was so utterly different from the run-of-the-mill girl nurses who came to work at the Mosse Memorial. Tall, well-shaped, remarkably attractive, Miss Chao had the tremendous advantage over most Chinese women of an inborn pride, which enabled her to gaze confidently at all the world around her. For she was a Manchu—one of the conquerors, one of the aristocratic families in the bygone days of the emperors.

Her strong personality made Miss Chao a leader amongst both boy and girl nurses; but her dearest treasure, and one she could not conceal, was her anticipation of becoming the bride of Shu Ching, Dr. Philip Li's second son. In this, at least, she was merely a woman in love—no more and no less than her Chinese sisters.

Indeed, she already thought of herself as a member of the Li family. When the Superintendent's wife was away in Peking, Miss Chao did not wait to be asked to take over her duties: she mended Philip Li's clothes, saw that his bedding was kept clean and, when she was off-duty, sometimes went to his office to act as hostess for him, pouring tea for his visitors. Thus she already saw herself as his near relation and bent her mind to thinking of the ways to please her fiancé's family.

Not long after Mary had the hospital running properly again, Miss Chao came to her.

"Miss Ball, I would like to become a Christian."

Mary was aware that the girl's engagement to Li Shu Ching might have provided the motive for her request, for all the members of the Li family were Christians.

"Do you really want that—for yourself?" she asked the girl.

"Yes, I do."

Mary still hesitated. She had observed that the Manchu girl had been quite rude to her fellow nurses who did not have the advantage of her family background. Still—Mary reflected—

though she was imperious in her manner to *them* she was not a cruel girl, for she was kind and thoughtful to the patients.

Mary said: "You realize if you go through with this it will mean giving up some of the things you have been doing? You will have to behave differently to some people."

Miss Chao nodded, almost with humility.

"I wish to be taught what to do," she said, adding eagerly: "Let me wait a month or two and prove by my new behaviour that I truly want to become a Christian."

But before many weeks passed, Mary became convinced of the girl's sincerity. Miss Chao had changed her manner towards her fellow nurses and she had begun to attend both morning and evening prayer in the hospital chapel.

"Would you like me to speak to Mr. Fox about you?" Mary offered.

"Oh, please do!" Miss Chao's eyes gleamed with pleasure. And the S.P.G. priest began to give her instruction. She was a most intelligent girl, and soon was translating the Christian ideal into the manner of her living. When a girl patient was brought into the hospital suffering from an exceptionally severe case of smallpox, the other nurses were too terrified to help her for fear of catching it themselves: only Miss Chao could be depended upon to minister to her needs. This impressed Mary more than anything else regarding Miss Chao's sincerity in turning Christian. The Manchu girl had always been proud of her clear skin and special beauty: if she were to contract smallpox it would be devastatingly tragic for her.

One day in mid-August a merchant from Peking named Wang, who had been caught in Tatung at the time of the expected Communist attack, came to the hospital. He asked to see the Superintendent on a matter—he insisted—of great urgency. When he was taken to the office of Dr. Philip Li he waited until he was alone with him.

Then he indicated a prominent wart on his forehead and a small scar on his left cheek.

He said nervously: "Please, doctor, will you operate for me

and take this wart away? And can you do anything to remove this scar from my face? Both of these are very painful."

"But—but neither of these sicknesses are of any great consequence," the Superintendent snorted. "I don't think you need an operation, Mr. Wang."

Wang cast his eyes on the floor and he put a hand on each of his knees to indicate the great depth of his humility.

"It is not what you think," he said. "It is not that I am vain and wish to appear better-looking than I am, but my heart is frightened. You see, some time ago I was a prisoner—and I am afraid *they* will recognize me and arrest me again."

In his fear, he had not identified his one-time captors, but there could be little doubt that he referred to the Communists. Out of pity—because the merchant was so obviously terrified—the Superintendent agreed to remove the wart and do what he was able to do with the scar.

In a few days, Wang's bandages were removed and the slight change the minor operations had given his appearance provided him with a disproportionate boost in confidence, so that he was no longer dour and nervously watchful but went about wearing a perpetual smile.

Only a few days before, Mary had been asked to attend a nurses' conference in Canton, which she considered to be important: but how could she go? The railway between Tatung and Kalgan had been cut by the Communists, but trains were still running north-westward to Sui Yuan; and from Ping Te Chuan, an intermediate station about a hundred and twenty miles distant, there was a motor lorry service through to Kalgan.

She mentioned to Philip Li her desire to try this roundabout route, but the Superintendent shook his head worriedly.

"I really cannot let you try it," he said. "Travelling in these wartime conditions is very difficult for a woman alone."

Wang had overheard the conversation, which took place in the men's ward.

"I am going as far as Ping Te Chuan myself," he interjected apologetically. "I owe the hospital very much, and I would be pleased to accompany Teacher Ball that far. I would help her to get accommodation in an inn as well as a ticket on the lorry convoy to Kalgan."

Before Philip Li had a chance to object, Mary gratefully accepted Wang's offer.

They started out, ten days later, at eight o'clock in the morning aboard a train crammed tight with local merchants who were travelling to Ping Te Chuan—where food was much cheaper—to buy meat and grain for resale in Tatung at a profit.

Twenty minutes after leaving the Tatung station, the train passed through a break in the Great Wall into Mongolia. Presently, it pulled into Ping Te Chuan.

Mary was surprised pleasantly when she was met on the station platform by an old friend, a Mr. Shang, a middle-aged man whose wife had died at the hospital some years before and whose son was now training there to be a nurse. The son had visited him the previous week-end and had told him of Mary's expected arrival.

After their greetings, and an introduction to Mr. Wang, Mr. Shang offered some bad news.

"I am sorry to tell you that the inns are all filled," he said. "They are filled with lorry drivers and their helpers. There is a strike. They won't do any work at all—and I don't know whether or not the lorries will be going to Kalgan tomorrow."

"The inns are all filled?" Mr. Wang echoed querulously. "Where are we going to stay the night?"

"We can still try," Mr. Shang told him.

There were no rickshaws or carts at the station, so they divided the luggage to carry between them and walked down the rough, earthen main street calling at one inn after another.

"*Mei yoa te faing, me yoa te faing.* No place at all, no place at all," they were told at each inn. Every courtyard was crowded with lorry drivers and travellers, sitting around smoking their long bamboo and jade pipes.

After trying at half a dozen inns with no success, Mr. Shang said apologetically: "Miss Ball, I'm so sorry I cannot ask you to my house. You see I live some distance away and you must not risk missing the lorries in case they leave at dawn."

"Of course, you are quite right, Mr. Shang," Mary agreed.

He bobbed his head. "I suggest that I ask the Salvation Army if they will let you and Mr. Wang stay in their preaching hall for the night. Do you have what you will need?"

Mary held up her canvas holdall.

"It's all here," she told him. In the holdall was the emergency kit she always carried when travelling in North China: two blankets, a cushion, toilet articles and a change of clothing. In a separate wicker handbag she had a thermos, sandwiches and cakes, as well as an electric torch.

They made their way to the Salvation Army Mission which was in the charge of a stout Chinese who excused himself to consult his wife regarding their request. As a result of that consultation, Mary was given their sitting room for the night and Mr. Wang was told he could sleep in the preaching hall. After Mr. Shang went home, they thanked their hosts and, leaving their luggage, went out to find a restaurant.

They found a small one in the main street and Mr. Wang went in first to ask if a foreign woman would be allowed to eat there. Presently the proprietor came to the door, bowing at Mary.

"Come in, honourable lady," he chirruped. "Our food is very bad, but perhaps you can eat a little of it. . . . But please don't sit near the window or else we will have too many children crowding around to see your red hair."

They had flat, savoury cakes, sprinkled with sesame seed, cabbage soup and a plate of vegetables. Mary split her cake first, filled it with vegetables, and ate it, following it up with the soup.

When she had finished, the proprietor came to their table and asked her anxiously: "Have you eaten enough?"

"I have been filled to the top," she replied, knowing what was expected of her.

Mr. Wang asked the proprietor if he knew what had stirred the lorry drivers up to striking pitch.

The proprietor shrugged. "They say it is too dangerous to take their loads of grain from here to Kalgan for the small pay offered by the Government."

Like everyone else, he, too, avoided the specific naming of the danger, but Mary needed no blueprint: he could only be referring to bandit gangs and to Red foraging parties in the surrounding hills.

Leaving the restaurant, they came to an oval-shaped open space in the heart of the town, surrounded by government buildings, a school and a run-down pleasure garden, this last a heritage of the Japanese occupation. At one end of the oval was the starting point of the road to Kalgan. The oval itself was packed solidly with lorries, about fifty of them parked in regular rows. Small clusters of men squatted on their haunches, discussing the meeting which was going on at that very moment between the committee of lorry drivers and representatives of the Government.

"When shall we know if the strike is to go on or not?" Mr. Wang asked one of the drivers.

"When the meeting ends at six o'clock," the driver said. "Are you going to Kalgan?"

"Well, I'm not travelling there myself," Mr. Wang said, "but this foreign lady with me is waiting to go."

The driver looked at Mary with a gleam of fresh interest. He bowed and introduced himself. He was a small-bodied, small-boned man, named Liu.

"She can come on my lorry," he said hopefully.

"Well then, what merchandise are you taking?" Mr. Wang asked cautiously. "No pigs, I trust?"

"Oh, no pigs, no pigs," the driver said. "I'm taking a load of grain."

Mary knew that the passengers were usually expected to climb on top of the load in the back of the lorry.

"Could you arrange with the driver for me to sit by his side in the cab?" she asked Mr. Wang.

The two men argued the point back and forth. At length the driver said: "To sit on top of the load is eight silver dollars. To sit in front will cost thirteen silver dollars. But if you pay that, I will take special care with the foreigner at inns when we stop."

Mr. Wang looked at her, eyebrows raised questioningly.

"I'd certainly rather pay the difference and sit in front," Mary said firmly. She paid two dollars on account, promised five dollars on departure and the remainder on arrival at Kalgan, the customary method of payment for a journey which might be hazardous. After she heard that the lorry drivers, having been promised higher pay, were now ready to set off in their convoy very early next morning, she returned to the Salvation Army compound and went to bed, spreading her blankets on two bare wooden benches which had been pushed together for her. Dogs kept barking irritably in the compound and she could hear children crying and it was about two o'clock before she dropped off to an uneasy sleep.

She was wakened by someone knocking at the window.

Mr. Wang called softly: "Miss Ball, Miss Ball. Four o'clock. Get up, get up!"

She had not undressed. For the journey she had put on a heavy blue skirt and jersey sweater over a cotton dress. In the high plateau in early September the nights were close to freezing, but the cotton dress was for Peking where it would be a great deal warmer. When she got there she would simply remove the skirt and jersey and be appropriately attired in summer-weight clothing.

Then she heard Mrs. Lien, the wife of the Salvation Army man, calling to her. "Shall I make you some hot water?"

"No, thank you—I have some," Mary called back. Though she had had her thermos filled at the restaurant the hot water was for tea, not washing: it was far too cold a morning for that and because the strong wind on the journey would cause chapping, she used face cream instead.

When she left the compound, there was still no sign of dawn. The air was sharp with frost. Mr. Wang took Mary's canvas holdall while she managed her wicker basket. They made their way to the lorries through the dark streets, and after searching around found the one she had arranged to travel in, loaded high with sacks of grain.

"Are you going to start right now?" Mr. Wang asked the driver.

"No," Liu told him. "It will be some time before the Government office is open to issue the petrol."

"Well, anyway, you get in the cab and sit down, Miss Ball," Mr. Wang urged. "It will be warmer inside."

She did so, observing through the rear window that Mr. Wang, swinging his arms across his body for warmth, was making friends with a passenger who had already seated himself on top of the bags of grain. After talking to him for a while, Wang passed up to him Mary's holdall, in which she kept her bedding.

Mary rolled down the side window of the cab and called back: "Please use my bedding to sit on."

"I'm really very comfortable as I am," the passenger called back. But he took the holdall and sat on it.

At about seven o'clock the petrol issue began. There were twenty-eight lorries for this particular convoy, all numbered. The one Mary was travelling in was number fourteen. But it was eight o'clock before the convoy pulled out, bumper to bumper down the main street of the town, each lorry carrying several paying passengers. But when it approached the town's gate, the convoy stopped. The driver turned to Mary and whispered quickly that one of the conditions made for paying the drivers a higher rate was that they would not take passengers.

"But you sit still—take no notice," Liu said. Then he called to the passengers sitting outside on the bags of grain to get off and meet him beyond the gate. Mary observed that passengers were scrambling down from all the lorries in the convoy.

The Government order, Driver Liu said, had stated that no lorry should be carrying passengers when it passed through the gate. Now, one by one, the vehicles passed through, under the watchful eyes of the police; but they did not notice Mary, sitting in the cab between the driver and his assistant—they were looking on the loads for laggards.

Just outside the gate, the convoy stopped again and picked up its passengers: the police had observed the strict letter of their instructions and that was quite enough for them.

The convoy travelled over rough dirt roads, pocked with deep potholes and during the morning they passed several broken-down vehicles that had started out nearer the front of the queue. This part of Mongolia was grain country. They passed through great fields of oats, some still standing, some being harvested, some in endless rows of stooks to dry.

They were four or five thousand feet above sea level. The air was bitingly crisp, the wind cold. Late in the afternoon they came to a series of salt-water lakes: Mary could see the glistening white crystals of salt on the barren shorelines. There were many birds, wild ducks and herons. There was a range of snowy mountains in the distance.

As dusk approached, the wide valley they were passing through cast long shadows and the great herons whirling overhead made weird silhouettes against the sky. They heard the distant roll of gunfire. Mary shivered. What had been quite a pleasant day had suddenly turned into the sinister foreboding of night.

It was made no more reassuring when the convoy stopped and the drivers, gathering to debate where they should end that day's journeying, spoke of their fears of an attack by bandits and that other nameless and somehow more deadly fear they all carried with them. Finally, they agreed to push on to a Mongol village some miles ahead.

When they reached it, Driver Liu was as good as his promise. He managed to find a place for Mary in the small local inn, though she had to share a k'ang with the daughter-in-law of the innkeeper and her child.

That night she had an experience shared by few Europeans.

"The k'ang was in a room with a mud floor," she later recalled. "Just beyond was the central room, containing the household gods, and beyond that was the k'ang occupied by the innkeeper and his wife. I had gone to bed early, tired and aching from the beating of the bumpy roads, having had millet gruel for supper. I was lying there, thinking over the sights of that day's journey when I heard movements and the shuffling of feet in the room of the household gods.

"Suddenly, there was what seemed, in what had been utter darkness, to be a blaze of light. Then I saw through the partly open curtains that two candles had been lit by the eldest member of the family, a venerable grandfather with a wisp of white hair.

"I peered through the slit in the curtains and observed that there was one candle on either side of a niche hidden by a faded red satin curtain. Then the old man used the candles to light thin sticks of incense, in bunches, and he placed them in an incense burner. He pulled aside the satin curtain and I saw the principal household god, a sitting buddha made of brass.

"I realized suddenly that this was the Moon Festival, the fifteenth day of the eighth month of the Chinese calendar—a very solemn occasion, indeed. I saw, too, that two dishes each of melon seeds, sunflower seeds, apples and pears had been placed on a table as offerings of thanksgiving.

"The old man knelt painstakingly down on the mud floor while his son, the innkeeper, knelt behind him and his small grandson, aged four, knelt behind him. The two women knelt on one side. By now I was up on one elbow, completely fascinated.

"The old man kow-towed, his forehead to the floor, and the others did the same. The women remained in that awkward pose while the males kow-towed three times. The distant gunfire which had been rumbling continuously, had now stopped.

"The grandfather intoned a prayer in a falsetto voice, but I could not make out his words. This went on for about half an hour. Then he struggled to his feet and drew the curtain over the god.

"The others rose.

"The old man pinched out the candles but left the incense to burn sickly sweet throughout the night. I had witnessed the ceremony of the Moon Festival, which had been performed unchanged for countless centuries.

"Presently, the innkeeper's daughter-in-law and small son padded into the room and slipped into the k'ang beside me. I was positive that she knew I was awake, but because she could not allow herself to think that I had witnessed their age-old ceremony, she pretended that I had been, and still was, fast asleep. But I did not drop off in fact for some time."

Next morning, the convoy started out in a soft grey drizzle of rain. The distant guns were rumbling again. The driver seemed less apprehensive than he had been the day before and eventually he admitted that it was because he felt the bandits were unlikely to attack the convoy in the rain. In the twenty-four hours since they had begun the journey so many lorries had broken down that theirs had moved up to sixth place in the line. Looking back through the rear-view window Mary saw how cold and wet and miserable the outside passengers appeared to be, huddling within themselves as if to capure the tiniest spark of warmth from their own bodies.

When the rain stopped at about ten that morning the driver uttered a sudden exclamation of dismay and pointed off into the eastern distance. There, along the crest of a hill, about a dozen horsemen were galloping parallel to the convoy.

"Bandits!" the driver muttered fearfully. He had turned quite pale and was chewing at his lips; but after surveying the strength of the convoy, the bandit gang must have decided the odds were not in its favour for it rode off. The driver sighed his relief heavily. He told Mary that now he expected to arrive safely in Kalgan by two that afternoon.

All that morning they had been rolling along the flat surface of a great plain, but now the road shot upward. The lorries growled in low gear through a winding pass, which narrowed down to a mountain defile. At the crest, the lorries were stopped by armed Nationalist guards who went through the cargoes for smuggled weapons. After a half hour's delay, they were signalled on. They headed down through the rocky pass until at last it opened up to give a far-reaching vista. Down below, tiny in the distance, Mary could see Kalgan.

Just outside the city they met a company of Nationalist cavalry and were ordered off the road by their officers until the horsemen cantered past, shouting boastingly of their mission. They had been ordered out of Kalgan to sweep a contingent of guerillas out of the hills. They would do it, they would do it!

Now the convoy was back in China again. Shortly after it entered the city, the horsemen came back at the full gallop, shouting at the cheering crowds in the streets: "We've conquered; we've conquered! We got rid of them!"

Mary was disinclined to believe this latest boast. Surely they had merely driven out for a short sweep and back again, for they would have had no time to do any more than circle around and raise a cloud of empty dust.

Next day she travelled on uneventfully by train to Peking, and flew on to Hong Kong in the comparative luxury of a Skymaster. She travelled to Canton on the last leg of her journey, by rail. The nurses' conference lasted for about ten days. When she got back to Peking, she found that she could not make the return journey to Tatung by the roundabout route she had followed on the way out. It, too, had now been cut by the advancing Communists.

While she was in Canton, Mr. Fox, the S.P.G. priest, had arrived in Peking and now, like Mary, was anxious to return to his Tatung post. Through a friend, he learned that an aircraft was being sent there to carry salaries for postal and railway employees. He managed to wangle seats aboard it for Mary and himself. For a while, an irregular air service was maintained between the two cities after this. In fact, Eunice Preece, needing a holiday, used it to fly down to Peking in mid-November; but by the time she was ready to return, the air service had been discontinued. She was still in Peking when it fell to the Communists in the last days of that year.

Some time before Mary's visit to Canton, Miss Chao had knocked at her office door in the hospital. When the Manchu girl entered, she smiled, showing her large, well cared-for teeth.

"I am to be baptized on Sunday, Miss Ball," she said happily. "Would you please be my god-mother?"

Mary was touched. "I'd like that very much."

They chatted for a while, and now the girl seemed inclined to confide in the older woman, sketching in hitherto unrevealed details of her background as well as breathless hopes for the future.

Her father, Miss Chao revealed, had been working at the Hill Murray Institute for the Blind in Peking when, because of a tubercular infection, he had had his left leg amputated. For this, he had gone to Dr. Philip Li's private hospital in Peking, and when she had paid him a visit there her father had introduced her to the doctor. This had led, a little later, to her accepting a nursing post there and, eventually, to her meeting and then becoming engaged to the doctor's second son. In her telling of it, the story gained an aura of importance, of singularity, as if no such thing had ever happened under the kind connivance of fate before. The girl's dark eyes shone when she spoke of her coming marriage: her voice turned liquid when she spoke her fiancé's name.

Shu Ching, Mary reflected, was a very lucky young man.

Unfortunately, a few weeks after her confirmation, Miss Chao became ill with typhoid fever.

"She was extremely patient and good in doing what the doctor told her," Mary recalled. "She was six weeks in bed, during which time I grew to be very fond of the girl. She was brave and uncomplaining. Towards the end of the fifth week, she started with a very bad cough and her temperature began going up each evening instead of settling down as it should have done. I thought she was developing TB. She was given streptomycin injections and another treatment. We had no X-ray equipment at Tatung, but directly her temperature settled down, Kay Porter took her to Peking where she was examined by a tuberculosis specialist who ordered two months rest for her.

"She came back to the Mosse Memorial and we warded her in one of the verandahs.

"Her young man, Shu Chin, was extremely bright in some ways, but even though his father was a doctor he had an unreasonably backward fear of disease. He was frightened at the thought of being engaged to a girl who might have TB. Miss Chao's X-ray, though it had shown some scars on the right lung, had revealed nothing active. We sent her down to Peking again and another X-ray proved her to be quite clear.

"She returned to duty. But in the meantime the young man had decided not to risk it and broke off the engagement. That was hardly to his credit but, even worse, he lacked the courage to tell her, face-to-face, of his decision. He prevailed on his father—who did not approve of his action—to tell Miss Chao that the marriage was off.

"At first she seemed to take it remarkably well.

"'My marriage is indefinitely postponed,' was how she announced it to me, though she must have known, as I did, that it was off for good.

"Then, in a kind of delayed reaction, it hit her. It hit very hard. She was a proud girl who had been brought up in a proud family; and she had been jilted in a land where her prospects for another marriage were made slim by the jilting.

"I often saw her off duty at that time. She would more often than not go into the garden and sit alone, brooding. Of course, her work went off: she became careless. She had once led all the others in the nursing exams: now she dropped down to the tail end of the list. I felt dreadfully sorry for her, but because of her great pride, which had been crushed, I could think of no way to show it without seeming to remind her of her loss of face.

"After that when Shu Ching came up from Peking to visit his parents it would upset her terribly—just knowing he was there. The other nurses, whom she had once looked down upon from an aristocratic height, would tease her simply by coming to her and smirking: 'Shu Ching's come, Shu Ching's come!'

"At first she would pretend not to notice, but I could see her back stiffen involuntarily against the teasing, like the automatic resistance to the lash of a whip. Later, she would forget her pride and burst out eagerly: 'He has? And what has he come for?'—as if she still nourished a serious hope that he had changed his mind and come to tell her so.

"Then the other nurses would say to her with cruel mock innocence: 'What has he come for? Why, to see his mother! Why else would he travel so far?'

"And Miss Chao's last lingering breath of hope was whisked away at last when Shu Ching was married to another girl in Peking. Dr. Philip Li did not attend the wedding. But none of us realized, just yet, how deeply the Manchu girl had been hurt and how bitterly she was soon to react."

Isolated from its source of supply after the fall of Peking to the Communists, the hospital was running short of money. In addition, though it carried on its services to the public, the number of patients fell off sharply, for the surrounding villages were quite cut off from Tatung. The people in the city were convinced that an attack was bound to come at any hour.

The trenches which had been dug around the city's perimeter nearly a year before had begun to collapse, and again the townsfolk were pressed into digging new defences. The population of the north suburb was evacuated by a military edict. The city's daily paper boasted editorially that Tatung had never surrendered to an enemy and would not do so now, even though Tai Yuan, Shansi's capital, had capitulated.

Doubtless the editorial sabre-rattling had been inspired by the military commander to stiffen the backs of the merchants who, grumbling about their closed shops and the absence of trade, argued that the city ought to bow to circumstance. Word had somehow filtered through the barricades that red troops with plentiful new equipment were assembling in attack positions, and the rumours did nothing to allay the fears of the citizens.

Mary saw many signs of this faltering morale amongst those who came to the hospital. One morning she looked up to see a middle-aged woman in black satin coat and trousers entering the outpatients' department. Of the Chinese upper class, she wore a black satin bandeau over her hair, encrusted with seed pearls. A small woman, she was unsteady on bound feet, but her scarlet lacquer walking stick with its dragon's head handle was meant as much for show as for use.

Mary asked the woman politely if she could help, for she seemed nervous and over-wrought.

"Yes, yes," the small woman said. "Come fetch my son who is ill in my cart at the gateway."

Mary went out to see if this was to be a stretcher case or if a carrying chair would do; for many Chinese objected to being carried prone, believing that this was only for the dead or dying. The cart was of the Peking style: wooden-wheeled, wooden-framed, with a canopy overhead. A blue cloth curtain hung from the canopy. The carter stood in his soiled blue coat and loose trousers, holding a long whip.

Mary was made aware that the small woman had followed her, for a shrill voice cried: "Take care! Take care! My son is very ill!"

Mary turned. She waited for the woman to catch up with her.

"Could he sit in a chair?" she asked.

"Oh, yes," the woman said.

Helped by the carter, Mary pulled up the curtain and pushed it back over the canopy. The youth inside was pale, emaciated and about nineteen years of age.

"How are you? " Mary asked. His right foot was bound up in a black cloth. "Is it your foot that's causing you pain?"

"Yes, truly it is my foot," he replied querulously. "You must be careful how you move me."

His reactions seemed slow; and to Mary he looked to be an opium addict. When the boy nurses arrived with the carrying chair, they helped him into it, one climbing into the cart behind him to move him by the armpits. The second boy took his legs.

"Be careful; be careful! " he whimpered.

"Slowly, slowly, don't hurry him," the mother cautioned.

He was taken into the doctor's office with his mother fussily trailing after. She bowed low to Dr. Philip Li.

"Honourable doctor, I have brought my son," she said to him. "He has been very ill for many months and, hearing of your skill, I came to ask you to save his life."

The doctor bowed his response.

"How old is the boy? What is he suffering from?"

"He has terrible pains in his feet and legs and cannot walk."

"I'll examine him," the Superintendent said.

A boy nurse laid him out on the examination table. Mary noted the results of the examination. The youth's temperature was sub-normal, which was to be expected of an opium addict.

His pulse, at 68, was a bit slow—also to be expected. The doctor looked at the pupils of his eyes.

Turning back to the mother, Dr. Li said: "Your son—he takes opium, does he not?"

She nodded, almost eagerly.

"Oh, yes: I do all I can for him. He has taken opium since he was a child."

Philip Li nodded his head gravely. He applied his stethoscope to the young man's chest.

The mother shook her head impatiently.

"It is not his chest I wish you to see," she snapped. And a moment later: "No: it is not his stomach. It's his *feet*." She unwrapped the black cloth bandage.

There was no discoloration, no evidence of swelling, no sign of any wound at all or even of a scar attesting the memory of an old wound.

"He needs these four toes off," the mother said, pointing to all but the big toe. "Then he'll be quite all right."

A dawning grin of comprehension spread over the doctor's face. He exchanged a knowing look with Mary.

He said: "Honourable lady, I can do nothing for this. He has been ill too long. You had better take him home."

The mother's façade of pride crumpled. She tugged at the doctor's sleeve.

"Have mercy," she whispered. Then, dropping her voice to the lowest of whispers, she murmured: "He's my only son, you see. I cannot have him conscripted into the army." She had bought the boy out of service more than once, she confessed, but the military situation in the city had gone too far for that method to work again. And now even this, her last-resort attempt to have her son maimed had failed.

Weeks passed—weeks of fearful and suspenseful waiting. One brisk but sunny afternoon, early in April, 1949, the Supertendent called a staff meeting in the outpatients' department.

"I have called you together to consider what you want to do in case the city capitulates," he said gravely. "I have heard that some of you want to leave with the retreating army. The hospital committee has discussed this and we would like to say that you must all feel completely free to do as you think best. However, though no one can guarantee what may happen, we will do all we can for those who decide to stay."

Then he asked for a show of hands from those who would stay on. There were now twelve boy nurses and nine girl nurses on the staff. To Mary's great relief, all the women raised their hands without hesitation. Of the twelve boy nurses, two were from Peking, and after they saw the women volunteer they hesitantly raised their hands.

One of the Shansi boys asked: "Do you guarantee us food and protection if we stay?" The Chinese were great believers in guarantees.

The Superintendent shook his head.

"We cannot guarantee any protection at all," he said in a low, unhappy voice. "We can only guarantee to do our best."

But he added that he wanted to put a few facts before them before the ten waverers made up their minds one way or the other. The first, he said, was that the hospital could not operate without staff. The second: had they considered their position if they accompanied the retreat? They would certainly not be provided with food like the soldiers. They were not fit for long route marches. If they arrived at some strange city, how would they find work? And, finally, according to reports only two cities to the west, Sui Yuan and Pao Tou had not yet been captured by the Communists. Where would they go?

One of the boys said, rather hesitantly, that they had made friends of some of the soldiers who were living in houses on the hospital compound: could they have some time to talk to the soldiers and make up their minds?

"Of course," the Superintendent said.

The Shansi boy nurses went out and button-holed their soldier acquaintances. What could *they* guarantee? But the soldiers told them not to be fools: they would be far better off to remain. The boys returned sheepishly and told the Superintendent that they had decided to stay, after all.

Towards the end of that month, however, when the massing of Communist troops around the city made it evident that the attack was imminent, the military and civil leaders of Tatung finally decided to parley with the enemy for terms.

The need for speed had become self-evident: a village, only three miles to the north, had been over-run and the ten Nationalists wounded in that hand-to-hand fighting had been brought in to the hospital for treatment. Besides, the tempo of patrol activity to the north had been greatly stepped up; the west gate had been sealed; tension in the city was close to breaking point. Mary was reminded of long ago—of that siege of 1926 when she was new to the country—for now, again, the hospital could get a pass for only one man at a time to go into the city to buy food.

The Nationalists sent a party of a dozen officers to a railway siding six miles to the north-east, where the Communists had their headquarters in several railway carriages. They questioned their besiegers: What would happen to the troops in the city? Would they be forced into the Red Army? How much ransom, in grain, would be demanded of the city? Would anyone be imprisoned? They tried to establish favourable terms for themselves, then they lowered their requirements a little and a little more: but the Communists listened to them impassively and at every overture shook their heads. Complete surrender—nothing less would do.

After four days of utterly futile manœuvring, Tatung's military commanders bowed to the insistent demands of the civil authorities and agreed to surrender unconditionally.

The news of the impending surrender aroused a great wave of activity amongst the Chinese members of the hospital's staff. Convinced that the Communists were harshly puritanical in regard to women's clothing, Dr. Philip Li suggested to the girl nurses that they discard the gay, flower-patterned gowns they wore off-duty. It would be much wiser, he thought, to wear dark and inconspicuous clothes in order not to attract undue attention.

As a result, the girl nurses filled their spare hours by stitching together dark, long trousers and short coats. The Superintendent busied himself nervously with packing away the porcelain vases and other colourful ornaments in his living quarters in order to make the rooms look austere and purely functional. He went out of his way to tell Mary and Kay Porter that it would be advisable for them to sweep and dust their own rooms from now on, instead of having it done by coolies. He certainly intended to do his own cleaning up, beginning that very day!

But the Communists had not yet accepted the city's surrender, so that the tension of waiting stretched itself still more dangerously thin. To ease this a little, Mary decided to give a party on April 29, which happened to be her birthday.

"In our part of China," she explained later, "nobody plans a party for you; you plan a party to give to everyone else. So I had to get cakes and sunflower and melon seeds and all the fixings.

"As for the cake, Kay Porter kindly made me one—a chocolate with chocolate icing. I didn't know it then, but on the 28th the nursing staff also got one of the Nationalist soldiers to go into the city and buy two sponge cakes.

"That day, it was Mr. Mei's turn to go into the city for supplies. When he came out again, he said to me: 'We must go and see the doctor. I have a very secret thing to tell.'

"I called Kay Porter and we went to the Superintendent's office. He was seated at his desk trying to repair a small alarm clock. There were wheels and sprockets and springs all over the desk top.

"Mr. Mei looked conscious of his importance. 'I have heard from the officer who gave me my pass that the Communists will enter the city tomorrow,' he said.

"I remember feeling relieved that the long wait was at last nearly over.

"The Superintendent nodded. 'Don't tell the soldiers in the compound,' he cautioned.

"At about six o'clock the following morning, Kay Porter came to my bedroom door. The first sound I heard that day was her sweet, clear soprano singing Happy Birthday. I leaped out of bed and opened the door, still in my pyjamas.

"Kay, in her white uniform and veil cap, said: 'Let's hope

you'll have a peaceful, happy day, Mary, whatever may happen later. But I can tell you one thing: I'm going to be at the gate when the Communists march in.' She loved to be in the thick of things.

"I got dressed and we both went to church, then I went round the wards. When the rounds were over, Miss Chang, the staff nurse, and Mr. Mei stepped up to me, smiling, and presented me with the two sponge cakes, each in a cardboard box. Of course, I had no idea what they were until I opened the boxes: the cakes, shaped like peaches, were dusted with pink sugar and trimmed with bits of green citron to look like leaves. I was terribly pleased and told them so.

"After they left, the boy nurses stepped forward, grinning, to give me a basket of fifty eggs, and, after them, the girl nurses with fifty more in a tray. Both basket and tray were lined with twigs of green yew, and bore labels on which were written in Chinese: 'We hope you live a thousand years.'

"At about eleven o'clock, cook came running. He was a very plump little man—from tasting, I suppose—with an unmanageable cowlick over one eye. He cried excitedly, the cowlick bobbing: 'The soldiers are starting to come!'

"That broke up the birthday ceremonials. The entire staff streamed out to the hospital gate. Groups of civilians were preceding the Communist troops with paste pots, posters and paint. One group had just finished lettering on the hospital compound wall: 'Welcome to the soldiers of Mao Tse Tung. May he live a thousand years.'

"Kay Porter was standing beside me. Grinning, she jogged my side with an elbow. 'That makes two today,' she whispered out of the side of her mouth.

"The first contingent of troops rode on horseback into the city. We walked down the roadway and saw them enter. Then we went back to the hospital gate. A second contingent of cavalry turned into the hospital compound. We followed. They dismounted. The unit's commanding officer was a short man with a weatherbeaten face. He looked around, frowning, as if for someone he knew.

"Then he said: 'Is there anyone here named Mary Ball?'

"I stepped forward, puzzled and a bit apprehensive.

" 'I am Mary Ball,' I said.

"He nodded, seeming to know me. 'Don't you recognize me?' he asked.

"I shook my head. 'No—I don't know you at all.'

" 'Are you *sure* you don't recognize me?'

"I told him I still felt I had never seen him before.

"Then he smiled. He had nice, regular teeth. 'My name is Chao—Major Chao,' he said. 'I was a patient in this hospital in 1926 with a wounded arm. You looked after me then, and I've always been grateful.' He had become very friendly, and he must have suddenly caught himself up and have begun to wonder what his fellow officers might think. Then he said, barking it out like an order: 'We will do all we can to protect your hospital so you can carry on.'

"I was tremendously relieved and bowed to him and thanked him. Then I turned to the Superintendent and, bowing again, first to the major and then to the doctor, I said: 'This is Dr. Li, the Superintendent of the hospital.' I wanted to make it quite clear who was in charge, for a Chinese would be likely to believe it was the foreigner. The major and the doctor exchanged low bows.

" 'I hope you will look over our hospital,' the Superintendent invited.

" 'If you lead the way, I will follow,' the major said.

"He and his five fellow officers clomped through the hospital in their heavy rawhide boots, inspecting the wards. Then, while the major continued to accompany Dr. Li, his officers broke away to make a more detailed reconnaissance of every nook and cranny. I think they suspected us of having a hidden store of arms and ammunition. Meanwhile, about fifty of the major's troops had been detailed to search the nurses' rooms, kitchens, outpatients' department and the houses in the compound.

"At last the Reds, who now seemed quite content that there was nothing further on the hospital property that might concern them, called the Nationalist troops from their quarters of the compound into the garden and took the rifles from the men and the bayonets from the non-commissioned officers. They were told to remain in the compound until further orders.

"After the city gate was opened, streams of Tatung people poured out as far as the railway station to look around. There were parties of school children conducted by their teachers, each child carrying a paper flag on which words of welcome were written—welcome to the Communists. The Chinese have learned that sometimes, in order to live, it is necessary to change their colours very quickly indeed.

"Late that afternoon, the sightseers began to drift back into the city. The major and his troops, leaving one man behind to guard the Nationalist soldiers, went inside the city walls. That was the last I saw of Major Chao, but he was as good as his word, for the hospital was not troubled by the Communist troops. The day we had all feared had come off very well—much better than we could have hoped. It was a great relief to us all.

"As far as I was concerned, it had been a most remarkable birthday."

*   *   *

CHAPTER XVI

UNLIKE their predecessors, the Communist Government officials did not look upon the Mosse Memorial Hospital as an independent enterprise; for it, and every other aspect of Chinese life was now expected to have its umbilical link to the state.

One morning in mid-May, a representative of the People's Party called on Dr. Philip Li to make this clear.

"This is the *new* China," he told the Superintendent with great earnestness. "Therefore it is necessary for you and your staff to understand the principles of the People's Party. . . . We will appoint two officers to come and explain things to your staff. Now then: what time would be most convenient? You see, the meeting may take several hours and we know the patients must also be looked after."

"We shall be very pleased to be better informed in all ways about the new China," the doctor said with a small formal bow, and he suggested ten o'clock the following morning as a convenient time. He had quickly accepted the fact that the change had come and that the sooner he learned the methods of the new government the fewer would be the difficulties put in the hospital's way. He circularized to the staff the time and place of the meeting, which was to be held in the outpatients' department.

At ten o'clock next morning the entire staff had assembled, murmuring. Awaiting them, in a navy blue tunic, was the representative of the new civil government. Beside him was his military counterpart in greenish khaki.

The man in blue cleared his throat, and the murmuring died away.

"I want to impress upon every single one of you," he crisply began, "that there is no need to fear us. We have taken charge for the good of the country and for the good of every man, woman and child. But, of course, we must have co-operation."

He paused to let that sink in, his eyes blinking; and then he went on to outline some of the Government's plans. Committees were to be set up—medical, educational, agricultural and so on—all kinds of committees for each department of life. Only through these committees could any approach be made to the Government.

But, he added with a brief smile, any person could appeal to the Government for redress of injuries received prior to the time they took over. [This plank in the Communist platform was later to result in a diarrhœa of public trials, many of which were instigated out of motives of personal revenge.]

But below the governmental level, the civil representative told his listeners, they would have their chance to participate in running their own affairs. Committees must be formed of hospital staff members—especially *Kung Hui*, the Workers' Party Committee, with a chairman and vice-chairman voted into office by all the staff, barring only the Europeans.

Also, he said, a lecturer from the Government of the new China would come and explain in greater detail the principles on which their government would function; how the hospital committees should be run; how the committees would co-relate with other committees in the city. For, indeed, every institution —the hospital, schools, factories—was to have its own *Kung Hui*, and the function of each would be, first of all to re-educate the minds of the people into the ways of the new China.

When the meeting was over and dispersed, Philip Li shook his head in a kind of stunned wonder.

He remarked to Mary: "They mean to run their own direct course, don't they? Nothing else matters! They are so sure of their aim, they will ride over anything that gets in their way!"

But for the moment Mary was more directly concerned with the world within the hospital compound. The meeting had made one thing very clear to her: it would be impossible for any member of the Chinese staff to remain uncommitted to the new government. And she had to admit to herself that so far, none seemed reluctant to follow the new leaders and the new concept.

As a result of that first meeting, Mr. Mei—now head of the hospital's nursing school—was voted chairman of their Kung Hui and Fan Shi Fu, the number one coolie, vice-chairman. Their installation meant that they had to assume some curious new duties, one of which was the teaching to the staff of a new dance through which they were expected to show their joy at the coming of the new government.

The dance, performed out of doors to the somewhat barbaric rhythm concocted by two drums and a set of cymbals, was quite simple: a few steps forward, then back again, each phrase ending with a kind of curtsy. Men partnered men, women partnered women. There had never been a national dance before and it was intended as another bond towards unity throughout the whole country. Mr. Mei taught the dance to the nurses in the outdoor basketball court in the hospital compound, and Mary became a fascinated onlooker whenever she could spare the time.

At first, the neophyte dancers were most reluctant, and they would practice only at dusk when they felt less conspicuous than under daylight's full candour. Even then, for some time, most of the girl nurses merely walked self-consciously in procession, unwilling to attempt the actual dancing.

Then, shyly, they made a stab at it and found, to their surprise, that they actually liked it!

They were dressed uniformly, boys and girls carbon copies of one another in navy blue trousers and short white coats with white turkish towelling round the head, rather like a turban. About the waist, each wore a cerise sash.

Once the Kung Hui was established it was divided into several sub-committees: one for food, one for coal and lighting, one for drug supplies and a student body committee again sub-divided into one for girls and one for boys. This last pair of sub-sub-committees had as their chief function what was euphemistically called 'self-criticism'—which in fact meant spying on one another and on any person with whom they came in contact in their work. Such splendid opportunities for trouble-making were not overlooked, particularly by those who felt justified, by reason of some recent and, perhaps, personal set-back, in lashing out at life which had been unkind to them.

So it was with Chao Tsun Lan, whose pride Shu Ching—the Superintendent's second son—had stamped under his heels when he had jilted her. She seized upon the opening the new order gave her to reassert, to the very people who had witnessed her shame, her own continued place of importance in their lives. She began by deliberately ignoring the long-standing hospital rules regarding the behaviour of nurses, and by influencing Nurse Tang, her closest friend, to follow her intransigent leadership.

Such insubordination, if allowed to continue unchecked, would soon seriously threaten hospital morale and—Mary well knew—her own authority. She was in a ticklish position. It was certainly her problem to deal with; yet—with the Communists observing every move of the foreigners remaining in China, distrustful, powerful, ready to find fault and act on their findings—was there any disciplinary action she dared to take? The last thing she wanted was to give the new leaders the excuse to make her leave her work and the people she so ardently desired to help.

Thus, daily, Mary helplessly watched the brazen rule-breakings by the Misses Chao and Tang. Once or twice she reminded them in mild reproval of the code of behaviour they had once undertaken to follow, but she dared go no further.

She later recalled unhappily: "How did they frustrate the rules? In countless small and irritating ways. They would not report as they were supposed to before going into the city. Though it was forbidden, they would go in and out of the men's wards at will. They would shout in the corridors, instead of maintaining hospital quiet. In fact, in any way they could, they deliberately showed their contempt for those of us who were supposed to be in authority.

"But this took place just after Miss Chao had learned that her young man, Shu Ching, had actually married that other girl in Peking. I knew what was eating into her; I knew that she was not really a bad girl but was simply hitting out at anyone and everyone because of her own deep hurt.

"And I honestly didn't know what to do. It seemed as if my hands were tied. I mentioned the problem to the Superintendent who (though for the sake of his own face he tried to pretend otherwise) must have felt every bit as helpless as I did.

" 'Take no notice, Miss Ball, take no notice,' he told me, wringing his hands. 'Let them both carry on: they are just as bad to me as they are to you.' "

A few days later, Mr. Mei trailed Mary out into the garden, where she had gone to reflect quietly to herself about the growing unrest of her staff and the seeming insolubility of her problem.

They exchanged greetings and Mary saw that Mr. Mei—licking his lips and looking anxiously around the garden to reassure himself that they were alone—was far from at his ease.

When, at last, he appeared satisfied that it was safe for him to speak, he whispered to her: "There was a Communist meeting today, Miss Ball, and there has been a criticism made against you. The girl nurses, led by Miss Chao, do not wish to report when they go out; and they object to being spoken to if they sing or talk loudly in the corridors."

Mary nodded. "Thank you for telling me this, Mr. Mei."

He had hardly slipped back inside the hospital building when one of the boy nurses hurried furtively out to her.

"Be very careful, Teacher Ball," he said in an urgent undertone. "The girl nurses made some complaints against you at the meeting and I'm afraid their criticisms may be taken to the big Communists in the city." He bowed hurriedly and fled.

This was what she had feared all along. She knew that if the nurses' complaints were forwarded to higher authority she would almost certainly be summoned for a public trial, and that could end in her expulsion from China. Even thinking of that possibility gave her a moment of panic. She so desperately wanted to stay! At the very best, if such a trial were held, with her in the dock, it would make her life in Tatung almost unbearable; and it could not fail to bring grave embarrassment to the hospital.

She went back into the hospital, pretending to be unaware of the threat hanging over her; but she took care not to be provoked into calling the misdemeanours of the Misses Chao and Tang to their attention.

Some days passed with Mary never knowing when the blow might fall. Then the Superintendent asked her to come into his office. He shut the door carefully.

Then he sighed—and suddenly grinned.

He said joyously: "Miss Ball, two nurses have been severely criticized by the rest of the nurses' committee for refusing to report when they went out and for coming in very late at night. Hardly anyone is speaking to them!

"I think things will be easier, now."

Feeling immeasurably relieved, Mary asked him how this about-face had occurred.

"Oh, the boy nurses had talked it over amongst themselves, and then at a committee meeting they spoke up. They said that during the difficult years the hospital had protected them and looked after them; and they said that both the trouble-making nurses were from Peking, visitors to a Shansi hospital; and they said that the hospital wouldn't have been here any more if *you* had not come back to make it live again, Miss Ball."

It seemed inevitable that some of the new committees—particularly those concerned with food, coal and heating and the supplies of drugs—would take out of Mary's hands some of the overload of responsibilities which had long been hers as the hospital's matron. In fact, now that the situation had again become easier, she found that she was faced, indirectly, with most of her former problems and countless new ones.

One day, Mr. Mei approached her with an air of apology.

"Oh, Miss Ball, last night we had a committee meeting and the nurses complained that the cook was not buying a great enough variety of vegetables and also that the steamed bread was heavy."

"I think perhaps it is true that the food is not quite so good now," Mary agreed, picking her words with painful care. "We have had some complaints from the patients about it—and only this morning I had some steamed bread that was quite inedible."

Mr. Mei shook his head unhappily. He had the appearance of an overburdened man.

"The committee would like to appoint one nurse and one coolie," he said, "to go to the shops and find out what vegetables they have; also to enquire if we can get a better flour for the money we're paying." His eyes were anxious. "Do you think it's a good idea?"

"Yes, a very good idea," Mary told him.

Mr. Mei looked around to make sure they were out of earshot. He dropped his voice to a thin whisper.

"Could you help me, Teacher Ball? How many *chin* are there in a bag of flour?"

A *chin* is about one and a third pounds.

"Usually forty-four to a small bag," Mary told him, her own voice obligingly reduced to conspiratorial dimensions.

"Ah, then how many steamed breads should be made from a *chin*, and how much should each bread weigh?"

"You ought to get about eight portions of bread, weighing about two *liang*, from each *chin*."

She knew that Mr. Mei was a very worried man: he told her he felt it was impossible for the staff members to keep a close watch on the cooks and do their own jobs as well.

"You must tell them to try," Mary urged him. She sympathized with Mr. Mei's reasoning, but she knew that there were very grave dangers for anyone trying to swim against the overpowering Communist current.

"I'll explain it to them if you think so," Mr. Mei said. But he was not at all happy.

Next day, Mary was in the kitchen when old Wong, one of the coolies, and Miss Lan, a girl probationer who had been in the hospital for only a few weeks, were trying to plan meals with the three cooks, all of whom remained tight-lipped and sceptical. The two sub-committee members, seeing that they were getting nowhere, finally gave up the attempt. They sent in a criticism about the attitude of the cooks who, they said, were not co-operating in the new venture.

Some days later, Mr. Mei again sought Mary out, coming to her office.

"Here I am again to worry you," he said, looking downcast.

"What is it, Mr. Mei? I know you have many difficulties. If there is anything at all I can do to help, I'd be only too pleased."

"It's the kitchen troubles again," Mr. Mei said, shaking his head. "Would you. . . . Do you think you could be kind enough to organize the meals and give out the flour and supplies—just the way you used to? "

After making his ward rounds one morning, Dr. Philip Li asked Mary: "Will you have some free time around six o'clock this evening, Miss Ball? I have what I believe is an important suggestion to make, but I don't want to write the Bishop before I consult with you about it."

"Of course I have the time." Mary saw that the Superintendent had something else on the tip of his tongue but was hesitant about expressing it. She was aware that there were certain phases of hospital business he preferred not to have his wife overhear, so she asked him: "Would you like me to come to your house? Or would you prefer to come to my room?"

"Oh!" he said, in pretended surprise at the suggestion. "Well, if it would be convenient, I'll come to your room."

Mary prepared tea for his arrival. When he came, she poured it and they chatted inconsequentially over the cups for a while; but then the Superintendent cleared his throat to indicate that he was ready to get down to business.

"With all the recent changes, I've been feeling very tired these days," he said. "I've been thinking that we ought to get another doctor to help out."

"That would be a very wise move," Mary concurred. "Your responsibilities are certainly much heavier than they were before."

And it was a fact that Philip Li now had very little free time. He gave lectures during the week, made his rounds of the inpatients, attended to the outpatients, performed operations in the afternoons—and, in addition to all these duties he had to make sure that the hospital was run in a way which would not rouse the ire of the watchdogs of the new order.

"In truth, I need a surgeon to help me," the Superintendent told her. "Is there—is there anyone you can suggest?"

Now she understood the game and pretended to consider the matter. Then she offered: "Well, your cousin, Francis, is a first-class surgeon. Besides, he is very well liked in the city."

"Ah!" said the Superintendent. "Yes—I would like to ask him to come here on the staff. But, of course, I know of the trouble there was, long ago. If you would consent to his coming back, I would be most grateful."

This, too, was why the Superintendent had wanted the matter discussed out of his wife's hearing, for she had no love for Francis's 'little' wife.

"I'd be very happy if the Bishop and the medical board in Peking approve," Mary said, smiling. She, herself, was fond of Francis; and she had always very much regretted the circumstances which had led to his departure.

The Superintendent arose. He seemed to shed a great weight of worry as he said: "I shall write to the Bishop, then. I should be pleased if you would write to him as well."

"Of course I'll do that," Mary promised, and went off to her office to keep her word without delay.

A week later she heard from the Bishop. He wrote to say that the medical board had been happy to approve of the appointment of Dr. Francis Li as Deputy Superintendent of the Mosse Memorial Hospital. Francis had moved to Peking some months previously, but—the Bishop said—he was overjoyed at the prospect of returning to the hospital in Tatung where he had worked for many happy years.

Francis stepped out onto the Tatung station platform at twenty minutes to eight in the morning of June 20th, a tall, slow-moving man. He was met by a delegation from the hospital.

"It was characteristic of him that he looked at us in shy astonishment," Mary recollected. "He lowered his eyes, bowed slightly—for in the new China there were no deep bows—and said: 'You should not have come to meet me. I am not worthy of your time.'

"But his cousin stepped up and said: 'Are you well, Francis? Did you have a good journey?' At times, Dr. Philip seemed to adopt a no-nonsense brusqueness which seemed more western than Chinese.

"Francis shrugged.

"I said: 'I'm very pleased to see you again, Dr. Li. I hope you're not too tired.' He was about fifty-eight then, and getting bald on top.

"'Miss Ball, I hope you're well,' he said, smiling gently. 'I shall see you at the hospital where we may talk.'

"Mr. Mei took his bedding and a basket of fruit he had brought from Peking. Then his cousin said: 'We have a rickshaw here for you, Francis—and one for me.'

"The two doctors looked at me apologetically. They took the rickshaws and the rest of us walked home, for things had changed a great deal. I didn't want to draw the attention of the Communists to a cavalcade of rickshaws—it would have been too apparent that the cousins had European friends. Of course, the top officials already knew this, but I thought it best not to flaunt the fact too forcibly.

"Francis still owned a chemist's shop in the city which his second son ran for him, and for the first couple of days he stayed with his son; but then he moved some furniture into a house in the hospital compound and made his home there. He settled in quickly to hospital work. It was very pleasant having him back.

"I was a little worried for fear he might feel he had lost face, but he didn't appear to mind being his cousin's assistant in the very hospital where he had once been Superintendent. To differentiate between the two doctors the staff began to call Dr. Philip *Yuan chang*, which means Superintendent, and Francis simply Dr. Li. Francis and his cousin agreed to divide the work so that Francis would care for the surgical outpatient and VD cases and all the surgical inpatients except for those with eye troubles. The Superintendent would perform all the eye surgery.

Children's nose, ear and throat, and all medical cases remained the responsibility of Dr. Philip."

The two doctor cousins began by working well together. Unfortunately, it was not long before jealousy eroded their seeming solidarity. Knowing them both, this came as no great surprise to Mary. What did surprise her was that it was Philip and not Francis who first revealed his envy.

Some weeks after Francis's return, he was scheduled to perform a Cæsarean section, the operation to begin at two o'clock in the afternoon. At ten minutes before the hour, however, the Superintendent arrived in the washing-up room, scrubbed his hands and came into the theatre where Mary was waiting to administer the anæsthetic. She wondered if there had been some change of plan of which she had not been informed. But such a thing had not happened before.

At that moment, Francis entered the washing-up room. He removed his long, outer gown and began to scrub his hands. Mary had heard him come in, heard him ask the nurse to change the water. The boy nurse was too frightened to tell him that the Superintendent was ready to begin the operation in his stead.

Mary turned to Miss Porter, who was waiting to take the baby when it was delivered.

"Will you go and tell Dr. Li that the Superintendent has scrubbed up?" she asked, remembering that Francis, usually mild and shy, sometimes allowed his temper to erupt when he was unexpectedly thwarted in an area of importance to him. Would there be a clash between the cousins?

Listening, Mary heard Miss Porter's voice in the next room: "Doctor, the Superintendent has already scrubbed up for the operation."

Mary held her breath. Glancing at the Superintendent she saw that his head was attentively cocked to one side in an attitude of listening. Then, again from the next room, she heard the scrubbing brush drop with a splash into the basin of water. She awaited the outburst.

But Francis strode through the door into the operating room with a smile for the Superintendent. It was Philip who now appeared disconcerted, Francis who appeared calm.

"Are you going ahead with this case, then?" Francis asked mildly.

Philip coughed. He coughed again with increasing nervousness.

"Shall we do it together?" he suggested, back-tracking quickly.

"Together?" Francis said in surprise. "Oh, no—if you want to do it, I have other business. I will go and attend to it."

He dried his hands, put his outer robe back on and departed.

Mary began to breath again. For her, the moment had been ticklishly tense, for an outbreak of open warfare between the two doctors could have resulted only in another serious threat to hospital morale—and there had been too much of that, already! This time, it had been Francis's diplomacy that had saved the day.

He had indeed learned a great deal in the wilderness.

Some weeks later, at a hospital staff meeting, Francis displayed a quite different sample of his foresight.

"I think we ought to do something about setting up better relations between ourselves and the new Communist hospital in the city," he suggested, his manner shy as usual.

The Superintendent asked him, rather brusquely, what he had in mind.

Francis murmured, smiling gently: "Why, Philip, I am merely proposing that I should go to operate for them any time they ask me to. You see, they still have no surgeon there, and if I help them now and then I will be able to stay on here: if I refuse, difficulties will surely be made and I will be forced to leave. I certainly don't want to do that. In the long run, it will be much more difficult for this hospital to remain working at all if we don't co-operate."

He paused thoughtfully. Then his eyes came to rest on Mary.

"I also suggest that I should give anatomy lectures at their hospital and—if Miss Ball is willing—she might give some English lessons there." In a soft aside to Mary, he said: "They mainly want to learn the names of the medicines and diseases in English, I believe."

His suggestions were examined from every angle and, finally, the wisdom implicit in them was agreed upon. In the past several weeks, with the new régime at the country's helm, the disturbing suspicion had been scratching at Mary's mind that the days were numbered when the S.P.G. could still run their hospital at Tatung. In that light, it seemed to her, Francis's proposals made great good sense. They might, if acted upon, ease the way for the Chinese staff to carry on with the Mosse Memorial if the Europeans were compelled to leave. . . . *Compelled to leave.* . . . The very phrase passing through her mind sent a chill of despair through her.

Soon after this staff meeting—in October, 1949—Francis and Mary did in fact begin their lectures at the Communist hospital; and whenever a serious operation was needed there, he was called upon to perform it. This service of his paid a supplementary dividend which Francis had foreseen but had been too tactful to mention: it ensured Philip of getting more than the minimal share of operating duty which earlier had activated his jealousy.

Thus, with a single stroke, Mary reflected, Francis had achieved two noteworthy results; on the one hand relieving the tension which had sprung up between his cousin and himself and on the other enhancing the hospital's position in the eyes of the Communist overlords who could, if they wished, destroy it.

But when winter again came to Tatung, it was Francis's turn to be unreasonable and Philip's to assume the diplomatist's role.

Behind this potential cloud of trouble, and stridently egging him on, was Francis's shrewish, gold-toothed, 'little' wife.

She complained incessantly and shrilly about their house in the hospital compound, and how cold it was, and nagged at him to get at least seven stoves to heat it—and, of course, the coal to feed them.

When Francis tried to object that coal, now terribly scarce, was being strictly rationed and that he could not demand more of it than anyone else, she snorted at his qualms. Was he not a very important man, both at the hospital and in the city? Should *she* have to suffer and shiver all the winter because he would not insist on his due?

At last, unable to withstand further domestic brow-beating, Francis demanded the coal—not from the coal committee directly, but from the Superintendent who, he hoped, would influence the committee to supply it.

"Coal for *seven* stoves?" Philip repeated, aghast. "But, Francis —you know I have only asked for coal for two stoves, and our houses are exactly the same size."

Francis must have been aware of the unreasonableness of his demand, but he had been effectively brainwashed by his wife's constant nagging. Stubbornly, he repeated that coal for seven stoves was no more than his minimum need.

It was useless for Philip to remind him that the mines, having been non-operative for many months during the recent civil war, could not now even begin to catch up with demand; that the hospital itself was suffering gravely as a result. They had cut off their running water because there was no coal to work the pumps; they were deprived of electricity and, indeed, had only recently run out of kerosene for their lamps so that now they had to take the edge off the night-time blackness in the wards by filling saucers with *hsang you*, the thick, yellow, acrid oil often used in Chinese cooking, and lighting the makeshift wicks of twisted cotton wool.

Francis, well aware of all this, thought again of the high, continuous whining of his 'little' wife.

"Coal for seven stoves," he repeated.

"Well, this is most difficult," Philip murmured. "Let me think about it."

Presently Philip came up with his simple solution: he had Francis elected to the coal committee, knowing that in this position he could not possibly have the face to force his exorbitant demands. As a result, a compromise was reached: Francis insisted that he still needed the seven stoves, but if the hospital provided the coal for three of them, he would try to obtain the rest privately. And the committee voted to supply coal for three stoves to both Francis—and the Superintendent.

"One night, quite late, a woman far gone in pregnancy was brought to the hospital, moaning in agony," Mary remembered. "She was carried in on a door which had been taken off the hinges of her compound entrance. With her was her husband, several of his friends and an old Chinese midwife. The pregnant woman looked as pale as paper; she was weak from prolonged suffering.

"Directly Dr. Philip came into the outpatients' department, the husband—a rough-looking farmer in a sheepskin coat and a sheepskin cap with ear flaps—knelt on the floor, bowing three times, touching his head to the boards.

"'Chao ming, chao ming,' he pleaded. 'Save her life, save her life.'

"The doctor hurried forward and helped him to his feet.

"'Come into my office and tell me all about your wife's illness,' he said.

"While they consulted together, I got the coolies to carry the patient into the examination room and examined her. We were followed by the midwife, who chattered on busily, explaining all that she had been able and unable to do.

"'I have been with her six days, now,' she said. 'I have done all I can but the child has not been born.'

"The mother interrupted.

"'You will save my life, won't you?' she begged of me, gasping it out between spells of laboured breathing.

"This, I learned, was her tenth pregnancy—and only her first child had survived. All the others had been difficult labours: the children had been prematurely born or were removed piecemeal by the village midwife. Her general condition was so poor that it was clear the only chance to deliver the child was by means of Cæsarean section. Her temperature was 102; her pulse 136; her respiration 30. Considering her history, plus the fact that she had some infection, the Cæsarean would be a dangerous undertaking. She had suffered from the common complaint—ostramalicia. But, with a stethoscope, I could hear the baby's heart beating and, now that we had penicillin, the chance seemed well worth taking.

"I reported her condition to Dr. Philip and he asked the husband for permission to operate, explaining the dangers. The husband agreed.

"We had, for our lighting, only the small saucer lamps flickering in the operating theatre and it was very dark. The scene could hardly be related to normal operating theatre conditions: the patient lay on the table, covered with white towels, the nurses in their white gowns and masks stood holding the saucers of oil, having to take great care not to move too close to the highly inflammable ether and chloroform, looking like fireflies in the gloom. The Superintendent had brought his electric hand torch, but in it were his last three batteries and more were unobtainable.

"All of the preliminaries were completed. Then Dr. Philip said: 'When I give the word, flash on the light.'

"He poised his scalpel.

" 'Now!' he cried.

"The light flashed on. The scalpel plunged.

"Within minutes, the baby boy was delivered. He cried and struggled at once. The doctor passed him to Kay Porter, who gave him his inaugural slap.

"The doctor finished his work as quickly as he could. Then the torch was flashed off.

"I looked at the doctor and he smiled in the flickering light from the saucer lamps. He seemed tired in the way a person shows sudden tiredness after great strain.

" 'The mother will be all right, too,' he said."

In March, 1950, a cheerful, middle-aged Chinese clergyman, Pastor Yang, came up from Peking to pass on to the Superintendent, Mary and their colleagues the official Government view regarding the hospital's future.

As the pastor rose to address the senior staff members, Mary in her anxiety, could distinctly hear the loud and hollow pounding of her own heart. She felt sure that the moment had now come when the Europeans were to be told that they had to leave. She knew that Pastor Yang sympathized with those now in power, and had been free in earlier days with his criticism of the corruption of the deposed Nationalists.

His first words reassured her.

"The Government says that if the Church professes all that our Lord teaches, it must be a social asset to the country," he began. "If you prove this in your work, they will not interfere with your religious beliefs."

But the pastor had not finished.

"As evidence of their loyalty to the Government," he said, "all foreign personnel must agree to be replaced by Chinese."

Mary stirred. The speaker glanced down at her with a reassuring smile.

"Do not be afraid, do not worry: if a foreigner's usual term of service is for, say, five years—even ten—the term can be finished. But when it is finished the foreigner must leave China and not return.

"Of course," he added with seeming regret, "no new foreign missionaries will be allowed into the country, except for certain approved persons in special categories, like professors for the universities and perhaps some medical specialists."

He half turned, looking down as if to resume his seat. Then he turned back quickly: "Oh, there is one other thing. All the church schools and hospitals in China must become fully self-sufficient within two years."

Mary saw what this last item meant: that the S.P.G.'s programme of handing more and more responsibility over to the Chinese would have to be drastically speeded up. She felt depressed over the underlying significance of what Pastor Yang had said, for she knew that he was a good man. It revealed to her in a way leaving no room for doubt that the Chinese attitude was hardening, not only to those at the hospital, but to all Europeans throughout China.

At about this time, she received a letter from Peking which

told her that many of her missionary friends were thinking of going home. And there was mention of an unnamed European woman teacher at the *Chung Te* boys' school who, through saying the wrong thing thoughtlessly at the wrong time, had placed herself in considerable jeopardy.

Some weeks before (the letter said) a Communist lecturer at the school had spoken critically of the way foreigners tended to treat the Chinese, even in their own land. With not unnatural bitterness he had quoted a notice posted in a park in Shanghai's international area: "Dogs and Chinese not allowed here." A few days after that lecture, the teacher was taking her class when one of the boy students cleared his throat and spat on the floor.

Offended by the vulgar act, she spoke up, angrily and certainly without forethought: "You should not spit! If you will behave in this dirty way, can you wonder that certain notices are put up?"

The class spokesman leaped to his feet, crying: "You have cursed China!"

A strike was called. By next day, all the Peking schools, in a demonstration against the unfortunate woman teacher, were demanding her public trial to avenge the insult.

The trial was held. When, after several days, the offending foreigner was judged guilty, she was sentenced to write an apology for publication in the newspapers and, in addition, to make a public apology to the school orally. When she arrived at the school to do her penance, however, the boys would not receive her. Very shortly afterwards, she was asked to leave the country.

The news from Peking further convinced Mary that it was just a matter of time before all foreigners who remained unaffiliated with the new order would be made to go. Then, early in July, the letter came from the Bishop—the one that advised the British staff at the hospital to apply for their exit permits.

And now, Francis—her dear and long-time friend—had spoken up for her to the new leaders so that she, at least, could choose whether to stay or to go. Was this why he had arranged for her to give English lessons at the Communist hospital—so the Government representatives could be shown that mark in her favour?

She remembered Francis's words—and her own—when he had asked her to stay on. . . .

She had said: *"There is more?"*

"Yes, there is more."

"Tell me, Francis."

"There are two things you would have to agree to carry out. You would have to give up your British nationality and become, instead, a Chinese citizen. And, I must warn you, after the age of sixty they would have no work for you."

"And the second condition?"

"You would have to become a professed Communist and give up your faith in God."

Yet, knowing her as he did, Francis must have guessed from the beginning what her answer had to be.

". . . and give up your faith in God. . . ."

In her mind, sadly, sadly, she had already said her farewell to Tatung and to China.

After many delays, early in September the man from the Bureau of Foreign Affairs office in Tatung told Mary that at last the papers were in order for the British members of the hospital staff to leave. With the news, the Chinese staff members decided to give them a farewell dinner.

This began with a hymn and a prayer and ended with speeches from many of those present, the Superintendent breaking the ground by expressing his personal sadness at this final parting of the ways.

He had no sooner finished when, to Mary's surprise, the one-time agitator, Miss Chao, sprang to her feet. She began to speak, but suddenly choked, and tears streamed down her lovely face and she was sobbing beyond control. Presently, standing unashamed before them all, she pulled herself together and dabbed at her eyes with her handkerchief.

Then, with the catch of tears still in her voice, she spoke directly to Mary.

"Put your heart at rest, Teacher Ball," the Manchu girl said. "We will do our best. But—come back quickly, come back quickly!"

But when Dr. Francis Li rose to his feet, he shook his head mildly.

"I disagree with anybody who finds this a time for sadness and crying. It is a day in which we have to start taking the responsibility for ourselves."

He smiled down at Mary, and it was a wistful smile.

"Until now," he said, "any part of the hospital's administration which was too difficult or too distasteful was always handed over to Miss Ball and she was glad to do it. Now we must do it all ourselves.

"I have worked with Miss Ball for many years. I know she has spent herself in working for the Shansi people and now she needs and deserves a rest. We should not begrudge her going or make it hard for her.

"Instead, let us rise to the occasion: prove that we are willing to take our responsibility of running the hospital. That is how we can thank her best!"

Mary, deeply touched, smiled around at Francis and all her friends. It seemed like a dream, a hazy and reluctant dream from which she would presently wake with a lingering, forgotten sadness, and wonder what had caused it.

On the Monday, carts were brought into the hospital compound to take their luggage to the station. By noon, the carts were loaded and ready to set out. Just as they were about to do so, two of the coolies came to Mary, red-faced and upset, wringing their hands.

"We apologize to you," one said, with a small, nervous laugh. "We have just had a telephone message to say that you cannot go this afternoon."

"Why not?" Mary asked. "Is the railway cut?"

"Oh, no—the trains are all right. But the Bureau of Foreign

Affairs has had a telegram from Kalgan. The man at the local Bureau now says your passes are not in order after all, and he's coming to see you at four o'clock."

"Have you any idea what the real trouble is?"

The coolie looked embarrassed.

"No," he said.

At four, three men came from the Bureau—the one they had previously dealt with amongst them.

"Are you frightened because your pass is stopped?" he asked, grinning. But his companions remained dour and serious.

"Not frightened," Mary said sharply, "but it's a nuisance to have all our things packed and nothing to use."

"Well, these passes I've already given you," he said, "are only travel passes for within China—not exit permits. Now—" he paused, teasingly—"I'm ready to give you exit permits."

He took the first set away and departed with his grim-faced companions.

At half-past eight that evening, Mary was called to the telephone and told to go with her friends to the office of the Bureau of Foreign Affairs where, at last, he gave them their proper papers.

The departing foreigners returned one last time to the hospital and, accompanied by all of the staff except for two nurses who were needed on duty, went to the railway station, some on foot, some riding bicycles, some on rickshaws. The last person Mary could see on the platform as the train pulled out was Miss Chao, standing alone, wiping her eyes.

Then, for a distance, she looked back at the receding, shadowy, wicked city which she had grown to love. It was hard to believe that, in the years ahead, no eager young new missionaries, earnest as she had been and—yes—dedicated as she had been, would come from the west to Tatung. She hated to go, for she knew that she was leaving part of herself forever behind; that this was the end of an era, and she had helped to make it.

*   *   *

EPILOGUE

A N D that was indeed the ending of an era as it was the ending of Mary's story in China. In the waning part of 1950 she returned to England, not knowing at first the drain her work in Shansi had made on her slenderly frail body : the tension and the enforced fasting of that first, far-off siege; the hardships of villaging; the using up of her reserves of energy when she so often willingly took upon herself the extra loads of work others found distasteful; the eroding years in the Japanese prison camp; and the final heart-breaking wrench of having to leave the place that had become her home.

In England, after a short rest, she asked the S.P.G. for further duty. For some months, she spoke up and down the country for the Society, helping to raise funds and recruit young missionaries for other fields than the China now closed to them.

Then, impatient to be doing again what she loved best, she asked for a new field assignment on her own behalf. Perhaps there was some small irony in the fact that she was sent to South Africa, where her father had begun as a missionary, where she herself had been born, and where she had so passionately desired to go when she volunteered for medical mission service in 1924. Her new posting—as a nurse—was to St. Michael's Hospital, Batlharos, Kimberley. She arrived in January, 1952. The heat there troubled her greatly, but she did not complain and did not mention her spells of great weariness. Indeed, her new friends delighted in her spirit and in her very human sense of humour.

"She told me, once, of a holiday she had in Johannesburg," a St. Michael's colleague recalled recently. "She was determined to go down a gold mine, so she made enquiries about where to apply. When she got to the office where she was to ask for permission, she was told very firmly that she could not go on that particular day.

"As she had to return to duty, she pleaded to be allowed to go. Mary could be very convincing, and eventually permission was given, though it came from a higher officer in the firm. Off she went, delighted at her success, and joined a party which was ready to start the tour.

"She had a wonderful time; saw everything; went wherever the party went; and finally ended up in a room splendidly set for luncheon. This seemed odd to Mary—that a free tour should provide for ordinary sightseers so lavishly—and she made a few enquiries of her companions. It was then she discovered that the others in the party were not, like herself, ordinary sightseers at all, but directors of the big firm that owned the mine. She took a vast delight in telling about that, whooping with glee at the end and telling it as a great joke on herself."

This same nursing colleague returned to St. Michael's from a long leave in mid-November, 1952. As she got out of the car that had driven her to the hospital, Mary was on the steps to greet her, looking tired and pale. Asked how she was feeling, for the first time Mary admitted that she found the hot weather very trying.

"On Sunday, December 1st she appeared to be as usual," her friend related. "She had been on duty in the morning and, as we usually do, had said Evensong at six o'clock that evening. After supper we were sitting in the garden and Mary was talking in her usual amusing, animated way. We separated for the night.

"About half-past six next morning, the catechist came up for me, saying Mary was ill. She had been going from her room to the mission house when she collapsed. We took her into a nearby room and she died soon afterwards. It was a great shock to everyone.

"The African priest took charge. Mary rested in our small hospital chapel until the funeral the following day.

"There was a large gathering in the church and several of her European friends came out from Kuruman, the nearest town. The nurses with whom she had worked were the bearers. She is buried at the east end of the church, inside the rail surrounding the

mission compound. The grave has a small marble stone. On it are
the words:

> 'Mary Ball
> Died on Duty
> December 2nd, 1952.'"

*   *   *